Abstract Pissarro

Planting the Seeds of Abstract Art

by Ann Saul

The Author

Ann Saul is an independent scholar specializing in the works of Camille Pissarro. Author of *Pissarro's Places* (2013), she has lectured at the Museo Nacional Thyssen-Bornemisza in Madrid, the American Library in Paris, the Newberry Library in Chicago, and for audiences in Philadelphia, New Jersey, and New York. *Pissarro's Places* was the only English-language book associated with the Festival Normandie Impressionniste in 2013. Sold in museum bookstores of the Thyssen-Bornemisza and the Philadelphia Museum of Art, it is in the permanent libraries of the Philadelphia Museum of Art, the Dallas Museum of Art, the American Library in Paris, The Frick Collection, the Fisher Fine Arts Library (University of Pennsylvania), the University of California, Davis, the Carnegie Library of Pittsburgh, and the Free Library of Philadelphia, among others. After several years living in Paris, she is now a resident of Philadelphia Center City.

. . . .

abstractpissarro@yahoo.com

Art Book Annex
2116 Chestnut Street
Philadelphia, PA 19103

Editor: Jane Watkins

Designer: Tina Laganella

First published: 2019

Printed by Lightning Source, La Vergne, TN USA

Library of Congress Control Number: 2019900533

ISBN -- 978-0-9885685-1-8

Front cover: Camille Pissarro, *Harvesting Potatoes*, Pontoise, 1874, Private collection [PDRS 360]

Contents

Note to the Reader

Pissarro Paintings

Most of the paintings reproduced in this book are the work of Camille Pissarro. Captions include the title of the painting, the year, the present location, and any additional credits.

PDRS number

Captions for Pissarro's paintings include a PDRS number that refers to the number of the painting assigned in *Pissarro: Catalogue Critique des Peintures* by Joachim Pissarro and Claire Durand-Ruel Snollaerts (Milan: Skira Editore S.p.A., 2005).

Paintings by Other Artists

Captions of paintings by other artists include the artist's name, the title of the painting, the year, the present location, and any additional credits.

Acknowledgments

In writing this book, I stood on the shoulders of many scholars who came before me. I was able to discover new information from the signposts they provided. This is particularly evident in my primary resource for this book: *Pissarro: Catalogue Critique des Peintures* (2005). The depth and breadth of groundbreaking information compiled by Joachim Pissarro and Claire Durand-Ruel Snollaerts allowed me to pinpoint the earliest known evidence of abstract elements in Pissarro's paintings and introduced me to dozens of paintings that are rarely seen in exhibitions, many more than I could include in this book. I will always be grateful for their extraordinary work.

Both Joachim Pissarro and Claire Durand-Ruel Snollaerts have offered me support, encouragement, and friendship for many years. Richard Brettell has also supported my efforts and offered advice and guidance. Christopher Lloyd encouraged me and provided valuable insight that helped me connect the dots. Richard Schiff lent much appreciated guidance and direction, Yve-Alain Bois provided important information, and Flemming Friborg provided answers at a critical juncture. My colleague Dana Gordon has been generous in sharing his knowledge and opinions of Camille Pissarro. He gave me an artist's viewpoint and helped me understand language I needed to describe abstract elements.

Special thanks to my editor, Jane Watkins, who brought her years of experience as senior art-history editor at the Philadelphia Museum of Art to this book, and to the designer, Tina Laganella, whose superior capabilities and creativity made this book beautiful and easy to read.

Many others provided day-to-day support, including Tamara Faulkner, adjunct lecturer at the Art Institute of Chicago, who patiently read every chapter as it emerged and offered guidance and advice. Bruce Satalof was the first to read the completed work, and his comments added clarity. Mitchell Satalof provided assistance that helped to preserve this book's integrity. Many others who listened, commented, and offered encouragement include Christophe Duvivier, Lionel and Sandrine Pissarro, Janice Witzel, Jane Whitehill, Allison MacDuffee, Patty Lurie, Ronni Gordon, and Daniela Galdi.

The research needed for this work would not have been possible without the help of the capable staff at Fisher Art Library, University of Pennsylvania; the American

Library in Paris; and also the Free Library of Philadelphia. Assistance was also provided by Alice Howard, Ashmolean Museum, Oxford; Susan Pacitti, Glasgow Art Gallery and Museum; Anna Kjaer, Statens Museum for Kunst, National Gallery of Denmark, Copenhagen; Fabio Sidler, Koller Auktionen; Julia Hayes, Toledo Art Museum; and Thomas Haggarty, Bridgeman Images. I am grateful for the advice and counsel provided by Harry Spiegler and Barry Worbin, Herrick Feinstein; and Ashley Catalano-Leckerman and David Perry, Blank Rome. There are countless others who lent help and encouragement to this project and to all of them, my heartfelt thanks.

Above all, I am deeply grateful to Marie O'Donnell, Anne Vogelmann, Bruce Satalof, Michael Vogelmann, and all of my family, without whose encouragement and support this book would not have been possible.

Preface

As a young man, Camille Pissarro chose to create a radical new art—one that defied French academic standards and the Paris Salons. He filled his paintings with obviously visible brushstrokes, flat forms with no volume, motifs of no special "importance" stripped to the bare essentials, and daring geometric compositions declaring their significance without any narrative framework. By signing his name, he made his intention clear that these were finished works. He was not making pretty pictures; he was making paintings.

This book identifies the earliest times that he began using each of these elements as unique abstract techniques and then shows how he developed these techniques in full. Similar methods had been used on occasion by older artists but always in the service of greater realism or romantic sentiment as well as to subtly remind the viewer that the work was art, made by an artist. Pissarro used these abstract elements to defy realism and romanticism. His goal was to make a new, fresh art, unencumbered by tradition or the academy, to embody the notion that the whole point of the painting was the exploration—What is art? As he shared his findings with younger artists, a revolution began, and Impressionism and abstract art were the result.

While Pissarro was an enthusiastic participant in Impressionism, he was never totally in that camp. Monet, Renoir, and Sisley used the new freedom of loose brushstrokes and pure colors to paint pictures of beautiful sites and lovely people. In contrast, Pissarro painted less beguiling subjects, like cabbage patches or plowed fields; the full reach of putting paint on canvas and expressing his "sensation" were more important to him. The purely artistic essence of Pissarro's paintings is more difficult to grasp as this work has been less often seen in exhibitions or museums. But those who take time to look closely at these unusual paintings by Pissarro are richly rewarded with a deeper art experience.

Dana Gordon, an abstract painter based in New York, has long understood what Pissarro was doing and sees its deep and direct (though not so well known) connection to the way contemporary artists work today. For years, he studied the works of Pissarro and wrote reviews and essays describing the artist's intentions and techniques. He believes that Pissarro was the first to consciously invent, deploy, and combine the pictorial means abstract artists have exploited ever since. Indeed, in his opinion, Pissarro was the first abstract artist, long before the word "abstract" entered the art vocabulary. Gordon's essays are compiled at http://danagordon.net/Dana_Gordon_wsj_writings.html. And his paintings may be seen at danagordon.net.

I hope this book will show you how Pissarro has been deeply underestimated and will take you beyond what has previously been generally accepted about this artist. And you will see that the abstract techniques he initiated had a major effect historically and continue to influence the art being created today.

*But persistence, will and **free** sensations are necessary, one must be undetermined by anything but one's own sensation.*[1]

Do not proceed according to rules and principles, but paint what you observe and feel.[2]

— Camille Pissarro

1. John Rewald, ed., *Camille Pissarro: Letters to His Son Lucien* (New York: Pantheon, 1995), 202.

2. John Rewald, *Camille Pissarro* (New York: Harry N. Abrams, 1963), 148.

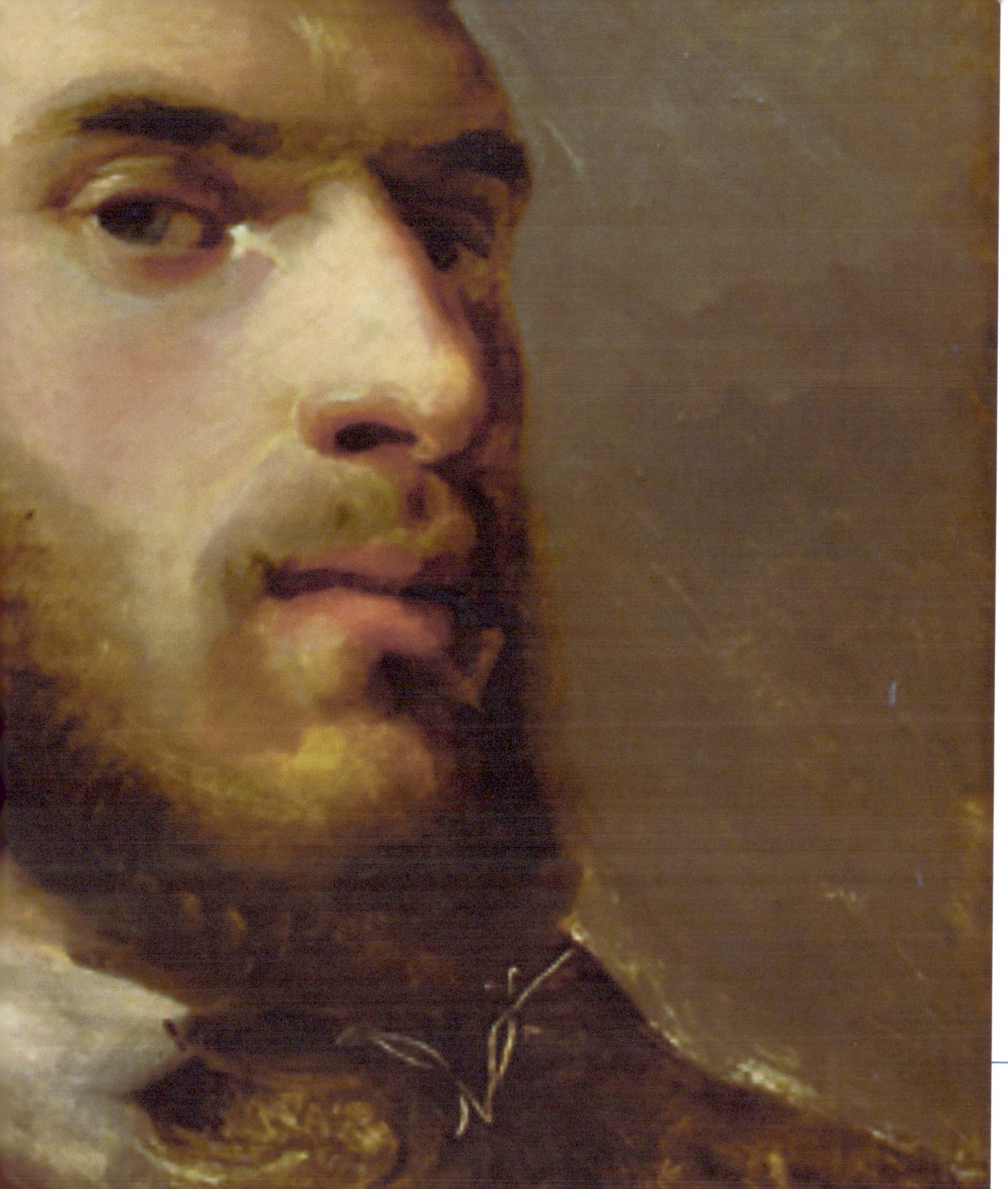

Fig. 1.
Self-Portrait, detail.
1852–54, National Gallery
of Denmark, Copenhagen

1 Pissarro–The Whiplash of Originality

He was, in essence, the first abstract artist.[1]

— Dana Gordon

1. Dana Gordon, "An Intimate Exhibition That Rewards the Keen Eye," *The Wall Street Journal*, October 17, 2007.

2. Rewald, ed., *Camille Pissarro: Letters to His Son Lucien*, 323.

   Pissarro used the term "whiplash of originality" to refer to the essential aspect of art that he found lacking in the paintings of Alphonse Legros. But it describes that element of prodigious inventiveness that characterizes his art.

3. Joachim Pissarro and Claire Durand-Ruel Snollaerts, *Pissarro: Catalogue Critique des Peintures*, 3 vols. (Milan: Skira Editore S.p.A., 2005), 1:144.

Camille Pissarro's early paintings—daring, radical, and uncompromising–challenge current beliefs about modern art every bit as much as they defied the Paris Salon in the mid-1850s. Bit by bit, Pissarro subverted academic art—flaunting his rough brushstrokes, blatantly placing colors side-by-side without transition tones, choosing unappealing motifs, using patches of color to create forms, pressing structures into flattened planes, and ignoring perspective when it pleased him. For Pissarro, art demanded no less than the "whiplash of originality."[2]

A close study of Pissarro's early paintings demonstrates that he was the first to use these elements **intentionally for what they represent**—marks in paint on canvas. In so doing, he made manifest the materiality of painting. This was nothing short of revolutionary, and he did all of this **before** the advent of Impressionism. Writing about Pissarro's paintings in the First Impressionist Exhibition, art critic Armand Silvestre said: "M. Pissarro . . . is basically the inventor of this style of painting."[3]

Indeed, other painters before Pissarro used rough brushstrokes, but their intent was to make features more realistic. Landscape paintings by Corot, Courbet, and the Barbizon School painters were gaining acceptability, but these artists depicted picturesque motifs not "common" views.

Occasional examples of these aspects can be found throughout art history prior to Pissarro, but they are isolated instances and are inconsequential to the overall narrative of the painting. And they were not done with the intent to focus viewers' attention on paint and canvas.

A Pissarro painting is often expected to fit the accepted definition of Impressionism—bright colors, loose brushstrokes, and picturesque motifs. Some of his best-known and loved paintings fit that description perfectly. But a large portion of his œuvre cannot be viewed through the lens of Impressionism. Some of his more radical works, those that cannot be easily categorized, are less wellknown and are seldom seen in exhibitions. These are the paintings that reveal Pissarro's genius—the innovations that paved the way for the Impressionists, modern art, and for what is now known as abstract art.

This book identifies the first use of these innovations by Pissarro, showing examples in his paintings. It documents the years

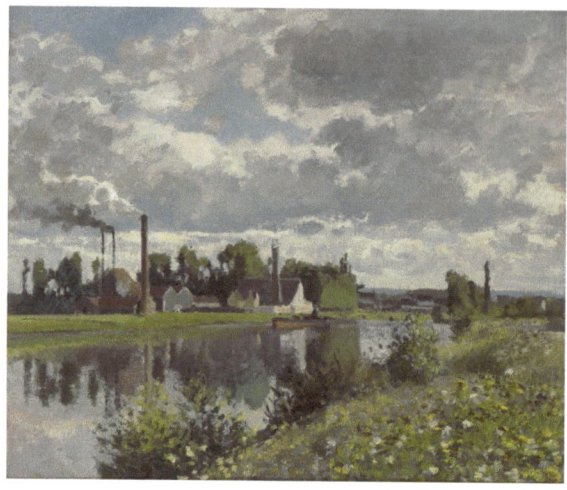

Fig. 2.
Factory on the Banks of the Oise, Saint-Ouen-l'Aumône, 1873, Sterling and Francine Clark Art Institute, Williamstown, Massachusetts [PDRS 300]

he initiated these techniques in relation to use of the same techniques by other artists. The examples shown of Pissarro's work are signed, indicating that he considered them complete. Did Pissarro know what he was doing and how different his work was? His letter to art critic Théodore Duret verifies that he knew exactly what he was doing: "If you could unearth for me the rare man who likes **modern painting** [my emphasis] and does not fear ridicule, I would be very grateful . . . ."[4]

While Pissarro does not fit easily into any art-history category, he has traditionally been known as an Impressionist. Some of

4. Ibid.

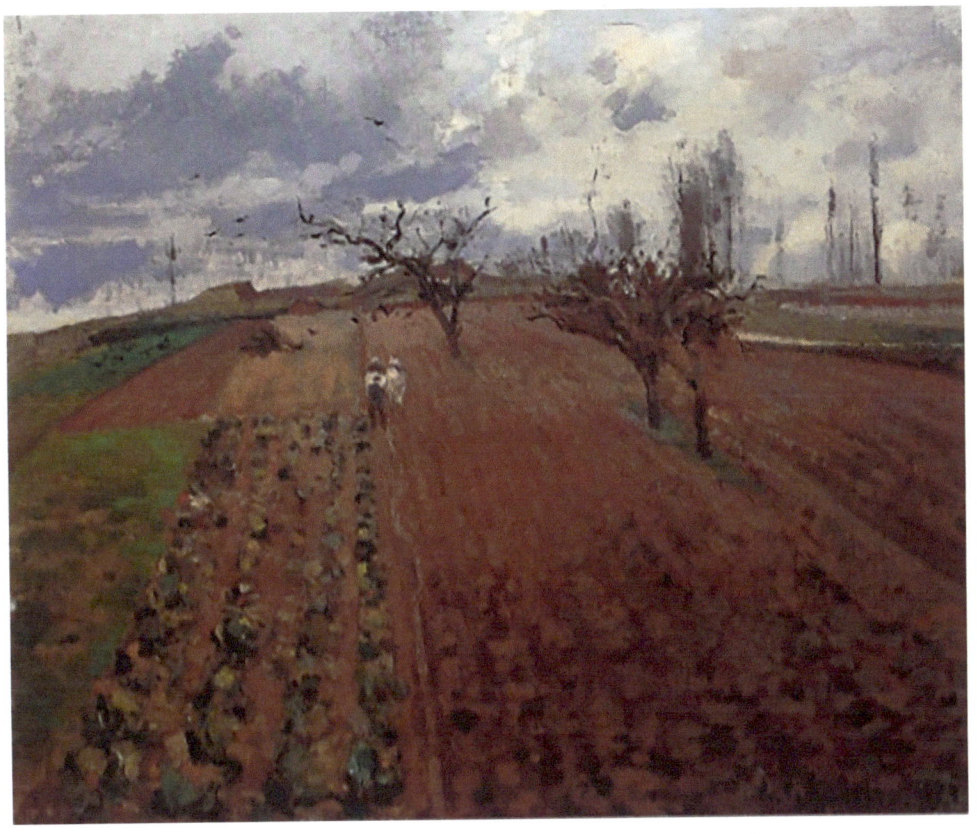

lining the banks of the Oise River, and the immediacy of the scene—all bespeak *plein air* painting.

Paintings like *Ploughed Fields near Osny* (1873), painted that same year, seem almost strange in comparison. While the latter also depicts an imminent change in weather, there is none of the lightness and "prettiness" generally expected from Impressionism.

What it offers is far more interesting—an earthy grid of color and texture with large rectangles—one of deep purple in the foreground fading into brick red and then into light salmon, with others in different shades of green. The areas are further delineated by varying brushstrokes—tiny repetitive up-and-down strokes are set next to circular forms, and in the next section, short puddles of paint create a mottled effect. The static framework of the field is accentuated by movement in the sky— flowing brushstrokes of dark blue invade grayish white clouds.

his paintings like *Factory on the Banks of the Oise* (1873) may be labeled quintessential Impressionism: the lavish portrayal of sunlight, the brightness of the colors, the consciousness of changing weather as gray clouds fill the intense blue sky, the modern presence of new factories

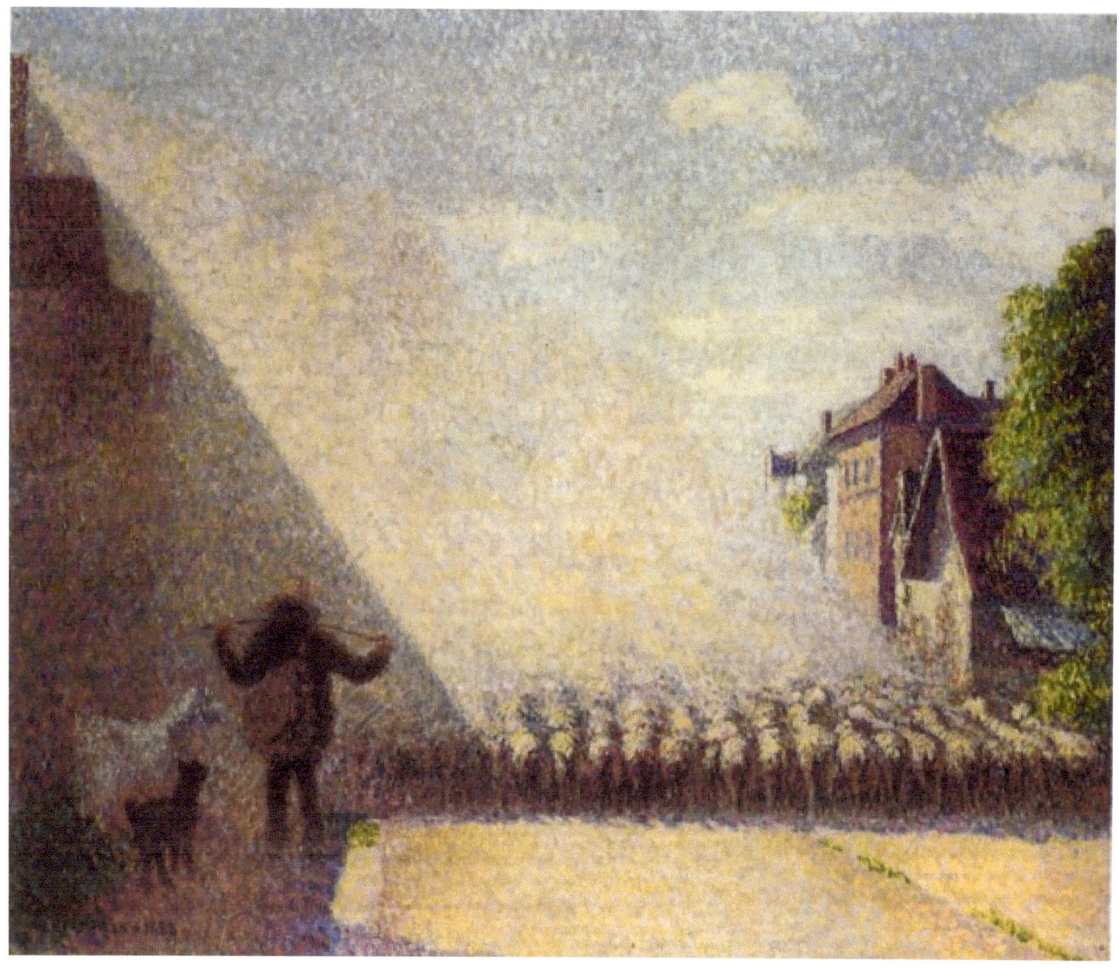

Fig. 4.
The Flock of Sheep, Éragny,
1888, Private collection
[PDRS 860]

While at first this appears to be a commonplace study in perspective, the genius of Pissarro is apparent in his placement of the view at a slight diagonal, and he curves the horizon line ever so gently. The farmer following two white horses and the three trees are just window-dressing for this captivating painting based on an abstract pattern.

Fifteen years later, Pissarro painted *The Flock of Sheep, Éragny* (1888), which can only be described in abstract terms. The canvas is dominated by geometric forms—the large bright rectangle covering three-quarters of the foreground and the dramatic diagonal that divides the shaft of light from the shadow. There is another pale diagonal ending at the house with the pointed roof that separates the light shaft from the cloudy blue sky. The backsides of the sheep form a straight horizontal line that is anything but realistic, and a tall house on the right provides a strong vertical. The dark wedge includes dark red, blue, and green dots, contrasting with the pink, cream, and gray dots of the light wedge. The sheep become a static line of identically rounded forms, and their legs form a dark line separating the upper wedges from the rectangle with its yellow and coral dots. The only legible figures—a herder, a goat, and a dog—are reduced to small sketches in the shadows. The image suggests no storyline but focuses on the paint texture and the geometric composition, creating a work that is undeniably abstract.

Pissarro's paintings that are less picturesque or those that do not fit the generally accepted notion of Impressionism are sometimes problematic for those expecting him to remain in that easily-defined category. Richard Brettell, curator and Pissarro expert, wrote: "Pissarro's art has been misunderstood and . . . this misunderstanding has been aided by the persistent clichés used to characterize the impressionist movement as a whole."[5]

Curators who choose to include his paintings in Impressionist exhibitions tend to pick images that work well with those of other artists. Museum visitors expect a

5. Françoise Cachin et al., *Pissarro* (Boston: Museum of Fine Arts, 1980), 13.

familiar look from Pissarro and may be disappointed if his more complex and difficult paintings are shown. Yet these paintings are the ones that are the most informative and interesting.

Pissarro was aware that people did not always understand his work. In 1883, he wrote to his son Lucien Pissarro: "It is only in the long run that I can expect to please, and then only those who have a grain of indulgence; but the eye of the passerby is too hasty and sees only the surface. Whoever is in a hurry will not stop for me!"[6]

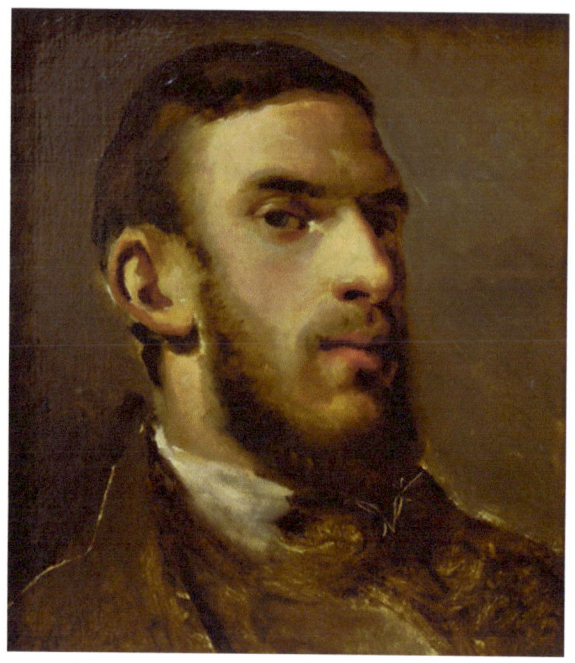

Fig. 5.
Self-Portrait, 1852–54, National Gallery of Denmark, Copenhagen

These issues are not paramount for most Impressionist painters. The characteristics of Impressionism are so familiar that they have become a brand. Who does not recognize the paintings of Claude Monet with their haystacks and waterlilies? The depiction of light, bright colors, a clear focal point, and picturesque motifs tend to epitomize Impressionism. Alfred Sisley painted similar *plein air* scenes that fulfill all the expectations of Impressionism. Pierre-Auguste Renoir combined his light palette with bright colors and feathery brushstrokes that easily convey the Impressionist brand. Even the ballerinas and laundry women of Edgar Degas are readily recognized by the public. These images can be easily captured, even as details, on teacups or bookbags and are often reproduced in advertising and illustrations. Pissarro's images are not so easily captured.

6. Rewald, ed., *Camille Pissarro: Letters to His Son Lucien*, 47.

Pissarro's Paintings Are Different

Art critics of the day recognized that Pissarro's paintings did not fit the familiar mold of his predecessors nor did they compare to those of his contemporaries. Théodore Duret, French art critic and friend of Pissarro, attempted to explain: "Pissarro's work was differentiated from that of the others [Impressionists] by a strongly marked individuality . . . . He never sought for rare motives in nature, ... He had no wish to embellish anything."[7]

Pissarro's difference was centered on his sense of individuality, his insistence on the freedom to make his own choices, and his determination to follow his own "sensations." This mindset was encouraged by his first drawing teacher, Wilfrid Savary, who favored the unorthodox practice of drawing directly from nature[8] over the academic practice of drawing from engravings or plaster casts.[9] Pissarro took drawing from Savary at a prestigious boarding school in Passy, then a suburb of Paris, where his parents sent him to get a proper education.[10] When he was summoned back at age seventeen to St. Thomas, his birthplace, Savary urged him to continue his visual exploration of nature, advising him, "Mind you, don't forget to draw [coconut] trees."[11]

His determination was demonstrated early on when he left home and the family business to go to Venezuela and paint with the Danish artist Fritz Melbye. Then, in 1855, Pissarro moved back to Paris to work as an artist and firmly turned his back on the formulaic painting directives of the Académie des Beaux-Arts and the Salon. He was certainly knowledgeable about academic painting: as a student in Passy he had visited the Louvre, the Salons, and the studio of his teacher's brother, the artist Auguste Savary, who regularly exhibited at the Salon.[12]

Pissarro's search for freedom or autonomy was "not so much the capacity to do anything, but rather the capacity to invent new rules and to experiment with them," according to Joachim Pissarro, art historian and great-grandson of the artist.[13]

7. Théodore Duret, *Manet and the French Impressionists*, trans. J. E. Crawford Flitch (London: Grant Richards, 1910), 130.

8. Pissarro and Durand-Ruel Snollaerts, *Pissarro: Catalogue Critique des Peintures*, 1:99.

9. Albert Boime, *The Academy and French Painting in the Nineteenth Century* (London: Phaidon, 1971), 24.

10. Pissarro and Durand-Ruel Snollaerts, *Pissarro: Catalogue Critique des Peintures*, 1:99.

11. Adolphe Tabarant, *Pissarro*, trans. J. Lewis May (London: John Lane; The Bodley Head, 1925), 9.

12. Ibid.

13. Joachim Pissarro, *Camille Pissarro* (New York: Harry N. Abrams, 1993), 8.

The self-portrait of the young artist reveals a resolute young man whose determination to assert his artistic independence would lead to revolutionary changes in mid-nineteenth-century art.

Even as a young man, Camille Pissarro had the inner strength and self-confidence (or stubbornness) to be uncompromisingly true to his own self, in his relations with other people and, most of all, in his art. While there were times when he doubted his capabilities, such as the time he felt afraid of "finding monsters where I believed there were precious gems,"[14] he tenaciously created art that reflected his own feelings, individuality, and temperament—his own "sensation."[15] He frequently referred to his "sensation" and often admonished his son Lucien that "one must be undetermined by anything but one's own sensation."[16]

These components—the resolve to draw from nature, his own personal autonomy, and his determination to follow his "sensation"—elucidate the primary reason that Pissarro's paintings were so different even from the beginning.

But another factor was equally important: Pissarro **saw things differently.** He said, "I can see only patches [*taches*]. When I start off a painting, the first thing I strive to catch is its harmonic form [*l'accord*]. Between that sky and that ground and that water there is necessarily a link. It can only be a set of harmonies [*relation d'accords*], and this is the ultimate hardship with painting."[17] In French, *tache* refers to an area of color distinct from its background,[18] so what Pissarro saw were **patches of color.**

When most people look at a scene in the country, they see hills and valleys, fields and trees, a river or road, and sky. When Pissarro looked at a similar scene, he saw greens, yellows, blues, and grays. It was his task to place those patches of color on the canvas in a harmonious relationship, and that task was what he found such an engaging challenge.

14. Rewald, ed., *Camille Pissarro: Letters to His Son Lucien*, 47.

15. Joachim Pissarro, *Pioneering Modern Painting—Cézanne and Pissarro, 1865-1885* (New York: The Museum of Modern Art, 2005), 25.

16. Rewald, ed., *Camille Pissarro: Letters to His Son Lucien*, 202.

17. Richard R. Brettell and Joachim Pissarro, *The Impressionist and the City—Pissarro's Series Paintings* (New Haven, Conn., and London: Yale University Press, 1992), xxxix.

18. Pissarro, *Pioneering Modern Painting—Cézanne and Pissarro, 1865-1885*, 36.

Following his own "sensation," Pissarro would choose colors of the appropriate value and apply them with a brush or palette knife to create unified compositions of forms, shapes, and lines on canvas. The motif itself was somewhat immaterial to Pissarro, and he more often chose innocuous scenes that had no special importance or meaning for anyone. He wrote, "Don't bother trying to look for something *new* [his emphasis]; you won't find novelty in the subject matter, but in the way you express it."[19] In other words, translating his own "sensation" onto the canvas with colors, brushstrokes, lines, and shapes was more important than the actual scene.

How Pissarro painted—how it was different—was not accidental but the result of his conscious intent. This is clearly evidenced by his signature, which is affixed to most of his works, even the most experimental ones. He knew that he was pushing against centuries of French academic art standards, and by affixing his signature, he made his intentions quite clear.[20]

Pissarro Made Materiality Important

Pissarro was the first artist to elevate the materiality of painting as more important than the narrative subject matter. Art historian Richard Shiff commented on this aspect in one of Pissarro's early paintings, *Still Life with Wine Carafe* (1867), noting the "roughness" of the brushstrokes, especially in the tablecloth, and the painting's materiality.[21] The brushstrokes on the tabletop and the overhanging tablecloth are highly visible as are those defining the bowl and the spoon hanging on the wall. The crisscross strokes on the apples are close to a herringbone pattern. The overlapping strokes, distinctly heavy with paint, distract from the actual image and force the viewer to focus on the paint itself.

This aspect set Pissarro apart from any of the artists who came before him and from most of his contemporaries, who utilized the new Impressionist techniques but were primarily still focused on their subjects. This explains why some of

19. Ibid., 39.

20. Mary Haus, "Sign Here!" *ArtNews* (2004). http://www.artnews.com/2004/07/01/sign-here/.

   Jack Flam, art historian and author, said that the artist's signature on a work declares: "It is mine, it is genuine, it is finished."

21. New York Studio School, September 26, 2018, "Joachim Pissarro in Conversation with Richard Shiff."

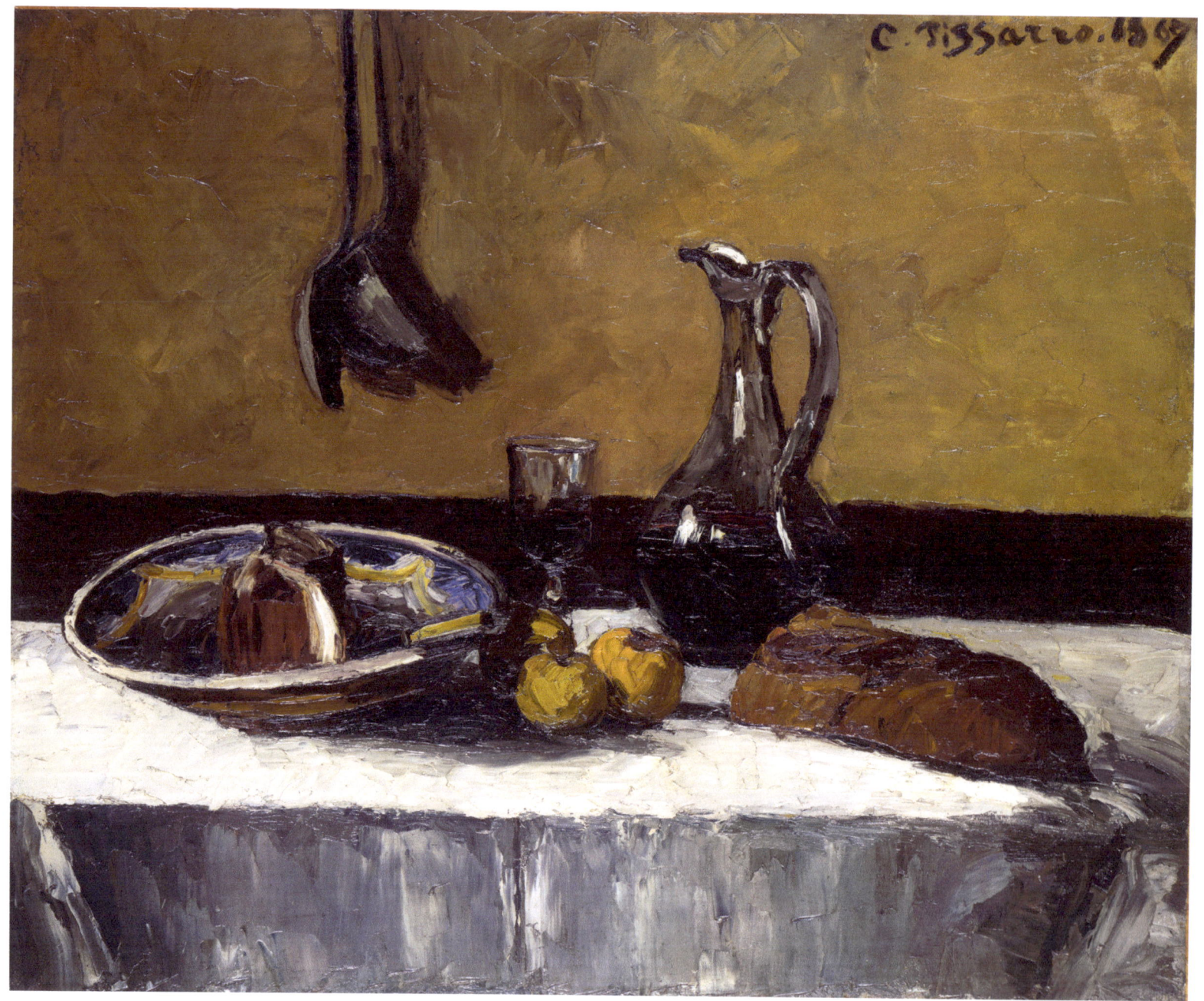

Pissarro's paintings are more difficult to understand and why those who are in a hurry might pass by a Pissarro to stand before a picture of something they can easily recognize. But this is Pissarro's genius. What he made were more than just pictures; they were paintings in the truest sense of the word.

As abstract painter Dana Gordon put it: "Pissarro discovered a new subject central to art: the nature of the medium itself. He showed that all of painting's basic qualities—colors, brushstrokes, materiality, lines, shapes, composition— were meaningful in their own right, and in their potential to transform paint into purely visual poetry, as well as into illusionistic pictures. He was, in essence, the first abstract artist."[22]

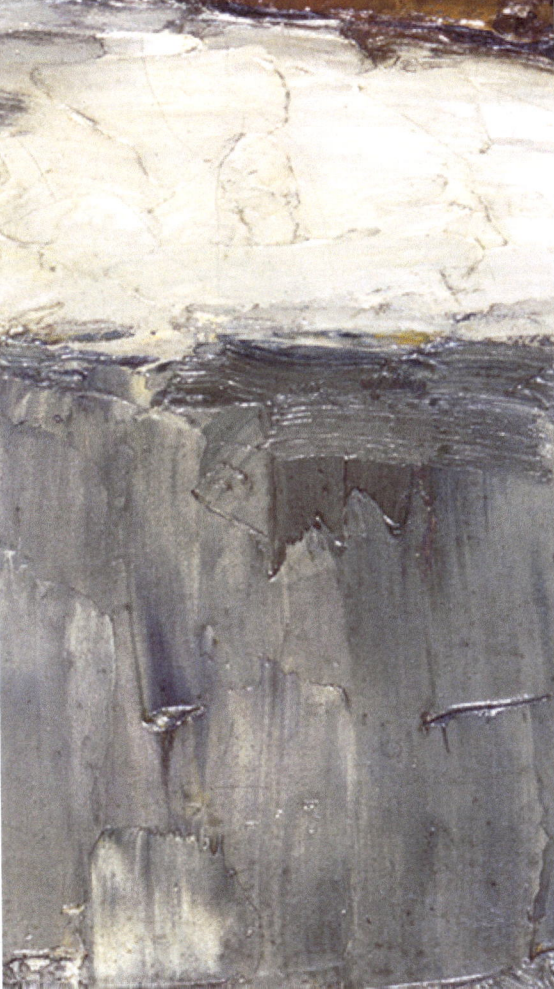

Fig. 6. (Left)
Still Life with Wine Carafe,
1867, Toledo Museum of Art, Ohio, Purchased with funds from the Libbey Endowment, Gift of Edward Drummond Libbey, 1949.6 [PDRS 114]

Fig. 7.
Still Life with Wine Carafe, detail, 1867, Toledo Museum of Art, Ohio, Purchased with funds from the Libbey Endowment, Gift of Edward Drummond Libbey, 1949.6 [PDRS 114]

22. Gordon, "An Intimate Exhibition That Rewards the Keen Eye."

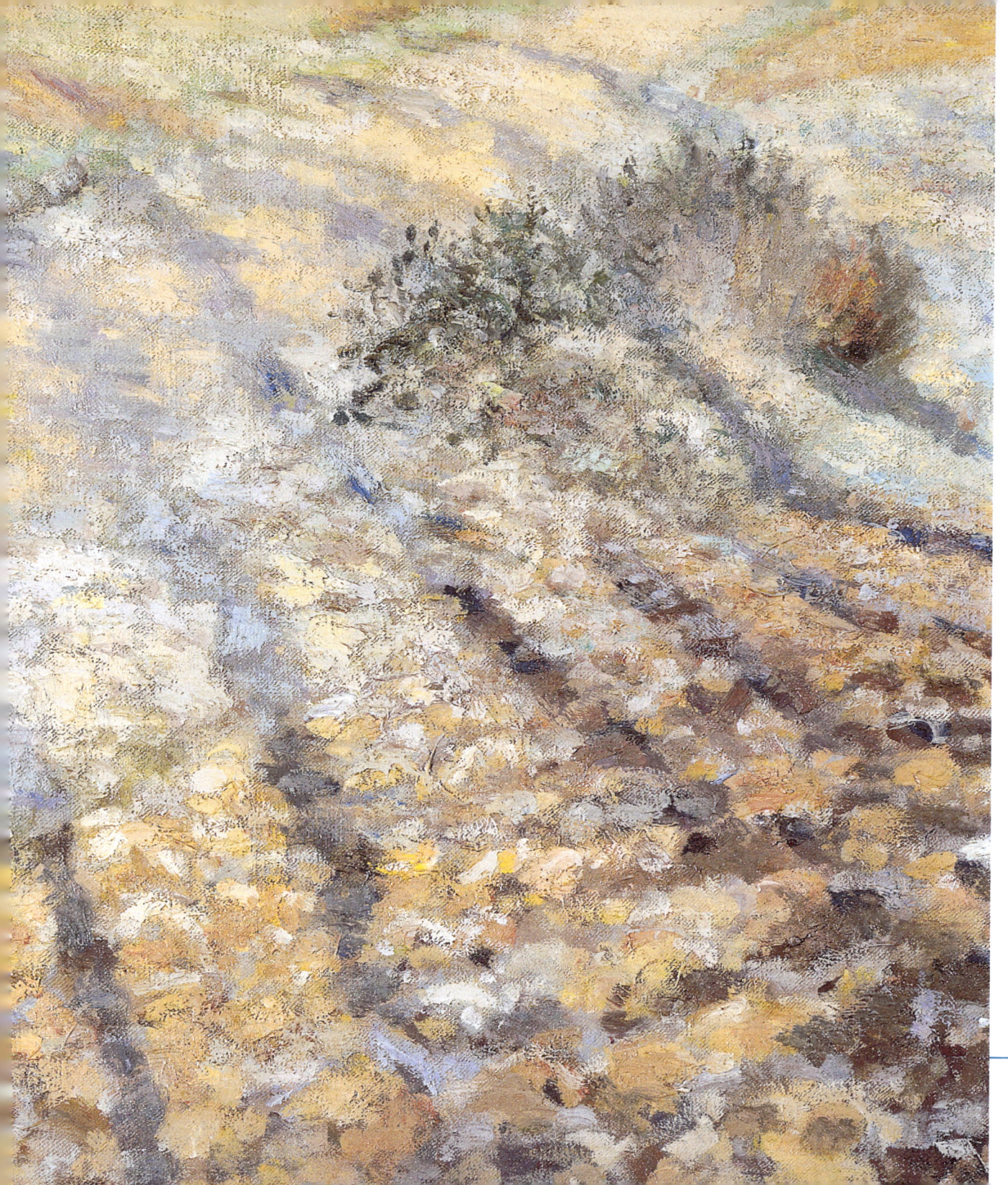

Fig .8.
Hoar Frost at Ennery, detail,
1873, Musée d'Orsay, Paris
[PDRS 285]

2 Abstract Elements in Pissarro's Paintings

To appreciate a Pissarro landscape, you first have to get over the fact that it looks like a landscape. Later, after seeing everything else that is there, you will be amazed that it does look like a landscape.[1]

—Dana Gordon

When Pissarro was a young artist there were no words to describe what he was doing in his paintings. Compared to the highly representational art of the mid-nineteenth century, his paintings were radical. He used elements that were unconventional, often unfamiliar, and generally unacceptable by the standard of French academic art. Dana Gordon said: "Even the early critics of the 1860s—Zola, Astruc, Redon, and Duret who acclaimed his paintings—did not yet have the language to describe his innovations."[2]

As early as 1852, before he moved to Paris, Pissarro began using abstract elements in his paintings. From the vantage point of the twenty-first century, many of his paintings seem traditional, while others are puzzling and inexplicable in Impressionist terms. However, when abstract elements are identified, the artist's brilliant creativity is evident. Some of the techniques Pissarro was the first to use as abstract elements, many of which were quickly taken on by other artists, are as follows:

1. Dana Gordon, "The Moses of Modernism," unpublished manuscript (2005).

2. Ibid.

- Absence of narrative or storyline
- Ordinary sites lacking importance and stripped to bare elements
- Lack of focal point; allover painting
- Accentuation of visible brushstrokes and paint texture
- Structures without volume, pressed into flattened planes
- Figures reduced to mere sketches
- Forms created from patches of color
- Blocks of color juxtaposed without transitional tones
- Nontraditional compositions based on geometric or other non-narrative framework
- Lack of depth, chiaroscuro, or shading; recession created by overlapping planes
- Focus on the materiality of the paint

the term "abstract" was applied in intellectual and religious terminology to describe something omitted or excluded; the word was in the contemporary vocabulary but not generally applied to art. By 1888 (long after the advent of Impressionism), the word "abstract" had been used in reference to art, as evidenced by a letter written to Émile Schuffenecker by Paul Gauguin: "A word of advice: don't copy nature too closely. Art is an abstraction."[3]

Nearly fifty years later, Alfred H. Barr, Jr., first director of the Museum of Modern Art in New York, provided a useful explanation: "For an 'abstract' painting is really a most positively concrete painting since it confines the attention to its immediate, sensuous, physical surface far more than does the canvas of a sunset or a portrait."[4]

Today, the elements that Pissarro was using 150 years ago have a name—they are called abstract. The word "abstraction" has been traced back to the thirteenth century, when it literally meant the removal of something. In the early 1800s,

While earlier artists had occasionally employed some of these techniques, such use was within the context of achieving greater realism. In contrast, Pissarro used these techniques **intentionally to draw attention to the materiality of the art.**

3. Terence Maloon, ed., *Camille Pissarro* (Sydney, Australia: Art Gallery of New South Wales, 2010), 33-35.

4. Alfred H. Barr, Jr., *Cubism and Abstract Art* (New York: The Museum of Modern Art, 1936), 11.

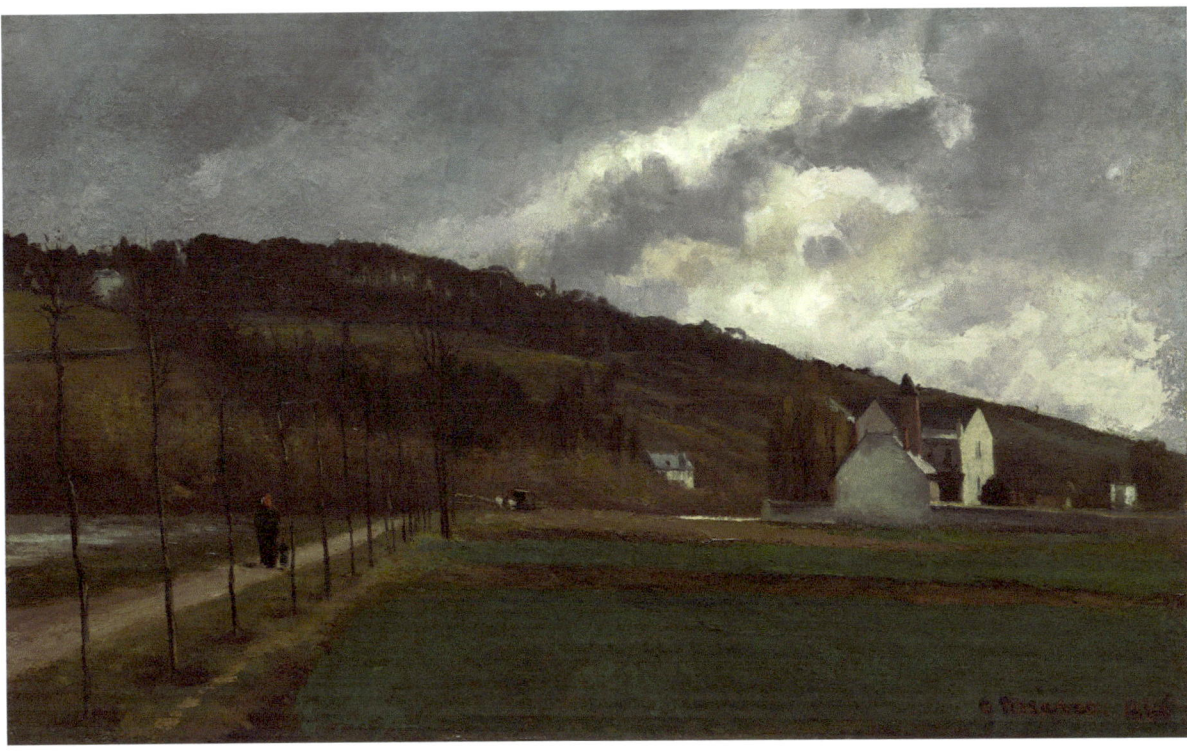

Fig. 9.
Banks of the Marne in Winter, 1866, The Art Institute of Chicago, Mr. and Mrs. Lewis Larned Coburn Memorial Collection [PDRS 107]

5. Author's note: While traveling on a train from Reims to Paris a few years ago, I saw a scene with this same contour of hill and green fields. I quickly located the site on my cell phone and realized I was on the banks of the Marne. Before I could take a photograph, the train had passed it by.

A close look at paintings throughout Pissarro's career shows that these abstract techniques are easily identifiable. One of his early paintings, *Banks of the Marne in Winter* (1866), exhibited at the Salon in 1866, shows that he had already developed these elements and was using them consistently.

The bleak, empty site is certainly insignificant and the exact site has not been identified as have many sites of Pissarro paintings.[5] Pissarro weaves the topographical features into a tight geometric structure, enmeshing the viewer in its web. A strong diagonal beginning with the two paths at the lower left makes a sharp angle with a horizontal line that looks like a road with a horse and carriage. In the midst of the dark-green ground cover, a shorter horizontal line of darker earth extends to the right.

The diagonal river and two paths are lined with spindly leafless trees. There are other diagonals, softer ones: the line of trees from the crest of the hill to a house below and a renegade dark line in the clouds above. The color field in the foreground displays the artistic use of a palette knife and brushstrokes in a flurry of bright green. The structures are flat as cardboard and are layered to give a sense of recession. A woman walking the other direction does not especially invite our attention, nor does the carriage with white horses whose only purpose is to indicate the presence of a road. This painting is intriguing because of its mystery—it does not tell a story or pamper the eye.

For Pissarro, however, this was enough. Upon seeing Pissarro's work for the first time, Émile Zola also believed that this was enough. He wrote a long, glowing review of the painting including the following comments: "You ought to know that you please nobody and that your painting is thought to be too bare, too black. So why the devil do you have the arrant awkwardness to paint solidly and study nature so honestly! . . . Not the least delectation for the eye. A grave and austere kind of painting, an extreme care for truth and rightness, an iron will. You are a clumsy blunderer, sir—you are an artist that I like."[6]

Many other Pissarro paintings were considered radical by any standard and remain puzzling today. One of the best known of these is *Hoar Frost at Ennery* (1873), which was shown in the First Impressionist Exhibition in 1874.

The site is even more insignificant; the bare fields are frankly unappealing. Pissarro created interest by constructing a giant "X" using diagonal lines from the treetops on the left through the bushes at the center and continuing to the right along the top of the dark-orange section. This diagonal is crossed by a line from the top of the tree on the right through the center bush and down the other side of the dark-orange section.

Within each triangular space are more diagonal lines, which, if they are interpreted

6. Pissarro and Durand-Ruel Snollaerts, *Pissarro: Catalogue Critique des Peintures*, 2:96.

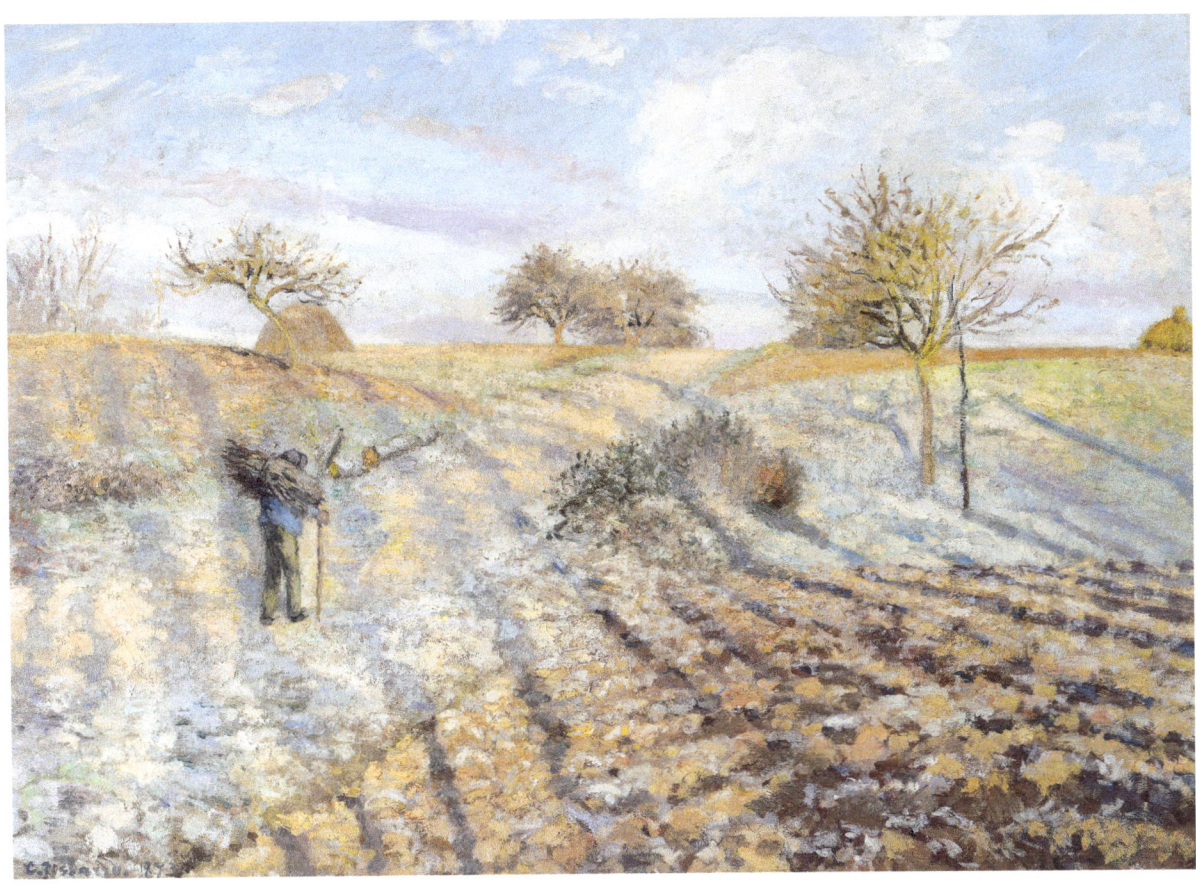

Fig. 10. *Hoar Frost at Ennery,*
1873, Musée d'Orsay, Paris
[PDRS 285]

as shadows are incredibly long shadows. The triangle in the foreground is filled with rosy-orange and yellow patches, overlaid by dark purple. In the two side triangles, lighter yellow is crossed by a bluish lilac, providing studies in complementary colors. The muddled brushstrokes create an uneven texture, focusing attention on the paint and canvas. The man with a bundle of sticks is a mere sketch, simply defining a pale pink diagonal panel that might represent a road. In the sky, loose brushstrokes depict clouds in a bluish gray sky and horizontal lines of blue and rose are somewhat perpendicular to the dark lines below. If the tree outlines and the sketchy man are ignored, the result is a complex abstract pattern that seems puzzling to someone looking for a traditional landscape. (Try using a piece of paper to cover the sky and another piece to cover the left side enough to block out the figure. The result is totally abstract.)

Needless to say, this painting was not fully appreciated by art critics of the day. Jules-Antoine Castagnary remarked: "He makes the serious mistake of reproducing on the ground shadows cast by trees that are placed outside the frame, and as a result the viewer, not being able to see them, is reduced to inferring them."[7] This was a serious breach of academic rules in those days. Another critic, Louis Leroy, wrote sarcastically: "Those are furrows! That is frost? But those are palette scrapings placed uniformly on a dirty canvas. It has neither head nor tail, neither top nor bottom, neither front nor back."[8] If Pissarro's intent was **to call attention** to the paint texture, color patches, and

geometric design of the painting, these words mark his success.

A later work, *Harvesting Potatoes, Pontoise* (1874), was painted the same year as the First Impressionist Exhibition, but it bears little resemblance to typical Impressionist style. Pissarro abstracted the scene to its literal basics with layers of vibrant colors, juxtaposing stripes of red, green, orange, yellow, and violet from the middle of the canvas almost to the top, showing only a sliver of sky. The bright colors of the highest layers do nothing to signify distance.

The foreground demands attention with its brushstrokes—little slabs of red, orange, blue, and green, overlapping in a pattern that foreshadows Pointillism. The people are reduced to visible patches of overlapping color. This is most obvious in the kneeling woman, whose body is shaped by a few strokes of blue paint and a patch of white for her kerchief. The reflection of the setting sun on her skirt is indicated by quick strokes of rosy red. The sketchiness of these figures reveals the depth of Pissarro's abstraction.

7. Ibid., 2:26.

8. Ibid.

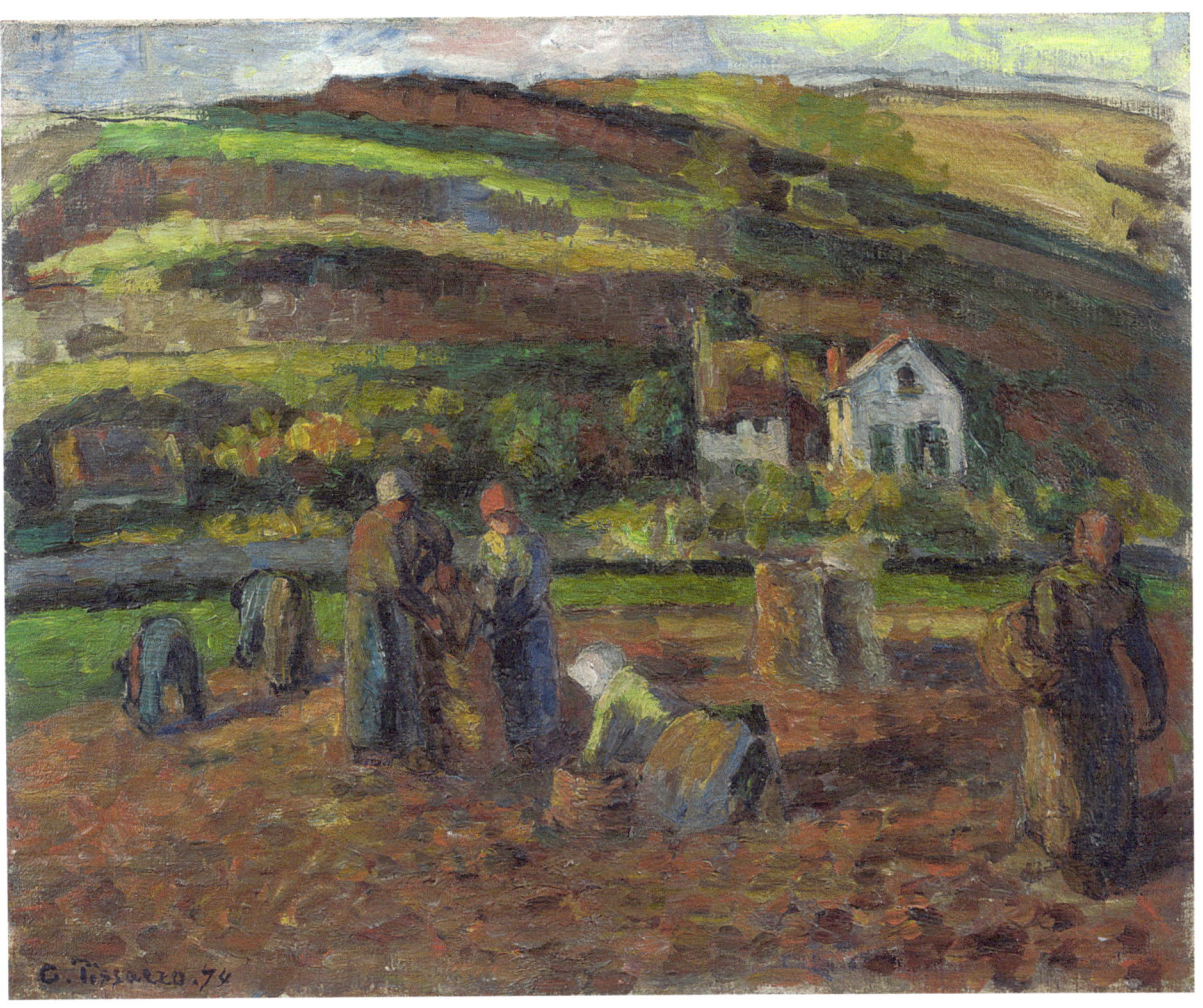

Fig. 11.
Harvesting Potatoes, Pontoise, 1874, Private collection [PDRS 360]

Richard Brettell, art historian and Pissarro expert, explains how Pissarro moved away from value shifts he learned from Camille Corot and then used color to create form as he applied areas of thick paint in almost color opposites side-by-side, creating an "optical brilliance" uncharacteristic of Impressionism: "Both its color and its contrived and constructed composition look forward to the anti-Impressionist esthetics of the 1880s and 1890s."[9] This painting in particular foreshadows the Fauvism of Maurice de Vlaminck and André Derain.

The little-known painting *Houses at Pontoise* (c. 1878)[10] is a dramatic example of abstract elements that focus on materiality—emphasizing the texture of the paint on the canvas rather than the scene itself. Light is contrasted with shadow in the brushstrokes, all set in a complex geometric structure that offers cues to depth alongside flat abstract form in the same structure.

The dark wall creates a sharp angle in the middle of the canvas, but while the vertex draws attention, there is no depth in the corner where the two walls meet. The angle is suppressed by strong opposing diagonal lines on the red roof, with its perpendicular chimneys. The bright-red roof compliments the dark-green leaves below. Patches of green suggest the foliage and wall, the lights and darks creating a

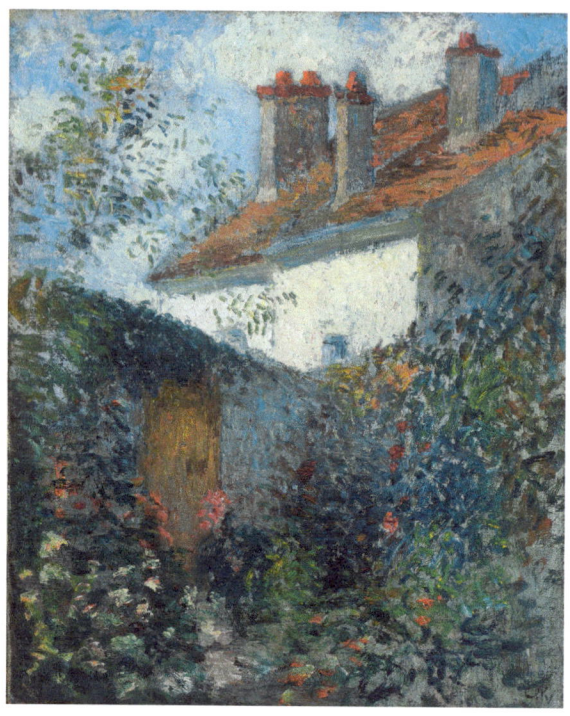

Fig. 12.
Houses at Pontoise, c. 1878,
Private collection [PDRS 546]

speckled pattern with red patches. The smooth surface of the front wall contrasts with the side wall, which is simply a flattened shadow merging with green foliage below. The sky, an airy design of circular white-and-gray brushstrokes against blue, is loosely stitched to the solid geometrics by a tall offshoot with fragile leaves. The excitement this painting creates is monumental compared to its small size (approximately 22 by 18 inches).

9. Richard R. Brettell, *Pissarro and Pontoise* (New Haven, Conn.: Yale University Press, 1990), 167.

10. Pissarro and Durand-Ruel Snollaerts, *Pissarro: Catalogue Critique des Peintures,* 2:376. Before 2005, this painting had been shown in only one exhibition in Bordeaux in 1974.

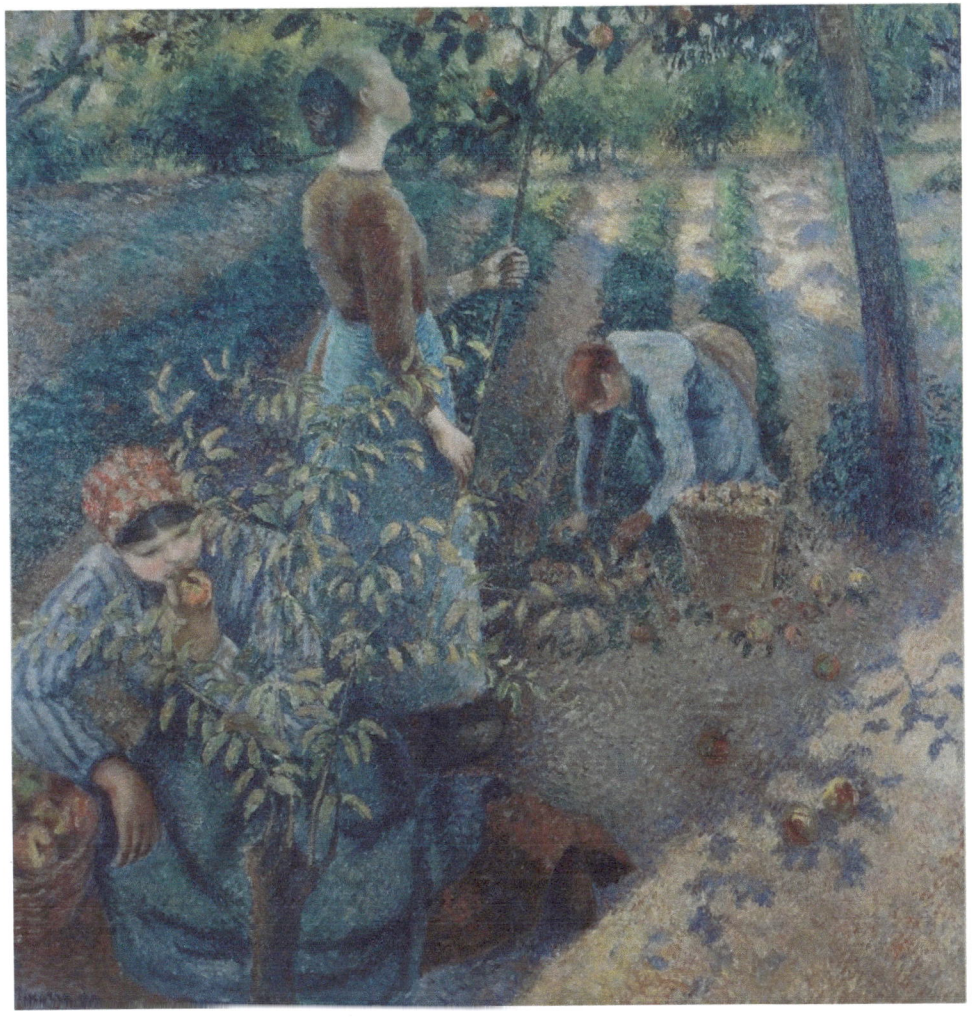

Fig. 13.
Apple-Picking, 1886, Ohara Museum of Art,
Kurashiki, Japan [PDRS 824]

11. Ibid., 3:540.

Pissarro worked on his painting *Apple-Picking* (1886) for two years in his studio. Then three years later, he reworked it using Pointillist technique and exhibited it in the Eighth Impressionist Exhibition in May to June 1886.[11]

This large and square painting (49 by 49 inches), with its intricate geometrical composition, is one of the most intriguing of Pissarro's œuvre. The lack of a horizon line creates instability, tilting the picture plane forward. Within the square, a large dark rectangle is diagonal to the square. Whether it is a shadow is not at all clear, since there seems to be no shadow on the women's faces. The rectangle is anchored on the right by a slanting tree trunk and pinned on the lower left corner by a full basket of apples.

Layered on the dark space is a triangle of three figures, one of them nearly touching the top of the canvas. The woman in the lower left is partially hidden by a large spray of leaves that curves toward the middle woman's hands and connects with her staff, forming a diagonal from the lower left to the top of the canvas. If the staff were extended, it would meet the tree trunk, forming another angle. Between the staff and tree trunk behind the kneeling woman are stripes of bluish green and pale orange, emphasizing the upward motion. The triangles in the upper left and lower right repeat the two pairs of complementary colors—the bluish green with pale orange and the green leaves with the red apples. The luxurious design of rich colors expressed in heavy impasto resembles a magnificent tapestry.

In 1885, when Pissarro met Georges Seurat, he began experimenting with Pointillism. However, Pissarro's paintings clearly show that for several previous years, he had been using the divisionist technique, placing small "points" of different colors close to each other. Though Pissarro did not fully adopt Seurat's method of complete separation of dots, he did experiment with the technique intensely for about four years. Then, discouraged by the loss of spontaneity and the time required for each canvas, he wrote, "I have had to call it a day—it was high time!"[12]

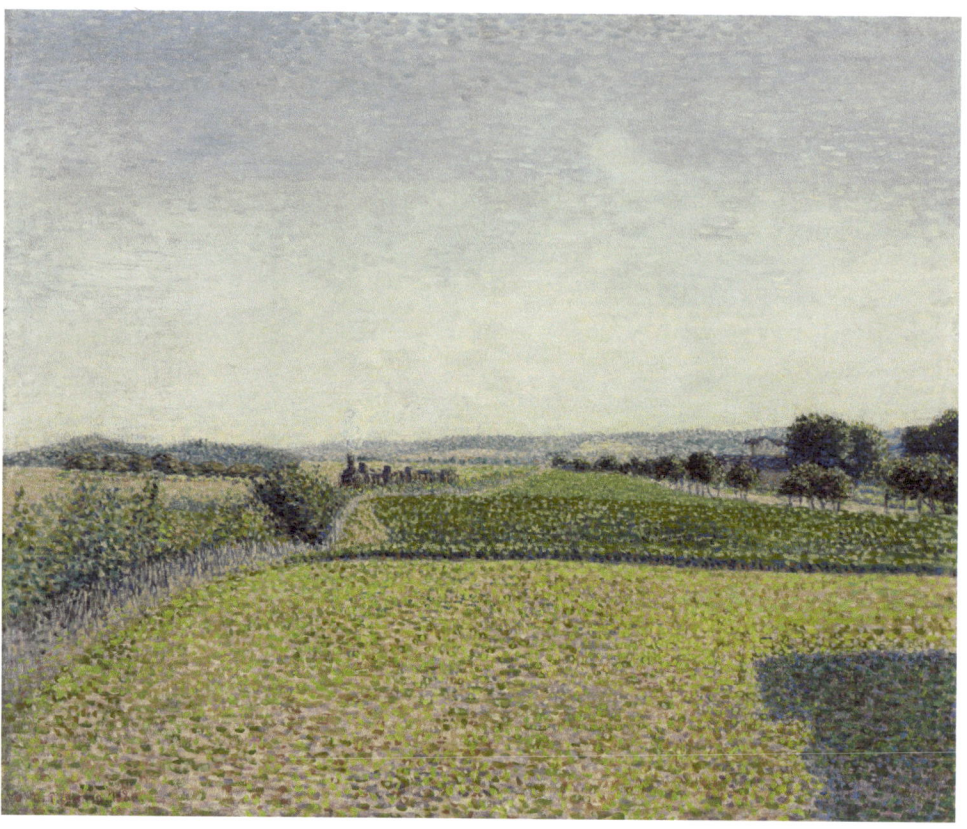

During those years, Pissarro created many Pointillist masterpieces. (More on Pointillism in Chapter 7.) *The Dieppe Railway* (1886) is classic Pointillism, constructed entirely of small dots placed side-by-side, most evident in the wide expanse of fields but also continuing up into the intense blue sky. Aside from

Fig. 14.
The Dieppe Railway, 1886, Philadelphia Museum of Art, Bequest of Helen Tyson Madeira, 2014 [PDRS 828]

12. Ibid., 1:217.

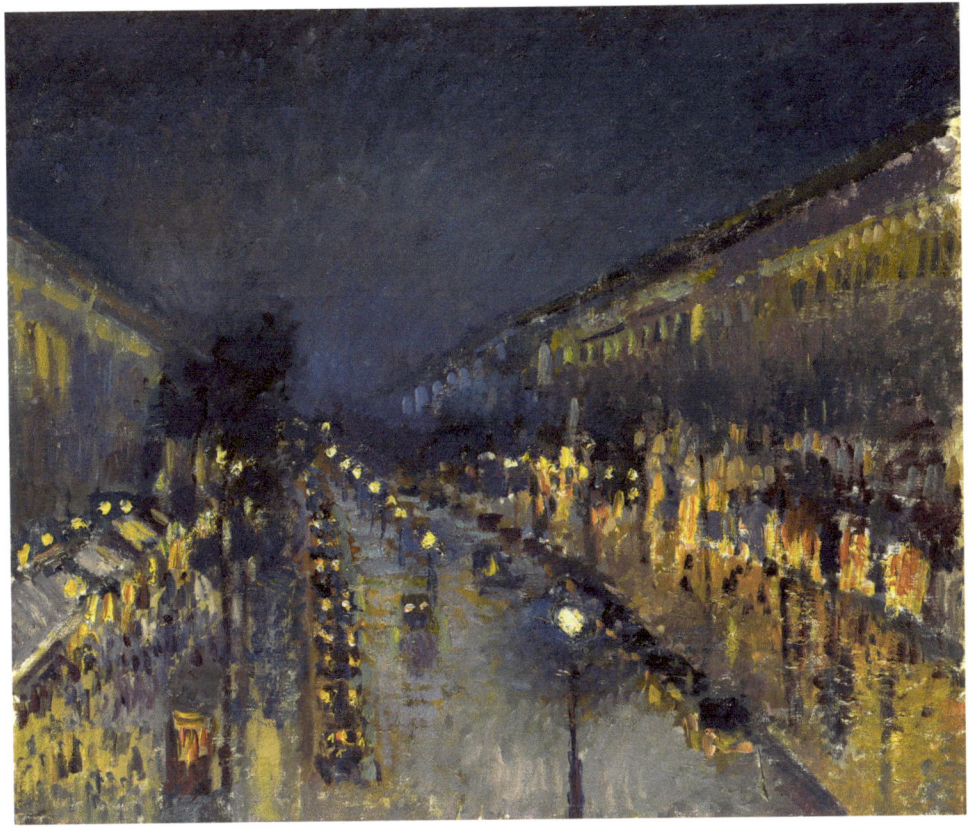

Fig. 15.
Boulevard Montmartre, Night Effect, 1897, The National Gallery, London [PDRS 1168]

interruption is the dark geometric form in the lower-right corner, perhaps a shadow from an unseen building. Right above it is a parallelogram of dark green and a strip of yellow-green interrupted by a dark-green wedge. On the left a diagonal of low bushes leads from the lower-left corner to the near center of the canvas, forming the path of the railroad tracks. The train itself is almost lost in the design of color blocks. The cloudless sky is another color block fading from intense blue to almost white before it meets the horizon. The emphasis on the color dots forces the viewer's attention on the texture of the paint, and while the technique is Pointillist, the overall effect is abstract.

the technique, this painting has strong abstract characteristics. The site itself is quite insignificant, but Pissarro stripped it bare of any complicating images. He constructed large color blocks—the dominant one in the foreground appears yellow but is actually composed of red, yellow, and green dots in various shades. The only

On his frequent trips to Paris, Pissarro painted boulevards and public places not as realistic reproductions of the scene but following his "sensation." The painting *Boulevard Montmartre, Night Effect* (1897) depicts a busy street on a rainy night. At the bottom, diagonal lines expand into three wedges. The side wedges are simply flattened images of tall buildings accented by patches of red and yellow, painted wet-on-wet. The center wedge is a shiny, wide, blue-green ribbon interrupted by little bug-eyed forms and a center line of bright white spots. The upper wedge begins near the center in dark blue and radiates to the top in increasingly darker shades of blue. Any indication of perspective is negated by the dramatic design of the colors and strong flat shapes. In fact, this painting can be viewed upside down, creating an effect that is just as pleasing to the eye. The painting itself is a celebration of brushstrokes painted wet-on-wet, short patches, and small dots of color overlapping each other, creating visual texture in an abstract pattern.

On his trip to Rouen in 1898, Pissarro made three paintings of the rue de l'Épicerie, a street near a large open-air market held every Friday. One of the paintings shows the street at midmorning, bustling with shoppers and vendors; another shows the same street on a rainy morning with few pedestrians about. Perhaps the most dramatic of

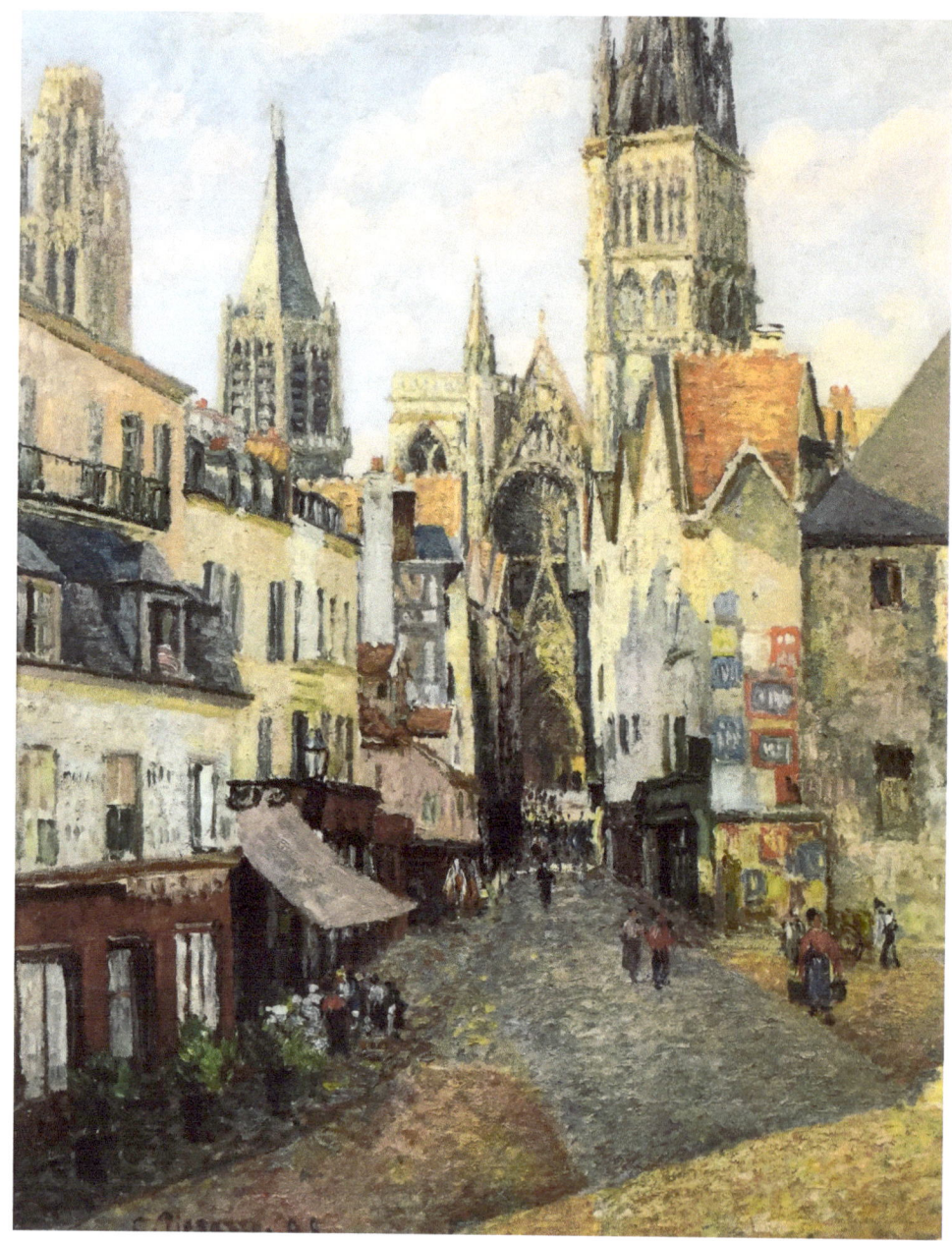

the three is this one, *Rue de l'Épicerie in Rouen, Late Afternoon* (1898). With the few pedestrians relegated to the sidelines, Pissarro focused on the cobblestoned street in the foreground. The flattened buildings on the sides act as theater flats, providing framework. The doorway of the cathedral, usually a major focal point for other artists, is reduced to simply brushstrokes, suggesting the Gothic arches Pissarro so admired. Rushing from its portals are a series of color blocks filling the foreground. The largest one, slabs of paint ranging from dark blue to gray, is nearly rectangular, extending from the cathedral door to the lower edge. A large triangle of red, dark orange, and tawny beige fills the lower-left corner. A similar segment lies to the right of the blue section. Slicing across the right corner is a small, bright-yellow triangle, shading into orange. The whole geometric effect is one of primary color blocks, giving importance to blue, bordered by reds, and accented by a touch of yellow—obviously the abstract pattern Pissarro wanted to highlight.

On his second trip to Dieppe in 1902, Pissarro wrote his son Lucien: "Dieppe is a wonderful place for a painter who enjoys life, movement, color. . . . In spite of the dense crowds, I have decided to go back there again this year."[13] He rented an extra room to use as a studio because of its excellent views of the fish market, the quai, and the basin.[14] He painted *The Fishing Port, Dieppe, Low Tide* (1902) showing a harbor for fishing boats in high tide and virtually empty of water at low tide. It seems a strange choice of motif, but Pissarro made it a study in abstraction, creating a composition that contrasts two different fields of paint—the sky above with the city and harbor below.

The basin sides create a geometric form that dominates the center of the painting. Tiny, dark brushstrokes line the near side. It is impossible to tell what they represent, though the variations suggest a row of people. Across the basin, dark pilings are driven deep into the earth. The basin is almost empty, except for a sliver of green that might be a shallow strip of water.

13. Ibid., 1:307.
14. Ibid., 3:878.

Fig. 16. (left)
Rue de l'Épicerie in Rouen, Late Afternoon, 1898,
Private collection
[PDRS 1223]

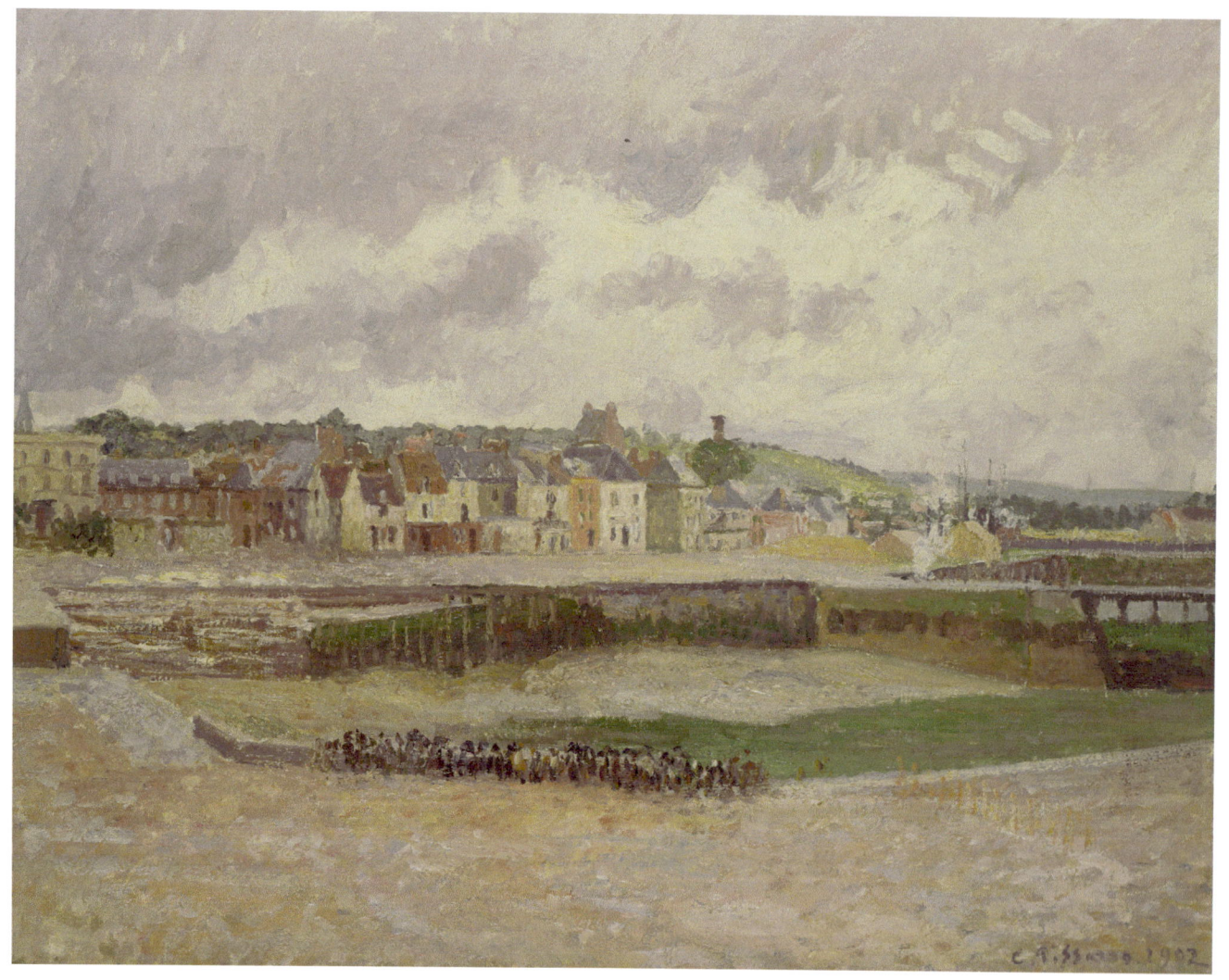

Beyond the basin, a sketchy row of houses, made with slabs of paint and dark lines for windows, provides a flat backdrop. In the foreground, large dabs of coral, gray, cream, and rose paint overlap. The drama occurs in the sky, where triangular dark clouds provide a strong diagonal to balance the rectilinear shapes below. This is the kind of painting that might be avoided by someone who is looking for a picturesque scene, but it offers rewards for the person willing to spend time with it and absorb its unique characteristics.

In choosing motifs for paintings, Pissarro was more interested in what he could do with the image than what it represented to other people. Richard Brettell explains this aspect well: "Pissarro was an intellectual painter. He analyzed forms and the relationships between forms in a detailed, almost grammatical fashion. His choice of a radically bounded landscape as *his* landscape gave him authority over a restricted range of form, from which using existing and invented conventions, he created new landscape worlds."[15]

In 1897, Pissarro described the process he had developed over a lifetime to the young painter Louis le Bail:

The motive should be observed more for shapes and colors than for drawing. . . . Precise drawing is dry and hampers the impression of the whole; it destroys all sensations. Do not insist on the outlines of objects; it is a brushstroke of the right value and color which should produce the drawing. In a mass, the greatest difficulty is not to establish a minute contour but to paint what is within. Don't work bit by bit, but take in everything at once by placing tones everywhere . . . . The eye should not be fixed on a particular point but should take in everything, while simultaneously observing the reflections that the colors produce on their surroundings. Keep everything going on an equal basis; use small brushstrokes and try to put down your perceptions immediately. Do not proceed according to rules and principles, but paint what you observe and feel.[16]

Fig. 17. (left)
The Fishing Port, Dieppe, Low Tide, 1902, Montreal Museum of Fine Arts, Canada, Gift of Mr. and Mrs. Paul Ivanier [PDRS 1452]

15. Brettell, *Pissarro and Pontoise*, 91.

16. Rewald, *Camille Pissarro*, 148.

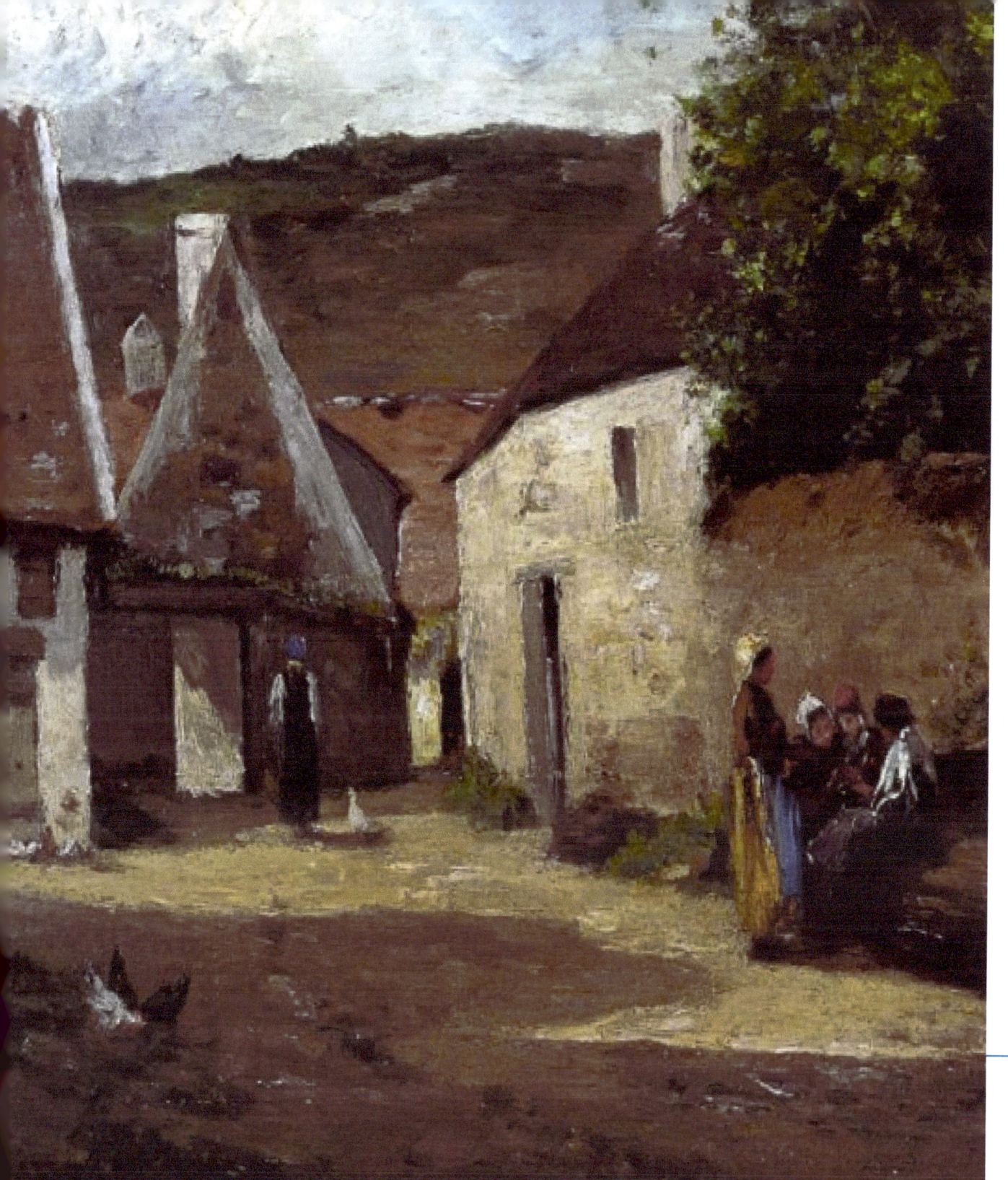

Fig. 18.
Village Scene, Women Chatting, detail, 1863, Private collection [PDRS 70]

3 Ahead of His Time from the Beginning

Pissarro was from an early age able to follow his own instincts in terms of style, subject matter, and technique, thereby defining for himself his role as an artist long before he went to France as an adult.[1]

— Christopher Lloyd

Many reviews and studies of Pissarro's work look only at his work in the 1870s, totally ignoring the paintings and drawings from St. Thomas, Venezuela, and his early years in France. This is misleading, because it implies that Pissarro was on a parallel level of expertise as other Impressionists. In fact, Pissarro was more advanced than his Impressionist colleagues; he was ten years older and already an experienced artist. By the age of twenty-four (or perhaps a year or two earlier), he was a working artist selling paintings, while Monet, Renoir, and Sisley were still in their early teens. In a drawing Pissarro made of the studio he shared with Fritz Melbye in Caracas from 1852 to 1854, there is a portrait bearing Pissarro's signature of a man in a tall hat, implying that Pissarro took portrait commissions.[2]

Proper consideration of Pissarro's early paintings has always been difficult because of their scarcity. During the Franco-Prussian War (1870-71), while Pissarro was in exile in Brittany and London, his home in Louveciennes was occupied by Prussian soldiers, who used his canvases

1. Katherine Rothkopf, *Pissarro: Creating the Impressionist Landscape* (London: Philip Wilson, 2006), 24.

2. Alfredo Boulton, *Pissarro in Venezuela*, trans. Stanton L. Catlin and Phyllis Freeman (New York: J.B. Watkins, 1968), 11.

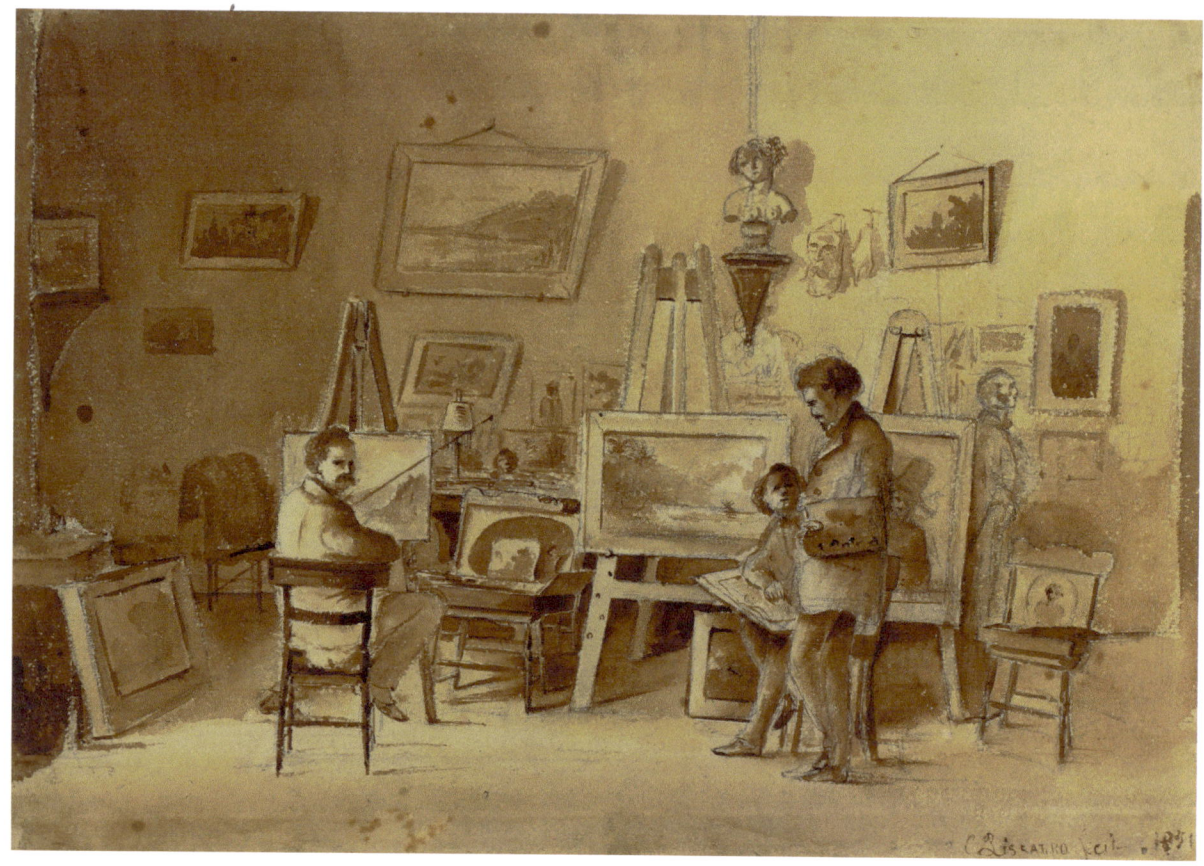

Fig. 19.
The Artists' Studio, 1854, watercolor, Banco Central de Venezuela, Caracas

3. Ralph E. Shikes and Paula Harper, *Pissarro: His Life and Work* (New York: Horizon Press, 1980), 101.

4. Pissarro and Durand-Ruel Snollaerts, *Pissarro: Catalogue Critique des Peintures*, 1:131.

5. Richard R. Brettell and Christopher Lloyd, *Catalogue of Drawings by Camille Pissarro in the Ashmolean Museum, Oxford* (Oxford: Oxford University Press, 1980), 5.

for aprons as they butchered animals or to cover mud in the garden.[3] The loss was immense for Pissarro: "I had between twelve and fifteen hundred—paintings, studies, sketches, the work of twenty years of my life."[4] This large number has been questioned, but if you consider that Pissarro had been a working artist for more than nineteen years by then and that he included studies and sketches in that number, it is not unrealistic.

Even as a child, Pissarro had a natural inclination for drawing.[5] His talents were encouraged at the Pension Savary, the prestigious boarding school near Paris

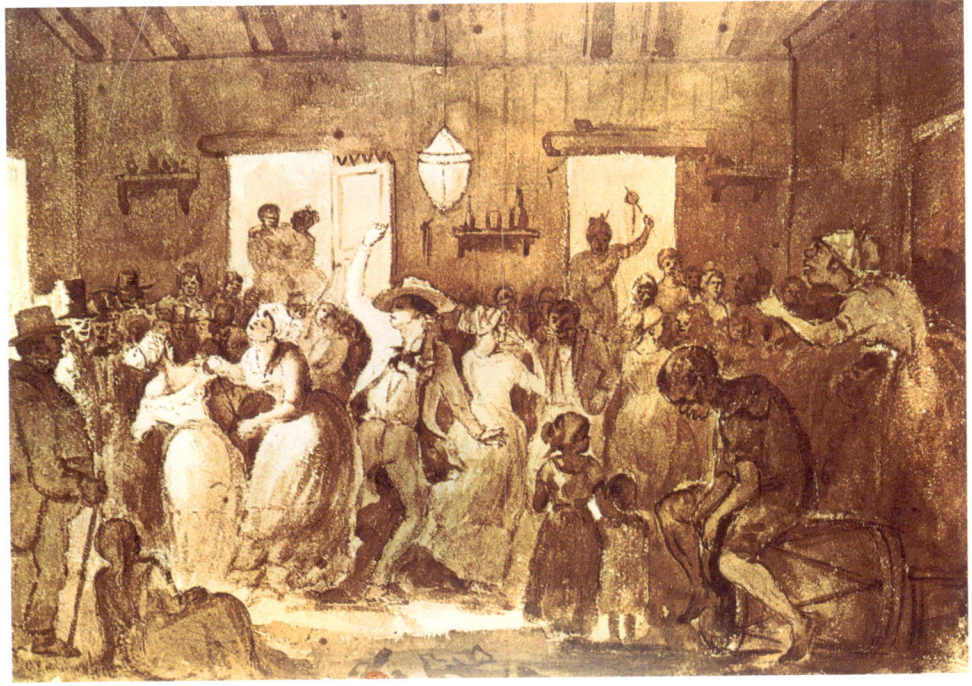

Fig. 20.
Carnival Dance, 1853-54, watercolor, Banco Central de Venezuela, Caracas

6. Pissarro and Durand-Ruel Snollaerts, *Pissarro: Catalogue Critique des Peintures*, 1:99.

7. Ibid., 1:101.

8. Richard R. Brettell and Karen Zukowski, *Camille Pissarro in the Caribbean, 1850-1855* (St. Thomas, U.S. Virgin Islands: The Hebrew Congregation of St. Thomas, 1996), 14.

where his parents had sent him at the age of twelve to get a proper education. When he returned to St. Thomas at the age of seventeen, he was required to work in his father's business. While he supervised the movement of merchandise in the harbor, he sketched sailing vessels and men unloading cargo. At that early age, he knew his own mind and confided to his cousin and a friend that he wanted to be an artist.[6] His opportunity appeared when

he became friends with the young Danish artist Fritz Melbye, who was visiting St. Thomas. In 1852, they went to Venezuela, where they established an art studio and worked together for two years. Later, Pissarro said of that adventure, "Without giving it a thought I dropped everything and ran off to Caracas."[7]

Few works of art remain from those early years in Venezuela and the Caribbean, but there is enough to demonstrate the advanced level of technique and artistic ability of the young Pissarro. Brettell notes: "The esthetic of Camille Pissarro emerged from a real dialogue with Melbye, a kind of shared or mutual artistic practice that Pissarro himself valued throughout his working life."[8]

In *Carnival Dance* (1853-54), the composition is quite sophisticated: Pissarro used bright light from the open doorway to focus attention on the dancers' movements, while shadowed figures provide a frame. The angled bodies of two women set the rhythm for the cavorting man, his arm flying high above his head. The onlookers in the lighted doorways respond with their own individual gestures. Dana Gordon says: "Clearly Pissarro must have studied Dutch painting and drawing while in school in Paris, but he goes well beyond this knowledge with his ability to portray the specific local nature and ferment in this scene."[9]

Pissarro was eager to learn from Melbye, who by that time had already mounted an exhibition of his own work in Copenhagen.[10] Together, they explored the mountains of Venezuela and worked in their art studio on the Plaza Mayor, overlooking the daily market. It was there, far away from Paris academies that Pissarro "penetrated into nature, into color, and into light. His lack of academic training enabled him to discern values in these realms even before he drew forms."[11] He watched as Melbye prepared his palette with "lilac, Veronese green,

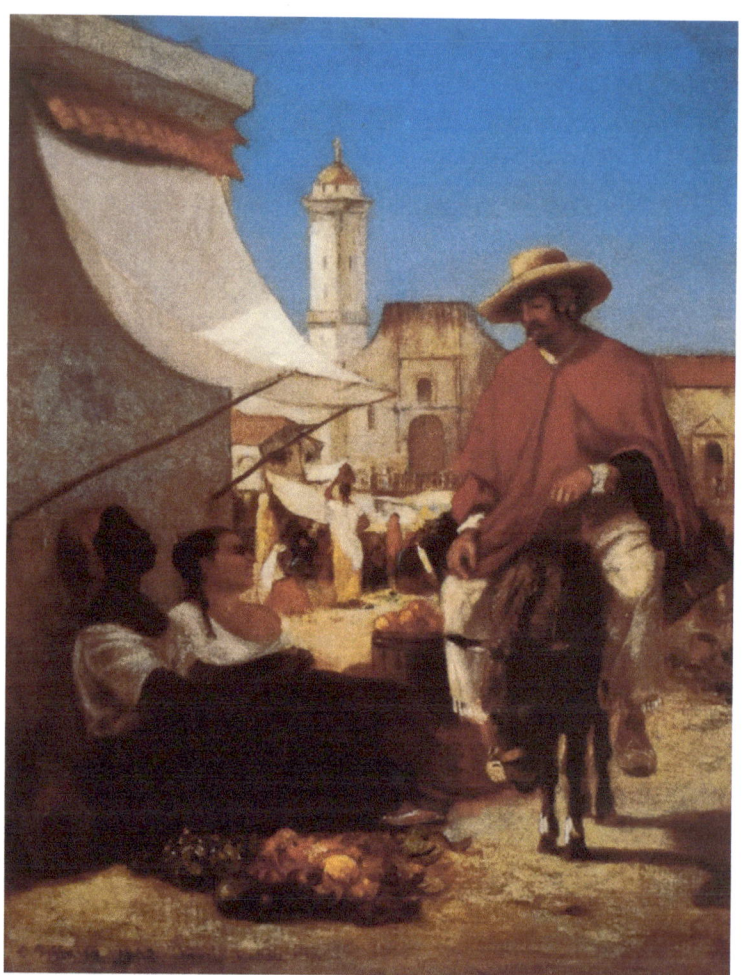

Fig. 21.
Market Scene on the Plaza Mayor, Caracas, 1852-54, Presidential Residence, La Casone, Caracas, Venezuela [PDRS 1]

---

9. Personal correspondence to author, May 3, 2018.

10. Boulton, *Pissarro in Venezuela*, 6.

11. Ibid., 18.

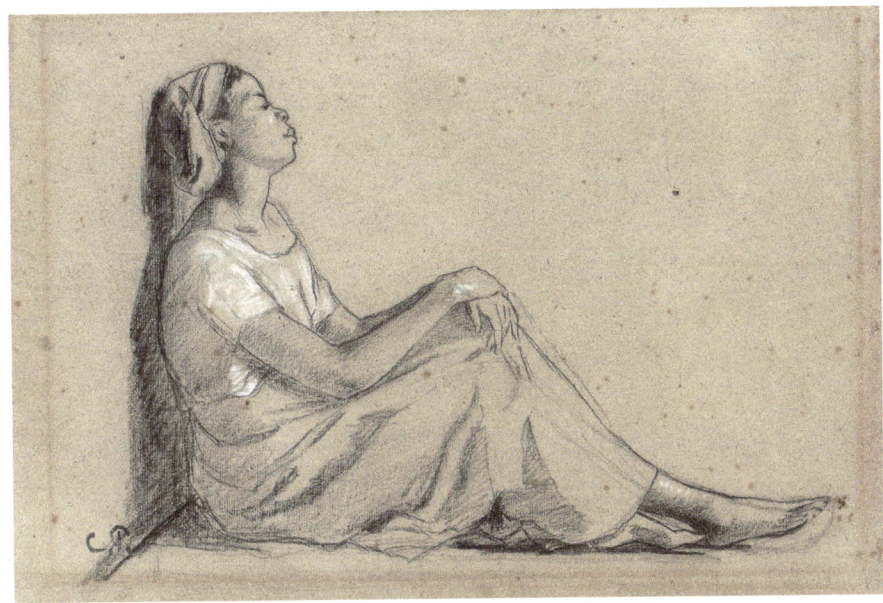

Fig. 22.
Young Woman Seated,
1852-54, charcoal
and white highlights,
Wildenstein Institute
Archives, Paris

depiction of the two women reclining under the awning. The young artist cleverly depicted intense sunlight beside pale shadow on the awning with bright yellow at the front and warm gray in the back, a startling contrast with the deep shadow underneath. Pissarro's sense of perspective is obvious in the distant figures and buildings lining the plaza, including the cathedral watchtower, a familiar landmark in Caracas.

Perhaps the most interesting elements of the painting are the dramatic colors: the intense blue sky, the man's bright-red cloak, and the brilliant yellow on the tent, which Pissarro used to emphasize specific shapes. These were not colors that artists of the French academy would have used, and they certainly would not have put them side-by-side as did Pissarro.

The drawing *Young Woman Seated* served as a study for the figure on the left in the painting. The technical ability of the young artist is apparent in the easy depiction of her posture, executed with

gray, ocher, and cobalt—pigments then considered outlandish in painting nature."[12] Pissarro's oil paintings of this period displayed "a plastic quality, an impasto of paint and a palette that were then considered to be the antithesis of academicism."[13]

All of this is evident in the painting *Market Scene on the Plaza Mayor, Caracas* (1852-54). The composition is tight and solid; the man in the bright-red cloak provides a prominent focal point. Pissarro's advanced ability to paint figures is evident in his

12. Ibid., 16.
13. Ibid.

43

numerous broken lines, the natural grace of her arms and hands, and the delicacy of the shadows in the folds of her skirt and at her back. This is a drawing of a highly skilled artist.

Pissarro arrived in Paris in 1855, just before the end of the immense and consequential Exposition Universelle. He had time to visit the Fine Arts Building, where some five thousand works of art were displayed, including paintings by Delacroix, Courbet, Ingres, and Corot. Courbet, incensed that some of his paintings had been turned down for the main exhibition, built his own exhibition space, where he displayed a large number of his own paintings.[14]

The exposition gave Pissarro a chance to compare his own work to that of artists currently being accepted by the Paris Salon. He chose to disregard academic painting formulas. Instead, he began investigating new methods that would allow him to submit paintings to the Salon without compromising his own integrity as a painter. These early images, such as *Banks of the Marne*

in Winter (1866) reveal that "he was painting innovative works earlier (than previously thought)" and demonstrate his "gradual evolution . . . toward modernism."[15]

During his first year in Paris, Pissarro made a group of nine paintings with tropical themes, some of which were taken to Lille for sale by a friend.[16] These were based on his sketches and memories of brilliant sunlight playing on tropical colors. The painting *A Creek with Palm Trees* (1856) looks very much like an Impressionist painting, but it was created **eighteen years before the First Impressionist Exhibition**. It has the characteristics of Impressionism: a picturesque motif, the play of sunlight on the bay, a slight mist enveloping the cliffs, colorful clouds, loose brushstrokes, bright tints of pink and blue with dark green, and reflections in the water. This painting proves that Pissarro had developed all the characteristics normally attributed to Impressionism and was using them in paintings long before the initial glimmerings of the Impressionist period.

14. Pissarro and Durand-Ruel Snollaerts, *Pissarro: Catalogue Critique des Peintures*, 1:106.

15. Rothkopf, *Pissarro: Creating the Impressionist Landscape*, 12.

16. Pissarro and Durand-Ruel Snollaerts, *Pissarro: Catalogue Critique des Peintures*, 2:49.

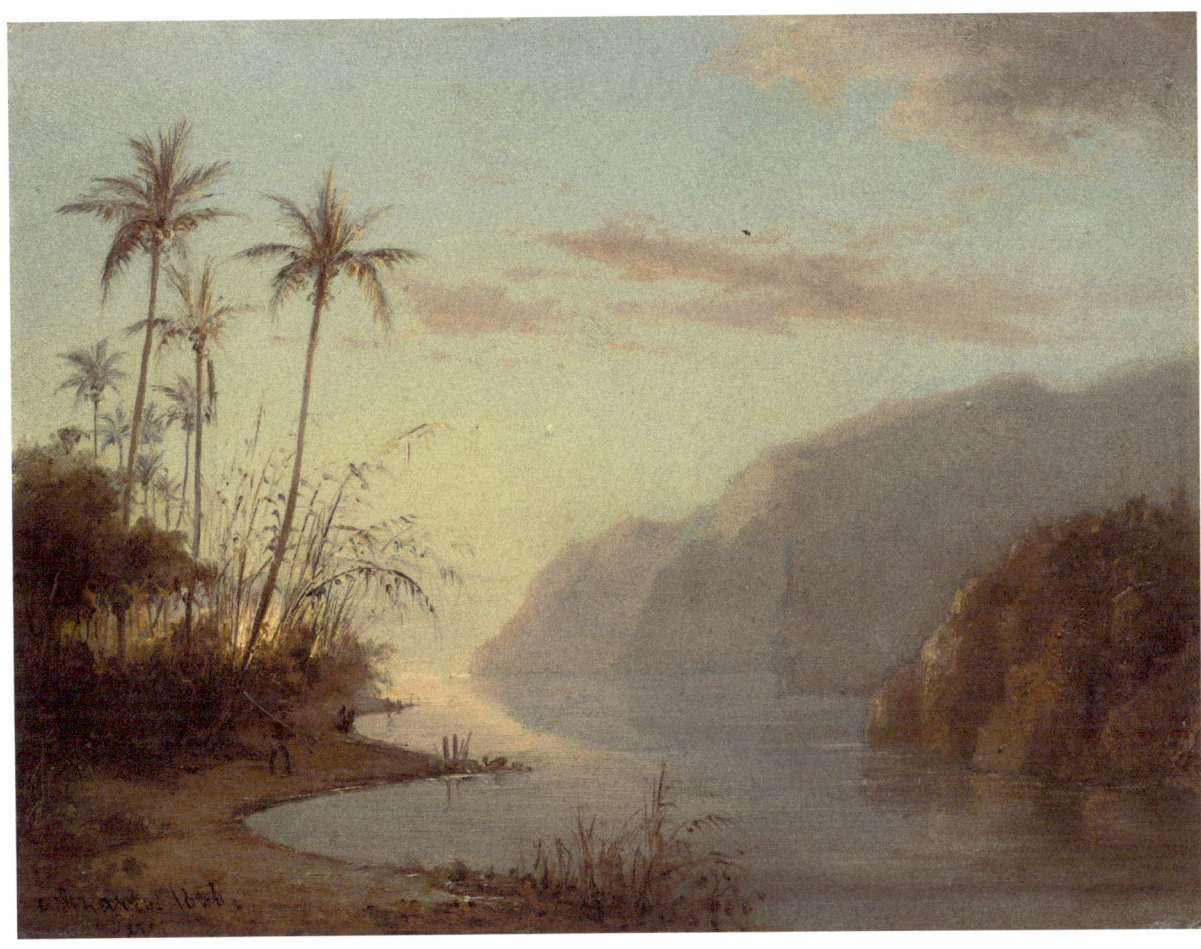

Fig. 23.
A Creek with Palm Trees,
1856, National Gallery
of Art, Washington, D.C.,
Collection of Mr. and Mrs.
Paul Mellon [PDRS 16]

17. Ibid.

Pissarro's earliest paintings that are shown in *Pissarro: Catalogue Critique des Peintures*[17] are almost all small in size. It is not until 1864 that a much larger canvas (32¼ by 42½ inches) appears. That painting, *Banks of the Marne* (1864; see fig 33), was the second painting by Pissarro to be selected for the Paris Salon.

When Pissarro painted *Ploughing, Bérelles* (c. 1860), he had been in France for several years and was familiar with the

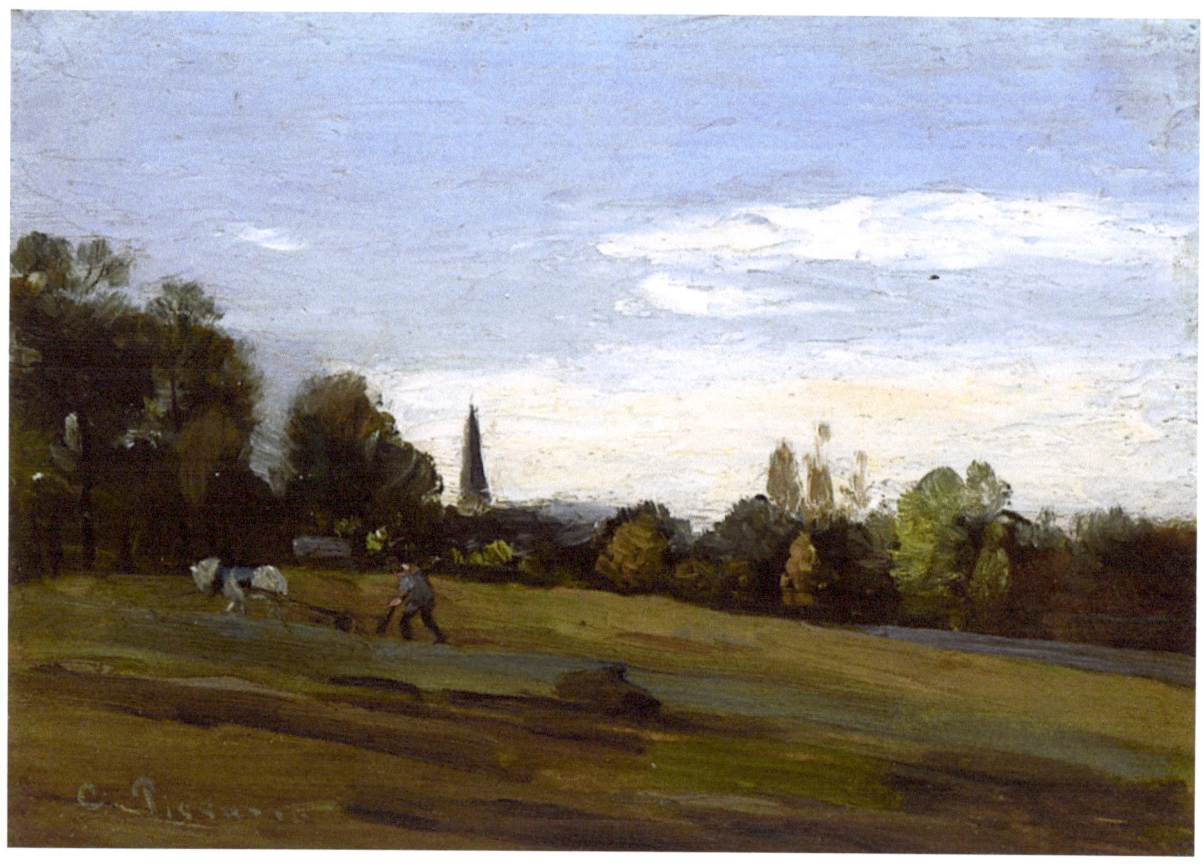

Fig. 24.
Ploughing, Berélles, c. 1860,
Private collection [PDRS 46]

work of other artists. He absorbed some of what he saw, but he refused to pattern himself after anyone else. Art historian Christopher Lloyd observed: "Although firmly committed to new developments in painting and in many ways pioneering them himself, Pissarro seemed to stand apart, as though preferring to monitor progress from a distance."[18]

All of the typical features are present: the church steeple, the farmer and his white horse, and green foliage. But none of these seem to make much difference compared

18. Rothkopf, *Pissarro: Creating the Impressionist Landscape,* 17.

to the large area of bare earth covering the foreground. With large, broad strokes and loads of paint, Pissarro's hand moved across the canvas, leaving streaks of brown, red, and green in its wake. The strokes, rough and irregular, move in a slightly downward diagonal, creating the illusion of a slope. Just below the middle of the canvas, Pissarro placed the horizon line, adorned with trees, bushes, and the omnipresent steeple. Here he created the structure for a more dramatic diagonal, beginning at the left with the tall trees, skirting the top of the steeple to the low bushes on the right. One tree, almost in the center, deserves special attention. Its crown is composed of short brushstrokes—the "constructive" strokes—that go in all directions. There is no attempt to create leaves or limbs. This little tree is decorated with strokes of paint.

The foreground is so important that the sky seems like an afterthought. The brushstrokes there are softer, more demure, and unassuming, lest they detract from the drama on the ground below. By emphasizing the brushstrokes in the foreground,

creating the trees and shrubs with slabs of overlapping color, reducing the figures to mere sketches, and creating strong contrast between the dark earth and light sky, Pissarro clearly intended to draw attention to the paint itself rather than the banal farming scene.

In France, Pissarro chose the same kind of motifs that he had selected in the Caribbean. At first glance, the painting *Village Scene, Women Chatting* (1863) seems like an ordinary street with people and chickens scattered about the canvas. But Pissarro used the bright sunlight to call attention to the structures, appearing as a series of color blocks. The large yellow house has no real door, only a slit, and one tiny window. Together with the wall, it forms a long rectangle that extends beyond the canvas edge. The building on the left has blocks of gray and red with large doors bisected by a diagonal line separating light and shadow. That shadow, together with the left side of the peaked roof, forms a long diagonal ending at the top of the small white block. The gray

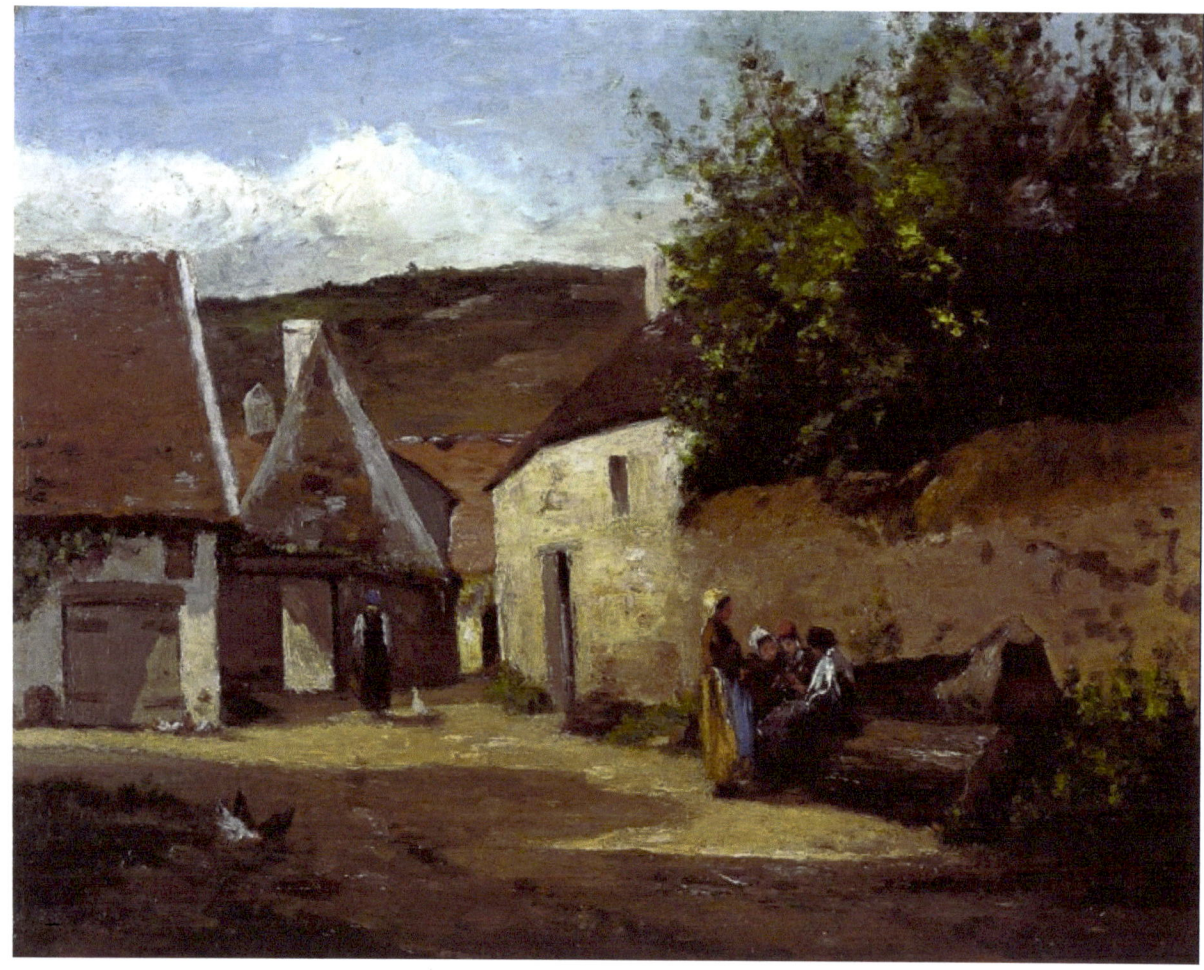

Fig. 25.
Village Scene, Women Chatting, 1863, Private collection [PDRS 70]

building with a pointed top should create depth; instead, it almost overlaps the structure on the left.

These flattened forms, jammed together and set against an indeterminate background, fill the canvas, leaving little room for the sky. The foreground is dominated by a large, dark shadow, its intensity conveyed by the white and black chickens.

The women are mere brushstrokes; it is hard to tell if there are three or four. Pissarro took an ordinary scene and used its innate geometrical shapes to make an assertive statement about form and color.

Looking at these last two paintings, some viewers might be tempted to think that Pissarro did not have the skills necessary to create depth, paint a detailed figure, or compose a painting in the traditional way. However, the paintings he made in Caracas clearly demonstrate his technical and artistic abilities to construct street scenes with perspective, to compose paintings with a dominant focal point, and to paint realistic figures. In these last two paintings, Pissarro is clearly experimenting with paint, brushstrokes, shapes, depth, and geometric composition.

Even though very few of Pissarro's paintings from this period are extant, there are sufficient examples to demonstrate his experimentation and inventiveness with the materials of art. He chose seemingly unimportant, even banal, scenes, and

eliminated all narrative or story-telling. He simplified the motif to its geometric frame and reduced buildings to flattened planes. He used color to create shapes and forms, overlapping them to deny depth, creating abstract shapes. He accentuated brushstrokes, calling attention to the canvas itself.

By the middle of 1865, Pissarro's career was well underway, and five of his paintings had been selected for the Paris Salon. The patterns of work that would continue throughout his life were already established. He was able to take simple landscapes and elevate them into uncommon works of art. He had discovered approaches totally unique to his time, techniques that we now term as abstract. He had already accomplished all of this **before** the birth of Impressionism.

Thadée Natanson, editor of *La Revue Blanche* in the 1890s, said: "Nothing of novelty or of excellence appeared that Pissarro had not been among the first, if not the very first to discern and defend."[19]

19. Christopher Lloyd, *Pissarro* (New York: Rizzoli, 1981), 5.

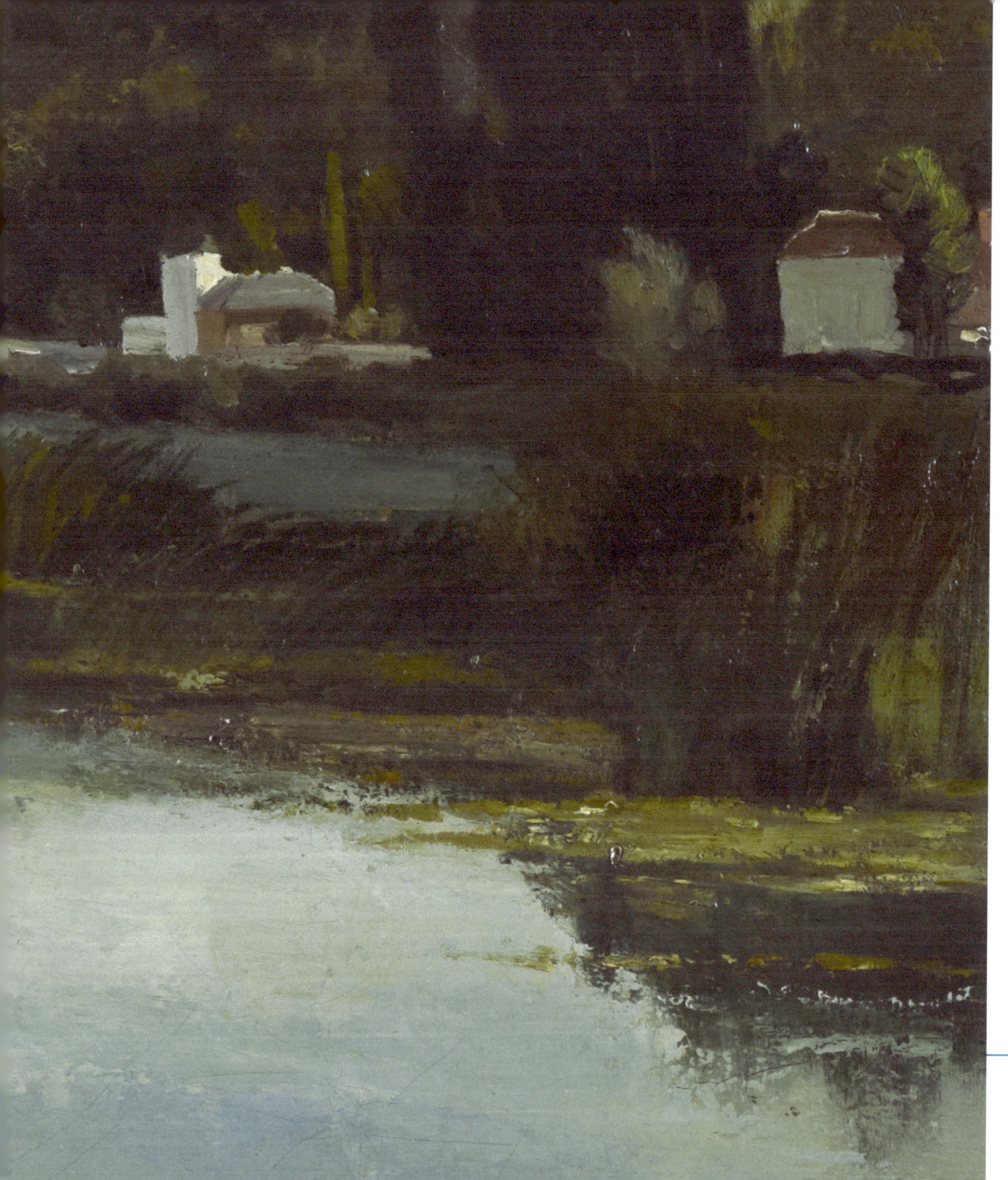

Fig. 26.
Banks of the Marne at Chennevières, detail, c. 1865, National Galleries of Scotland, Edinburgh [PDRS 103]

4 Pissarro's Tradition of Modern Art

Pissarro was twenty-five when he returned to Paris from the Caribbean, already an experienced landscape painter and free of the stultifying conventions of the French academies. During the late 1850s, he sought out his great predecessors in French art: Corot, Courbet, Delacroix, and others. Influenced by them but never a disciple, he integrated what he learned into his own vision.[1]

—Dana Gordon

Pissarro was developing a new way of painting; but at the same time, he respected the tradition of French painting, acknowledging the works of David, Ingres, Delacroix, Courbet, and Corot. He explained his artistic legacy in an 1898 letter to his son Lucien: "We have today a general concept inherited from our great modern painters, hence we have a **tradition of modern art** [emphasis mine], and I am for following this tradition while we inflect it in terms of **our individual points of view** [emphasis mine]."[2] Throughout his life, Pissarro was not afraid to learn from anyone; but he took that knowledge and applied it in his own way, following his own sensation. From the very beginning, he was artistically independent, forging his own path and inventing new artistic elements and techniques. However, a review of those who influenced him in his early years is informative.

1. Gordon, "An Intimate Exhibition That Rewards the Keen Eye."

2. Rewald, ed., *Camille Pissarro: Letters to His Son Lucien*, 329.

Wilfrid Savary

From 1842 to 1847, the young Pissarro studied at a boarding school near Paris and learned to draw from the headmaster, Wilfrid Savary.[3] It was from him that Pissarro acquired one of the fundamental aspects of his artistic life, the importance of working *en plein air* and drawing from nature. Not much is recorded about Pissarro's early years; however, a book written by Adolphe Tabarant and published in 1925 provides important insight. The author, who became acquainted with Pissarro in 1890, may have asked him directly about his first teacher.[4] Tabarant says that Savary, impressed with Pissarro's genuine gift for drawing, encouraged him. At a time when drawing from statues was the standard method of teaching art, Savary himself had "conceived a taste for drawing from nature, and did not hesitate to impart it."[5] When Pissarro returned in 1847 to St. Thomas and his father's business, he was "a very passable draughtsman, according to the most approved principles of direct observation."[6] The story has often been repeated that when Pissarro left, Savary told him more than once, "Mind you, don't forget to draw [coconut]-trees."[7] This important lesson, at the time considered to be radical and anti-academic, was perhaps the first notion about art that the young Pissarro ever absorbed.

At the École des Beaux-Arts, in Paris, students copied engravings or drew from plaster casts, learning the "correct" way to draw body parts and facial features. As they mastered the human form, they were taught fixed proportions and stereotyped positions that were considered noble and classic.[8] They learned punctilious modeling, using a minimum of six half-tones side by side, rendering the passage from one tone to another virtually imperceptible.[9] In his early years in Passy, Pissarro was almost certainly exposed to these formulaic methods of French academic teachers. When he was not in school, he visited the Louvre, the Salons, and the studio of Auguste Savary, a landscape painter and relation of Wilfrid Savary, who was a regular exhibitor at the Salon.[10] He obviously was familiar with the

3. Pissarro and Durand-Ruel Snollaerts, *Pissarro: Catalogue Critique des Peintures*, 1:99.

4. Tabarant, *Pissarro*, 61.

5. Ibid., 9.

6. Ibid.

7. Ibid.

8. Boime, *The Academy and French Painting in the Nineteenth Century*, 24-26.

9. Ibid., 38.

10. Pissarro and Durand-Ruel Snollaerts, *Pissarro: Catalogue Critique des Peintures*, 1:99; Tabarant, *Pissarro*, 8.

academic principles of painting. His earliest drawings and paintings show that the young Pissarro rejected academic standards and held fast to the concept of working from nature. He was so adamant about this that he later entreated his son Lucien "not to seek formulas, . . . not to fix the proportions in advance, . . . learn to see for yourself and to draw without relying on a ready made system."[11] This strong commitment to the concept of working before nature and painting *en plein air* probably attracted Pissarro to Corot, Courbet, and Daubigny during his first years as a working artist in France; hence, this early influence at the Pension Savary was a seminal event in his career.

Fritz Melbye

When Pissarro returned to St. Thomas in 1847, he took his place in the family business but spent much of his time drawing whatever was in front of him—sailing ships in the harbor, tropical landscapes, and people at work and leisure.[12] In May 1851, when he met the painter Fritz Melbye, who was commissioned by the Danish government to record the flora and fauna of the Danish Antilles and Central America,[13] Melbye was impressed by the expertise and vitality of the younger artist's drawings and convinced Pissarro to accompany him to Venezuela. Direct comparison of drawings of this period by Melbye and Pissarro demonstrates that "in nearly every case Pissarro's own artistic instincts were already comparatively well developed before his association with the Danish painter."[14]

Melbye's prior experience in the artistic circles of Copenhagen surpassed what Pissarro had experienced at that time. Melbye was four years older than Pissarro and had studied with his older brother, Anton Melbye, an academic artist known for his marine paintings. The younger Melbye became a competent landscape artist and had his first exhibition in Copenhagen in 1849.[15] Pissarro's first experience as a professional artist occurred when Fritz and Camille went together to Venezuela and established an art studio in Caracas.

11. Rewald, ed., *Camille Pissarro: Letters to His Son Lucien*, 34.

12. John Rewald, *The History of Impressionism*, 4th rev. ed. (New York: The Museum of Modern Art, 1973), 14.

13. Charles Kunstler, *Pissarro: Landscapes and Cities*, trans. Eva Kramer (New York: Justin K. Thannhauser Foundation, 1967), 10.

14. Brettell and Lloyd, *Catalogue of Drawings by Camille Pissarro in the Ashmolean Museum, Oxford*, 6; Richard Brettell has made extensive studies of Pissarro's work in the Caribbean and Venezuela and his collaboration with Melbye. For more, see Brettell and Zukowski, *Camille Pissarro in the Caribbean, 1850-1855: Drawings from the Collection at Olana*, 1996.

15. Boulton, *Pissarro in Venezuela*, 6.

Pissarro used that opportunity to observe and question everything that Melbye did, including how to develop the composition of a painting through a series of preparatory drawings. As Pissarro trekked through the forests and mountains of Venezuela with Melbye, he learned to observe the effect of changing light on colors and to experiment with new chromatic values in his paintings. Observing the colors Melbye used for his palette, Pissarro felt free to use a wide range of colors that he had not observed in Paris. Melby's skies were said to be luminous with "their grays, yellows, lilacs, clouds with a tropical brightness."[16] Dana Gordon said: "Perhaps the 'tropical brightness' stayed with Pissarro in the guise of pure, abstract color."[17]

This painting by Melbye shows a matter-of-fact recording of the topography of a new road leading to a town near Caracas. The contours of the mountains are as distinct as the planks on the side of the hut. The path of the newly carved road is carefully delineated by numerous detailed figures. Different kinds of foliage are meticulously

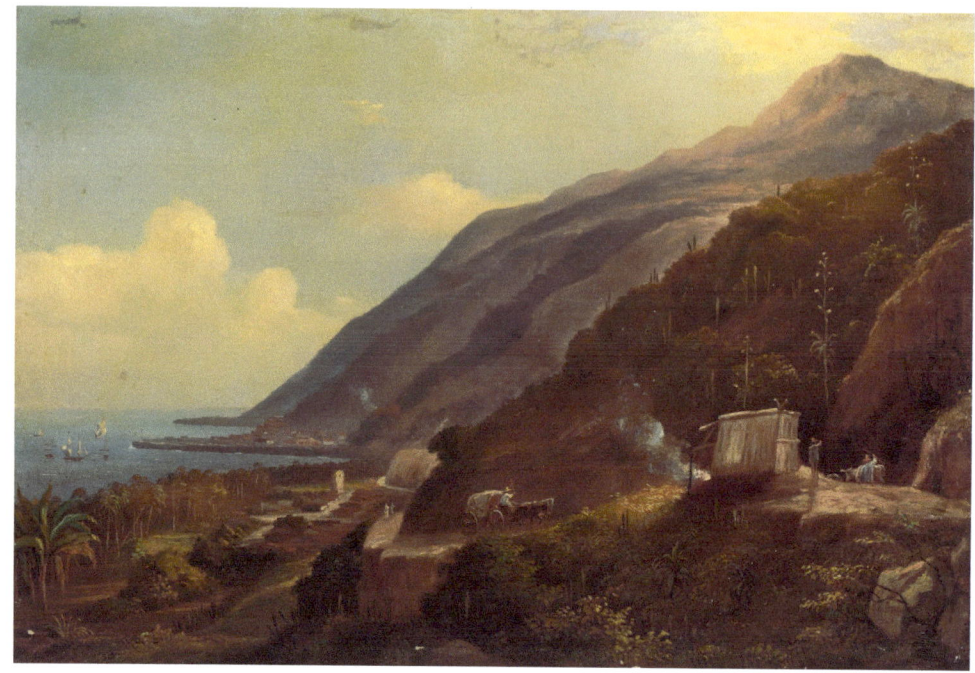

described in the foreground. Tiny sailing vessels in the bay are making their way toward the town at the foot of the mountain. In contrast, Pissarro's landscape *Mountain Landscape with a Hut* (c. 1854) has a different character altogether. Pissarro's composition is more complex, employing a series of diagonal lines, a technique the artist used throughout his career. The indistinct foliage in the left corner provides a small diagonal from the foot of the tree to the

Fig. 27.
Fritz Melbye, *Camino Nuevo de Maiquetia*, c. 1854, Private collection

16. Ibid., 14.

17. Correspondence with author, May 3, 2018.

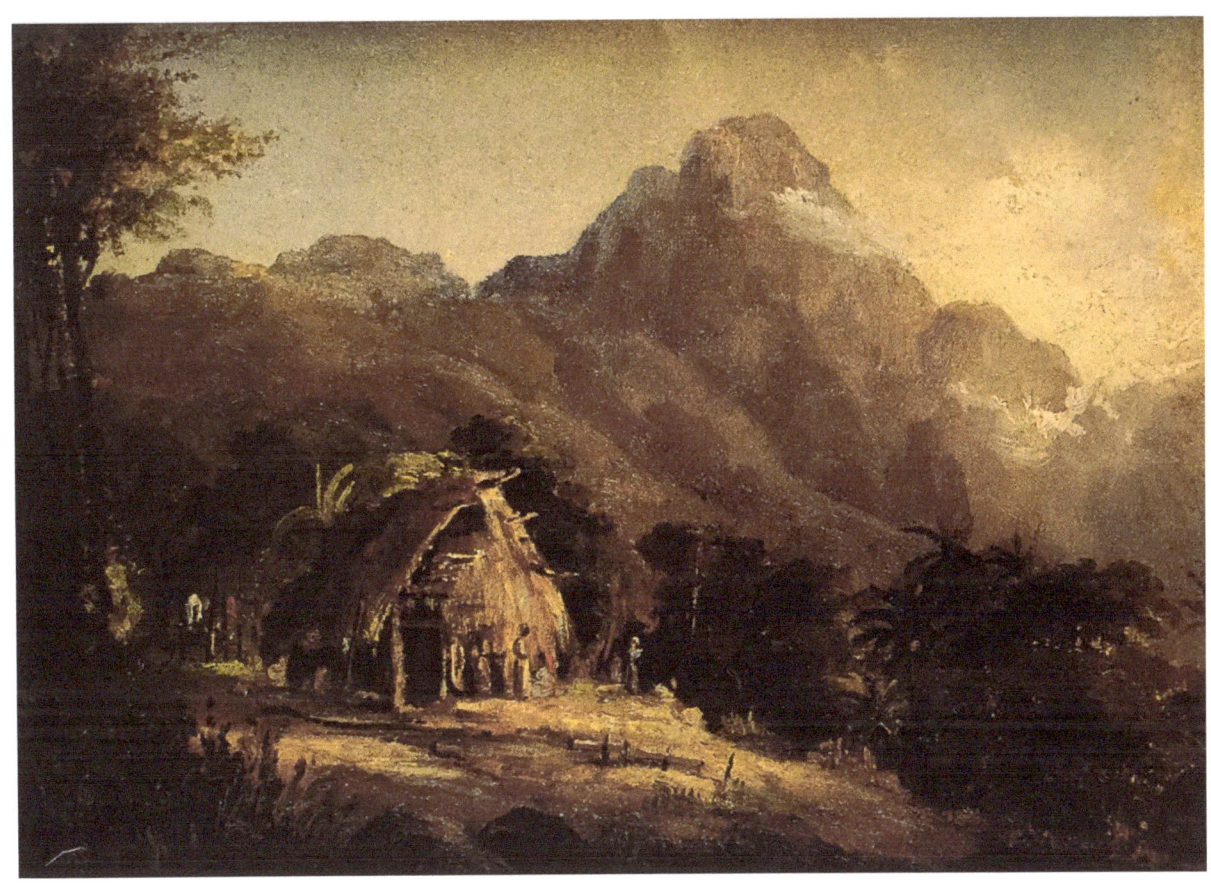

Fig. 28.
Mountain Landscape with a Hut, c. 1854, Private collection [PDRS 5]

18. Pissarro and Durand-Ruel Snollaerts, *Pissarro: Catalogue Critique des Peintures,* 2:43,

rocks. The second diagonal may be drawn from the top of the tree on the left to the crest of the two palm trees on the right. All of that leads up to the most dramatic diagonal, the right slope of what is probably Mt. Avila, which Pissarro and Melbye climbed in July 1854.[18] To ensure that the steepness of the mountain is noticed, Pissarro pierced the diagonal line with a white wispy cloud. The small hut, on level ground, surrounded by figures, provides safety and stability in these precipitous surroundings, and Pissarro focused attention on it with warm sunlight.

When Pissarro moved to France in 1855, he met Fritz Melbye's older brother, Anton Melbye. The young artist worked in his studio for a time and listed himself as a student of Anton Melbye for his Salon entries of 1859, 1864, 1865, and 1866. Anton Melbye introduced Pissarro to other artists in the city and supported his early efforts by purchasing a number of his paintings.[19]

Exposition Universelle of 1855

One of the first things Pissarro did upon his arrival in Paris was to visit the Exposition Universelle of 1855, where he saw works by Delacroix, Ingres, Corot, Courbet, and others.[20] He probably saw *The Stream* by Gustave Courbet, depicting a dark forest with glimmers of light reflecting on a small stream,[21] and *Souvenir de Marcoussis* by Corot, which was purchased by Napoleon III for his personal collection.[22]

The exposition provided the perfect platform for one of the most controversial debates in art history—classicism (Ingres emphasizing line) versus romanticism (Delacroix emphasizing color).[23] Evidence for both sides was presented in two special galleries: there were forty paintings and many drawings by Ingres and forty-two canvases by Delacroix.[24] Seeing so many works by these artists must have made a lifetime impression on the young artist, who had just arrived from the Caribbean. In 1891, he wrote his son Lucien about distinguishing between true and false art, "The art of 1830 is that of Corot, Courbet, Delacroix, Ingres. And it is eternally beautiful!"[25]

Eugène Delacroix

Pissarro recognized the importance of drawing and frequently reminded Lucien: "Are you drawing? —Don't waste time, try to improve your work. . . . Don't strive for skillful line, strive for simplicity, for the essential lines which give the physiognomy."[26] But over the long term, he was probably influenced more by Delacroix, who was already known for his unconventional use of color in which lines tend to be dissolved. He must have seen Delacroix's magnificent *Lion Hunt* (1855), which

19. Ibid., 2:47

20. Ibid., 1:106.

21. Mary Morton and Charlotte Eyerman, *Courbet and the Modern Landscape* (Los Angeles: J. Paul Getty Museum, 2006), 4.

22. Gary Tinterow and Henri Loyrette, *Origins of Impressionism* (New York: The Metropolitan Museum of Art, 1994), 354.

23. Arlette Sérullaz et al., *Delacroix: The Late Work* (London: Thames and Hudson), 97.

24. Rewald, *The History of Impressionism*, 16; Eugène Delacroix, *The Journal of Eugène Delacroix*, trans. Lucy Norton (New York: Phaidon Press, 1951), 275.

25. Rewald, ed., *Camille Pissarro: Letters to His Son Lucien*, 177.

26. Ibid., 37; Dana Gordon suggests that Pissarro may have been referring to the physiognomy of the picture as well as of the figures. Correspondence with the author, May 3, 2018.

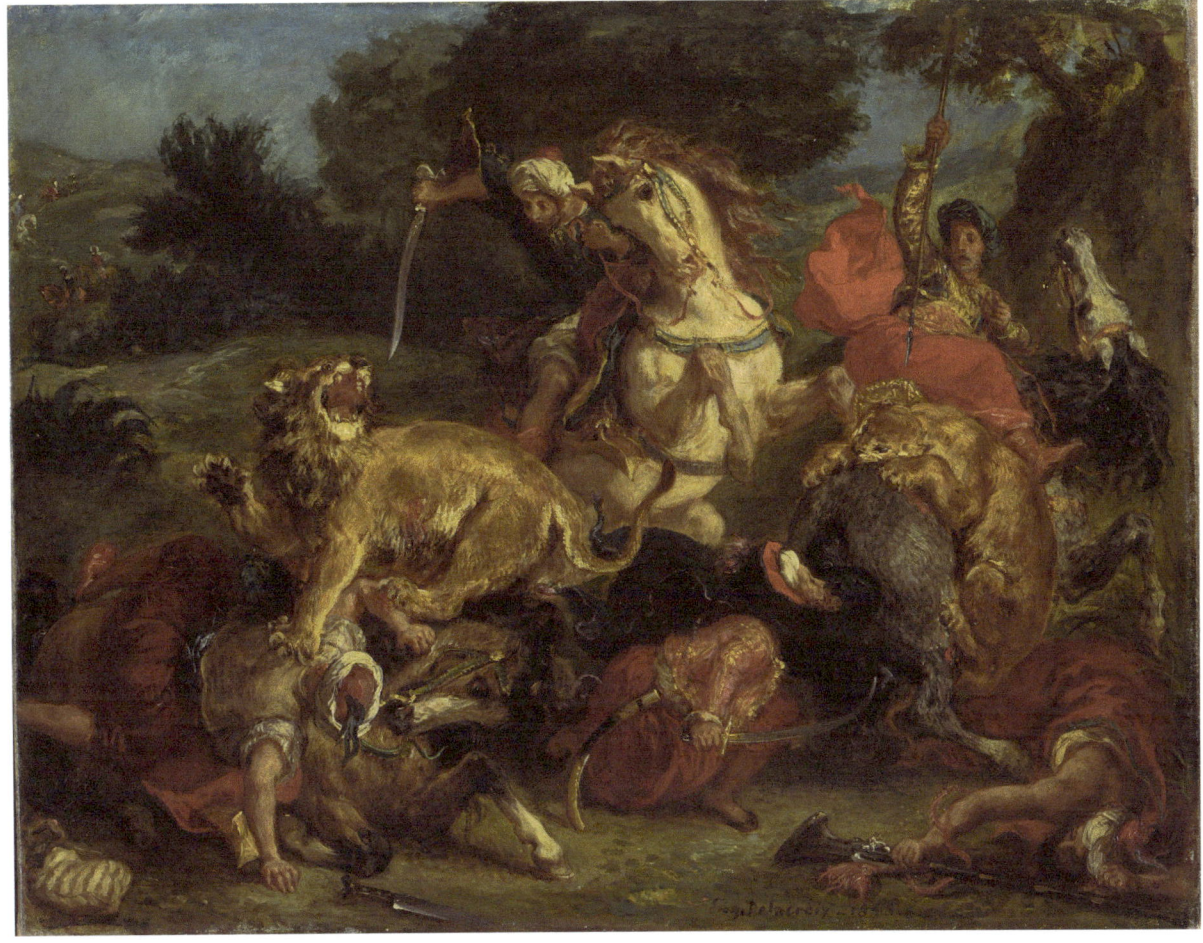

Fig. 29.
Eugène Delacroix,
The Lion Hunt, 1855,
Nationalmuseum,
Stockholm, Gift 1970 Grace
and Philip Sandblom

27. The original painting that appeared in the exhibition was nearly destroyed in a fire in 1870 in Bordeaux and only a fragment remains. This reproduction is a highly finished study and may be one the artist planned to submit for approval from his patron. See Sérullaz et al., *Delacroix: The Late Work*, 99-102; ibid., 37.

28. Ibid., 38.

was commissioned especially for the 1855 exposition.[27]

Delacroix's first painting in the Salon of 1822 caused critics to deride his use of color, labeling his painting a *tartouillade:* "jumbled and slackly drawn in which one sacrifices all for a bit of color." With his submissions to the 1855 exposition, one critic proclaimed him to be "a violent master, a passionate colorist, a tireless inventor."[28]

Pissarro must have heard his theories, many of which were later published in Delacroix's journal. As early as 1850, Delacroix wrote about brilliant light causing cold, blue shadows.[29] When Delacroix admired the green in Constable's landscapes and was told it was created with several different greens, he wrote: "What Constable says of the green of his prairies can be applied to all the other tones as well."[30] In his writings, he foreshadowed what Pissarro and others would do during Impressionism: "It is good not to let each brush stroke melt into the others; they will appear uniform at a certain distance by the sympathetic law which associates them. Colour obtained thus has more energy and freshness. The more opposition in colour, the more brilliance."[31] And more famously in 1857, Delacroix wrote, "Banish all earth colours,"[32] an admonition that Pissarro took seriously. As Cézanne noted, Pissarro was the first to give up black and eliminate earth colors from his palette.[33] Pissarro may also have gained confidence from some of Delacroix's other ideas, such as his insistence on "the free manifestations of my personal impressions, my estrangement from the standards practiced in the schools and my repugnance for academic recipes."[34] While there is no documentation to prove it, Pissarro could have visited Delacroix and discussed these ideas. Delacroix's studio was at 58, rue Notre-Dame de Lorette (from 1844 to 1857),[35] and Pissarro lived with his parents at 49, rue Notre-Dame de Lorette when he came to Paris in 1855.[36] Delacroix's influence on Pissarro was such that, in later years, the younger artist likened Delacroix's work and that of other artists to the work of Shakespeare, calling them "men of genius."[37] Nevertheless, Pissarro did not copy him—not the romanticism, not the realism, and especially not the literary narrative.

Art of the Dutch Golden Age

Other new influences affecting the Paris art environment were creating change in a different way. Dutch art of the seventeenth-century Golden Age had become popular, and French collectors were buying those genre paintings and landscapes of common villages and densely wooded areas.[38] Even the Louvre had a reasonably balanced collection of Dutch paintings by

29. Delacroix, *The Journal of Eugène Delacroix*, 138.

30. Willard Huntington Wright, *Modern Painting: Its Tendency and Meaning* (New York: Dodd, Mead, 1922), 38.

31. Ibid.

32. Delacroix, *The Journal of Eugène Delacroix*, 333.

33. Joachim Gasquet, *Joachim Gasquet's Cézanne: A Memoir with Conversations,* trans. Christopher Pemberton (London: Thames and Hudson, 1991), 164.

34. Patrick Noon and Christopher Riopelle, *Delacroix and the Rise of Modern Art* (London: National Gallery, 2015), 16.

35. F. Robert, "9ème Histoire [Paris]," http://www.neufhistoire.fr/articles.php?ing=fr&pg=1505&tconfig=0

36. Pissarro and Durand-Ruel Snollaerts, *Pissarro: Catalogue Critique des Peintures,* 1:107; Further research on Delacroix's influence on Pissarro and on the Impressionist movement would be very welcome.

37. Rewald, ed., *Camille Pissarro: Letters to His Son Lucien*, 26.

38. Sheila D. Muller, ed., *Dutch Art: An Encyclopedia* (New York: Routledge, 1997), 327.

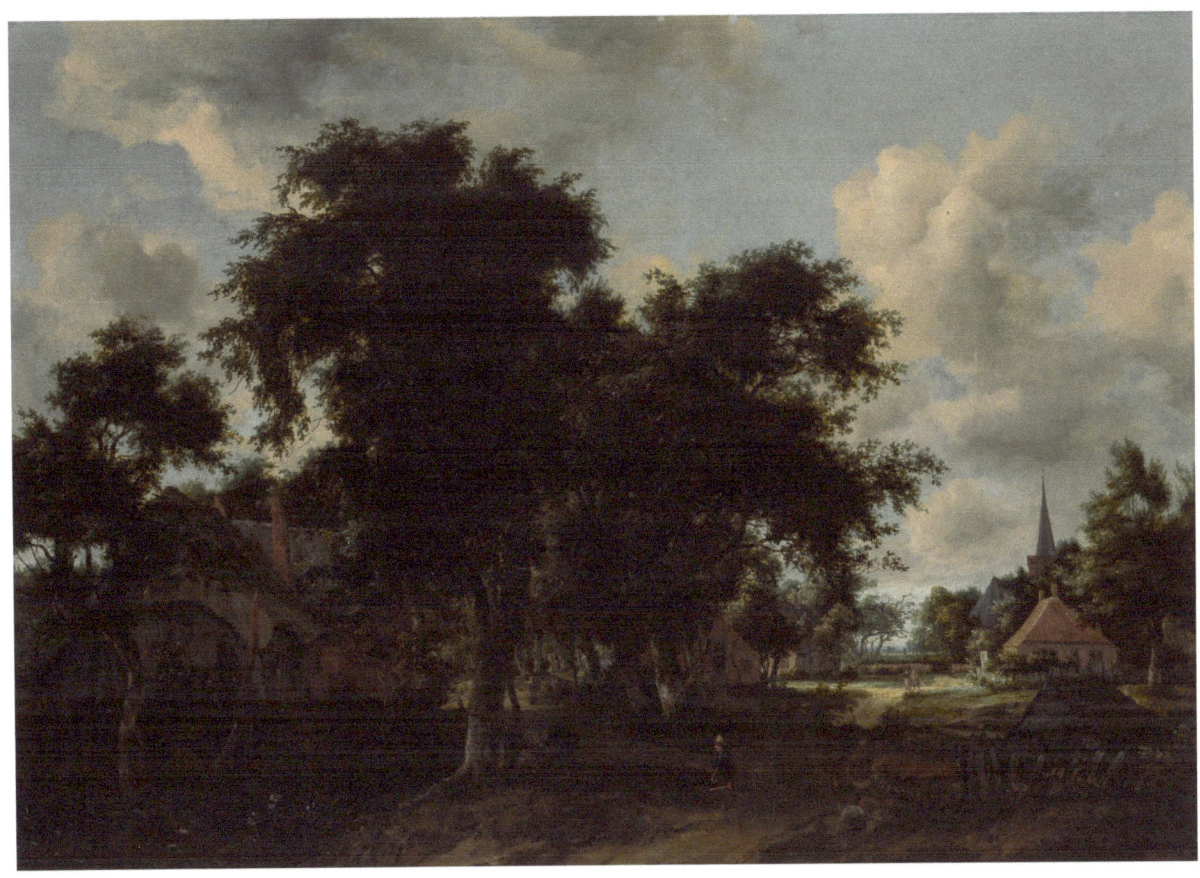

Fig. 30.
Meyndert Hobbema,
Entrance to a Village, c. 1665,
The Metropolitan Museum
of Art, New York, Bequest of
Benjamin Altman, 1913

39. Petra ten-Doesschate Chu, *French Realism and the Dutch Masters* (Ultrecht: Haentjens Dekker & Gumbert, 1974), 2, 12.

40. Ibid., 28.

1830, and by 1848, their acceptance had grown considerably.[39] Dutch landscape paintings had a significant influence on French artists, enabling "the Barbizon painters to free themselves from academic trammels and . . . redefine their attitude towards nature."[40] While these painters may have influenced Pissarro, it is important to remember that years before, in St. Thomas and Venezuela, he made drawings and paintings of the countryside and peasant life. Unlike Pissarro's art, the Dutch paintings frequently depicted storylines.

The influence of Dutch Golden Age paintings was evident in the works of Corot, who adopted some of the Dutch genre's compositional elements: for instance, the motif of a road going into a village or woods.[41] Corot even made a visit to Dutch museums in 1854 to see the Dutch paintings for himself.[42] Courbet is said to have studied the work of Frans Hals and copied one of his paintings.[43] While Rousseau, Millet, Diaz de la Peña, and Daubigny were all influenced by Dutch paintings, it was Boudin who felt the greatest impact. A self-taught artist, he copied seventeenth-century Dutch and Flemish paintings.[44]

The Barbizon School artists were beginning to turn away from the Académie des Beaux-Arts to paint realistic landscapes, dispensing with historical or mythological references. This must have seemed natural for Pissarro, because that is what he had done previously in St. Thomas and Venezuela. Since he had been using bright colors before, it must have been a big adjustment for Pissarro to change his palette to include the dark greens, browns, black, grays, and tans of the Barbizon School. He experimented with this darker palette, probably feeling pressure from his father to have a painting accepted by the Salon. But he never went as deep into the darkness as did Courbet and other artists. Pissarro used bright skies to contrast with dark earth spaces, building his compositions with forms defined by color. While Pissarro learned from other landscape painters, he used that knowledge in new and different ways.

Camille Corot

Pissarro must have seen the paintings of Corot at the Exposition Universelle of 1855, but he did not meet the older artist until 1857, when he visited Corot's studio to get a critical review of his own work. Corot encouraged him, saying: "Since you are an artist, you don't need advice. Except for this: above all, one must study values. We don't see in the same way: you see green and I see grey and blond! But that is no reason for you not to work at values, for they are the basis and the background of painting."[45] Pissarro's confidence in his

41. Ibid., 22-23.

42. Ibid., 6.

43. Seymour Slive, "On the Meaning of Frans Hals' 'Malle Babbe,'" *The Burlington Magazine* 105, no. 727 (1963):432-36; Muller, ed.; *Dutch Art: An Encyclopedia*, 328.

44. Chu, *French Realism and the Dutch Masters*, 24-29.

45. Lloyd, *Pissarro*, 28.

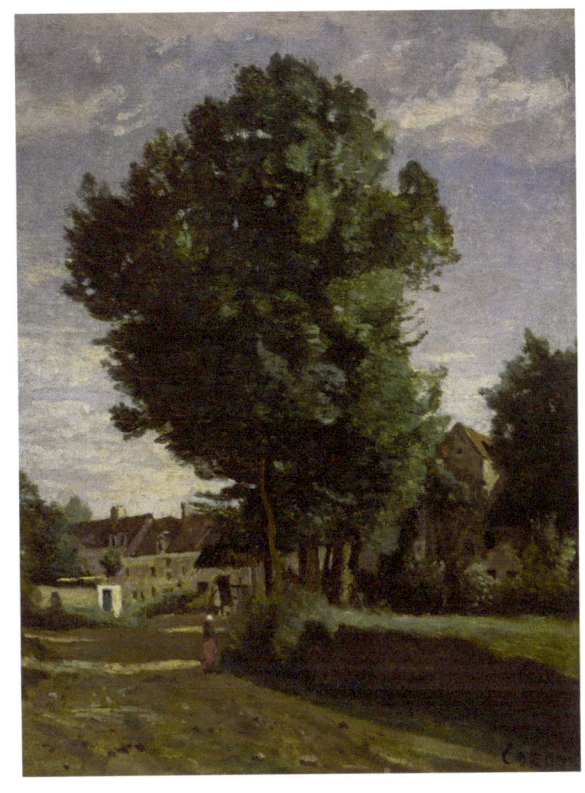

Fig. 31.
Camille Corot, *Environs
de Beauvais, du Côte de
Voisinlieu*, 1850-55, Musée
du Louvre, Paris

Corot's practice was to spend his summers painting small studies *en plein air;* then in the winter, he used elements from those studies to compose larger Salon-type paintings that included historical or mythological figures. The small studies had more immediacy, brighter colors, and looser brushstrokes than did his larger paintings that were finished according to Salon standards. It is likely that Pissarro was drawn more to Corot's studies than his Salon paintings, using them as examples for his own *plein air* paintings. Art historian Christopher Lloyd noted, "Corot's sympathy for nature and his stress on tonal values were obvious points of contact between the two men."[47]

Pissarro could have seen the small painting *Environs de Beauvais, du Côte de Voisinlieu* (1850-55) in Corot's studio. It is undoubtedly a study (only 15 ¾ by 11 ¾ inches) executed *en plein air* and painted with lively brushstrokes and animated sky.[40] Bright sunlight illuminates one side of the large tree and glances across the road, landing on the white cottage. The blue sky is filled with playful gray and white clouds.

own good judgment and strong sense of innovation was revealed when he attached himself to Corot, according to Théodore Duret, the French journalist, author, and art critic: "Corot, painting in a very individual manner, was as yet appreciated only by a small number of painters and connoisseurs."[46]

46 Duret, *Manet and the French Impressionists*, 126.

47. Lloyd, *Pissarro,* 28.

48. Gary Tinterow, Michael Pantazzi, and Vincent Pomarède, *Corot* (New York: The Metropolitan Museum of Art, 1996), 222.

Pissarro used some of these devices in his own early paintings—a curving road entering a village with a shaft of sunlight across the road. The most striking examples are Pissarro's study for *Banks of the Marne* (c. 1864) and his finished painting *Banks of the Marne* (1864), which was selected for the Paris Salon of 1864. They show that Pissarro examined not only Corot's *plein air* studies but also his method of preparing a painting for the Salon.

This small study (9 ½ by 12 ¾ inches) includes the curving road with a shaft of light that Corot often used. It also employs the dark greens, browns, and tans favored by artists of the Barbizon School. But there is a lightness in the execution in its exuberant brushstrokes, especially in the sky. The bright wedge of the river on the right pierces the dark colors and, with the road, forms an abstract angle pointing toward the base of the large tree.

The painting Pissarro submitted for the Salon is more studied, less spontaneous. The greens and tans are darker, the tree is

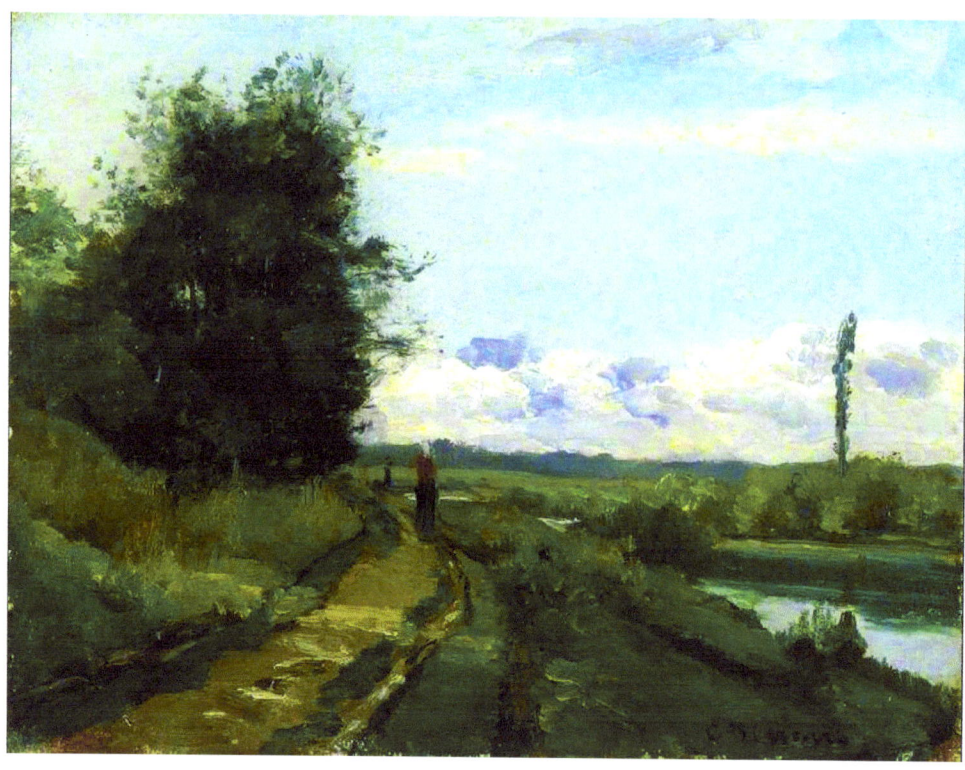

more contained, and the sky seems static compared to the study. In keeping with Salon standards, this painting is much larger (32 ⅛ by 42 ½ inches). That year, Pissarro was listed in the catalogue as "a pupil of MM. A. Melbye and Corot."[49]

In his later years, Pissarro acknowledged his gratitude to Corot: "I knew Corot very intimately. I passionately admired

Fig. 32.
Banks of the Marne, Study, c. 1864, Fitzwilliam Museum, Cambridge [PDRS 89]

49. Pissarro and Durand-Ruel Snollaerts, *Pissarro: Catalogue Critique des Peintures,* 1:114.

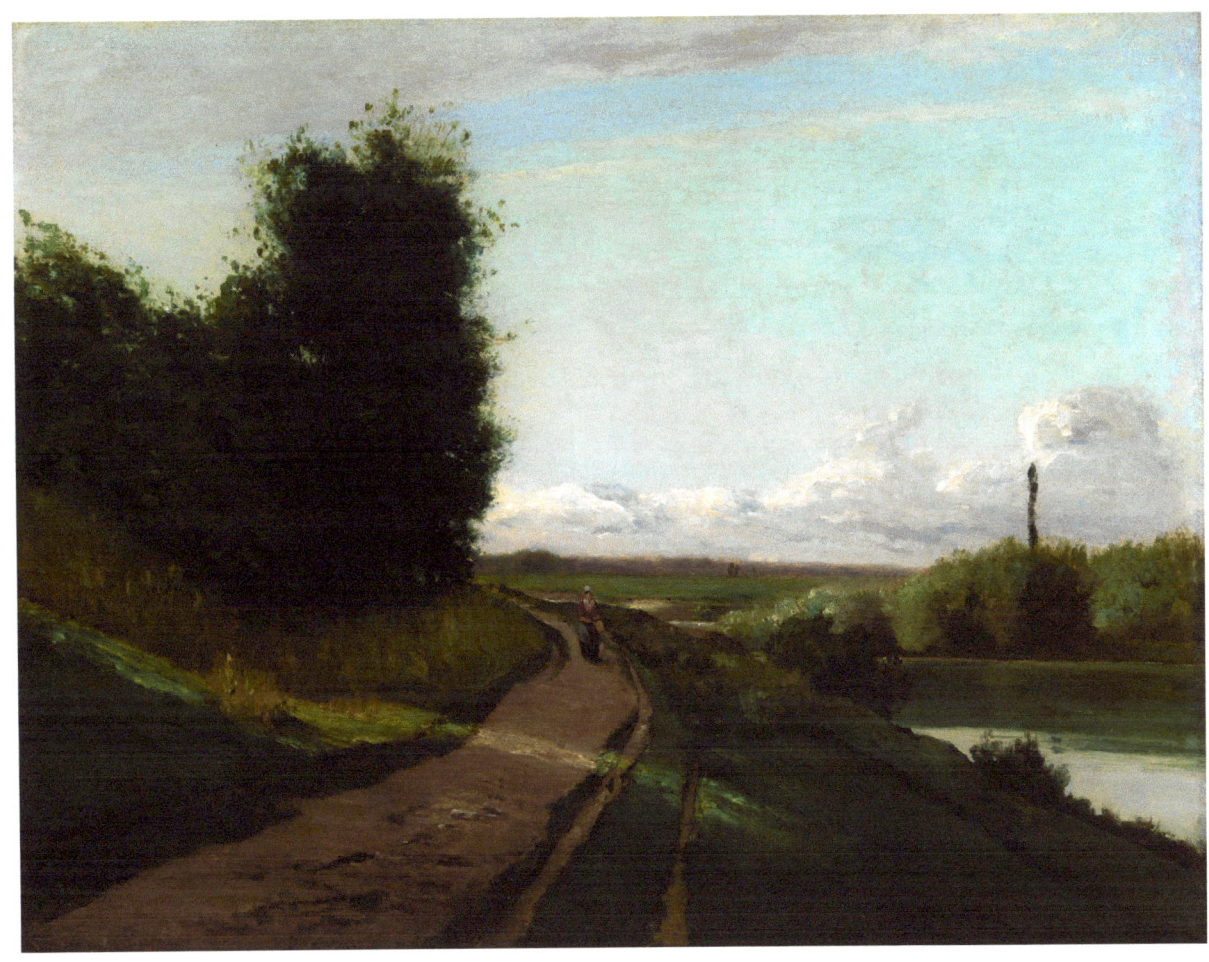

50. Rothkopf, *Pissarro: Creating the Impressionist Landscape*, 45.

him, and it's not surprising that his influence can be felt in my early work."[50] But Pissarro quickly had enough of the dark-green, brown, and tan colors that characterized Corot's paintings and was ready to return to the bright, pure colors he had used in the Caribbean. Cézanne described this: "In 1865 he was already cutting out black, bitumen, raw sienna and the ochres. That's a fact. 'Never paint with anything but the three primary colours and their derivatives,' he used to say to me."[51]

Charles François Daubigny

How Pissarro first met Daubigny is unclear, but it may have been through Corot, since those two had previously worked together.[52] Daubigny became known as a realist because of the exactitude with which he depicted trees, plants, seasons, and weather. He was adventurous in his use of colors, employing newly invented pigments in pink, violet, turquoise, blues, yellows, and greens. He used both the palette knife and brushstrokes to enhance the realism of his motifs.[53] He was best known for the *plein air* landscapes he painted from his studio-boat, "Le Botin."[54]

There are many similarities between the paintings of Daubigny and Pissarro, especially in the choice of motifs. Daubigny's painting *Washerwomen at the Oise River Near Valmondois* (1865) gives a realistic portrayal of the quiet waters of the Oise with perfect reflections of trees

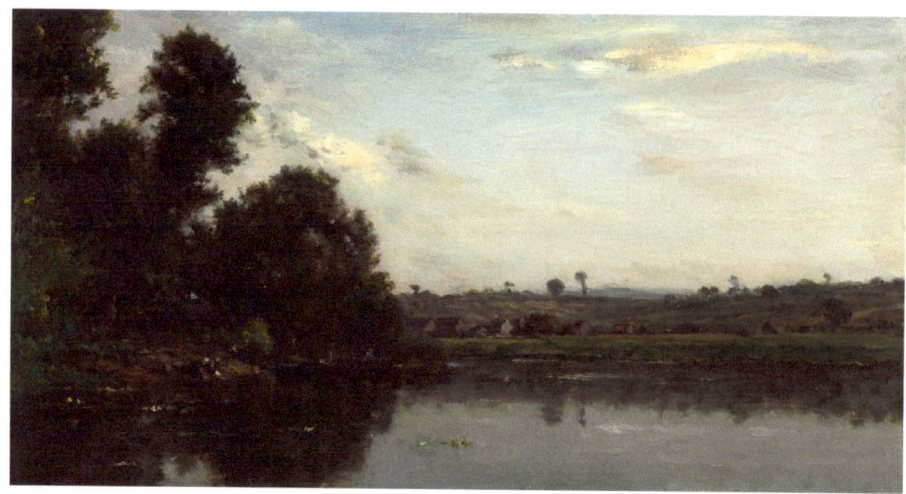

Fig. 34.
Charles François Daubigny, *Washerwomen at the Oise River Near Valmondois*, 1865, National Gallery of Art, Washington, D.C., Gift of Horace Gallatin

and houses. On the stony bank, under the large trees, two women wash clothes. Nearby, in the shade, are two fishing boats. Across the river is a cluster of houses, their volumes carefully rendered with light and shadow. The receding hillside is lighter, giving perspective to the carefully composed scene.

A similar painting by Pissarro, *Banks of the Marne at Chennevières* (c. 1865), exhibited at the 1865 Salon, was seen as an homage to Daubigny.[55] Its selection was probably promoted by Daubigny, who was a member of the Salon jury that year.[56]

51. Gasquet, *Joachim Gasquet's Cézanne: A Memoir with Conversations,* 164.

52. Lynne Ambrosini et al., *Inspiring Impressionism* (Edinburgh: National Galleries of Scotland, 2015), 16.

53. Ibid., 17-19.

54. Ibid., 25.

55. Ibid., 50.

56. Pissarro and Durand-Ruel Snollaerts, *Pissarro: Catalogue Critique des Peintures,* 1:118.

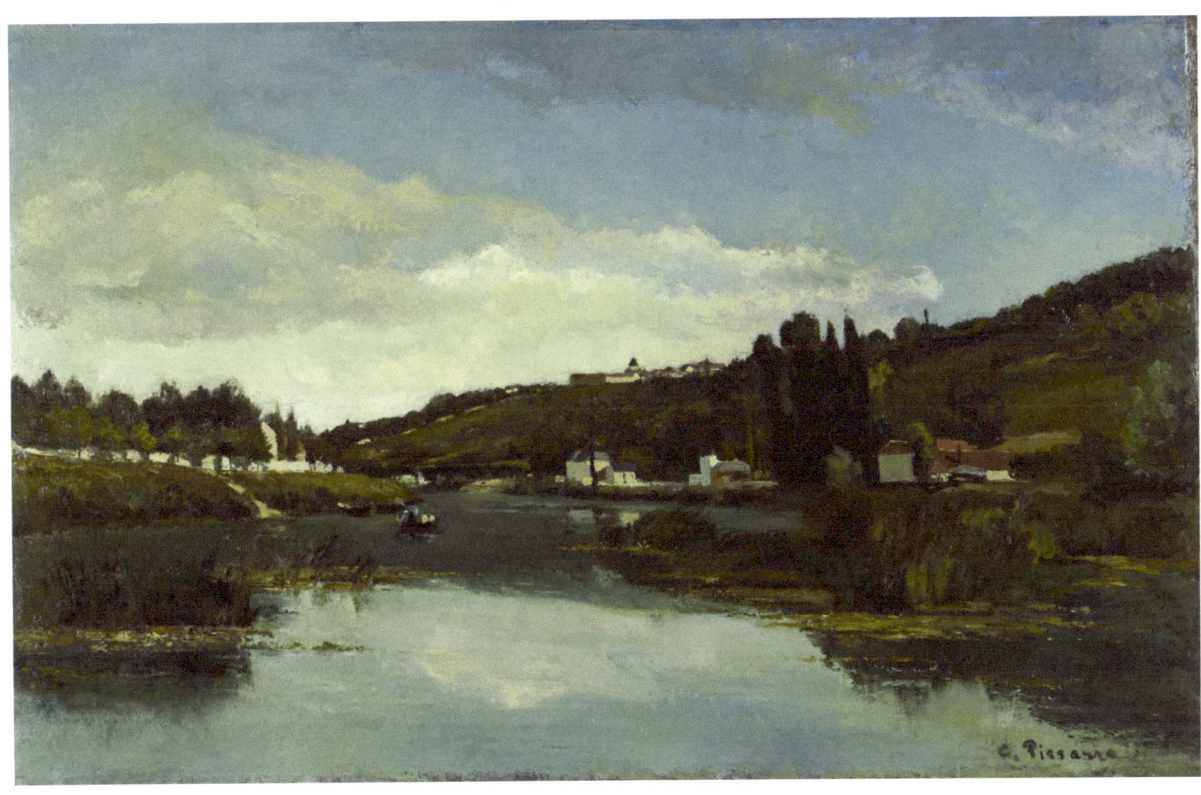

Like Daubigny, Pissarro painted a village by a river. His use of the palette knife is forceful, spreading thick impasto on the canvas. The houses are just slabs of paint sitting on the flat canvas surface. The reflections in the water are mere suggestions of the village. Pissarro constructed trees with back-and-forth strokes ("constructive" strokes, discussed in Chapter 6) and grasses with thick, heavy streaks of paint. The tiny boat crossing the river is too insignificant to be a focal point, which leaves the painting without a narrative.

Pissarro used this scene not to portray a narrative or storyline, but to contrast three distinct abstract shapes—the bright-sky layer at the top; the darker center section including the village, the mountain, and the dark part of the water; and the light, reflective band of the water. The darker center section creates a "negative" space in this abstract composition. This effect demonstrates that Pissarro was focusing on forms and the surface of the canvas, revealing movements of the paintbrush and palette knife. The landscape merely provided a design pattern for his unconventional execution. Joachim Pissarro said of this painting: "In fact, his treatment of much of the landscape and the buildings moves very close to abstraction."[57]

Gustave Courbet

Courbet, along with Corot and Daubigny, was one of Pissarro's earliest influences. At the 1855 Exposition Universelle, Pissarro saw twelve paintings by Courbet, including *The Stream*.[58] Most certainly, he also went to see Courbet's "Pavilion of Realism," the artist's private exhibition of forty additional paintings.

In spite of Courbet's flamboyant personality, or maybe because of it, his paintings

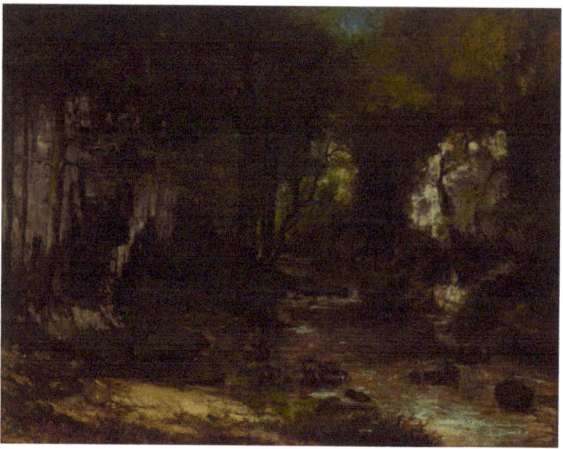

Fig. 36.
Gustave Courbet, *The Stream*, 1855, National Gallery of Art, Washington, D.C., Gift of Mr. and Mrs. P. H. B. Frelinghuysen in memory of her father and mother, Mr. and Mrs. H. O. Havermeyer

were acknowledged and widely acclaimed. His landscapes, known for their "boldness, dynamic energy, masculine vitality, and originality,"[59] demonstrated his eagerness to experiment with different techniques. His brushstrokes were authoritative, leaving their visible mark. With a palette knife, he plastered paint onto the canvas, then scraped and scumbled to achieve the desired texture.[60] He made his compositions solid and strong, pitting sharp diagonals against horizontals and tucking eye-catching elements in between. The result is as realistic as looking out of a window.

57. Pissarro, *Camille Pissarro*, 48.

58. Morton and Eyerman, *Courbet and the Modern Landscape*, 68.

59. Ibid., 6.

60. Ibid., 7.

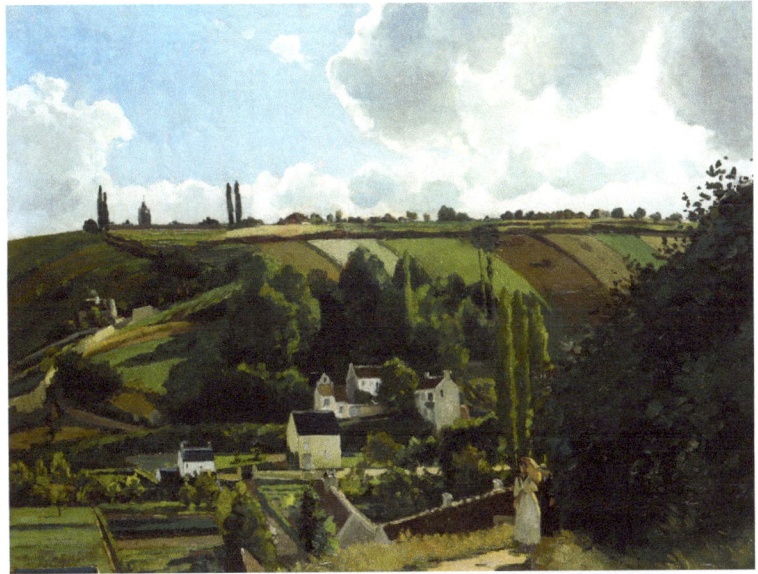

Fig. 37.
La Côte des Jalais, Pontoise, 1867, The Metropolitan Museum of Art, New York, Bequest of William Church Osborn, 1951 [PDRS 116]

Pissarro was certainly influenced by Courbet's paintings. As he gained confidence, the young artist explored new motifs and different techniques. Even though he rejected the idea of a smooth finish and an obvious narrative, he managed to make paintings that were accepted by the Salon.

The painting *La Côte des Jalais, Pontoise* (1867) was exhibited in the Paris Salon of 1868 and received favorable notices from critics of the day.[61] Its composition is strikingly similar to Courbet's 1858 painting *The Valley of Ornans.* Pissarro used strong geometrical structure, playing the sharp diagonal of the hill on the right against the horizon. Like Courbet, he filled the center with characteristic elements. But Pissarro pushed the composition a few steps beyond by adding curved color blocks just below

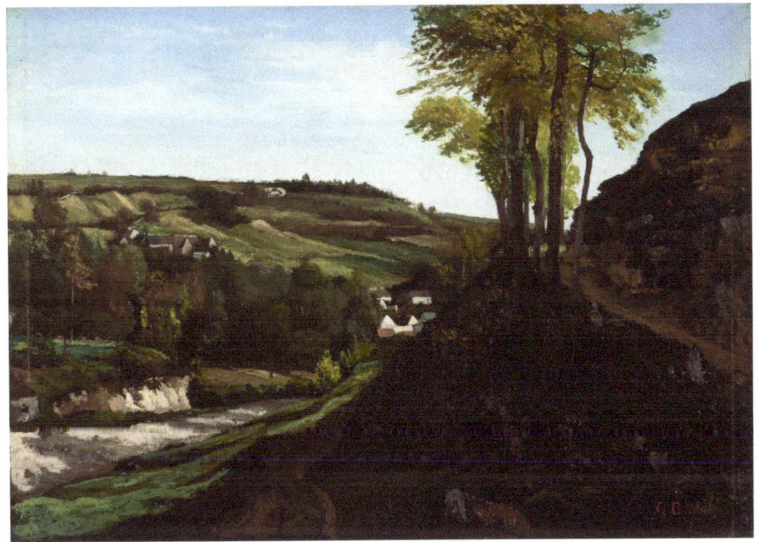

Fig. 38
Gustave Courbet, *The Valley of Ornans,* 1858, Saint Louis Art Museum

61. Pissarro and Durand-Ruel Snollaerts, *Pissarro: Catalogue Critique des Peintures,* 2:108.

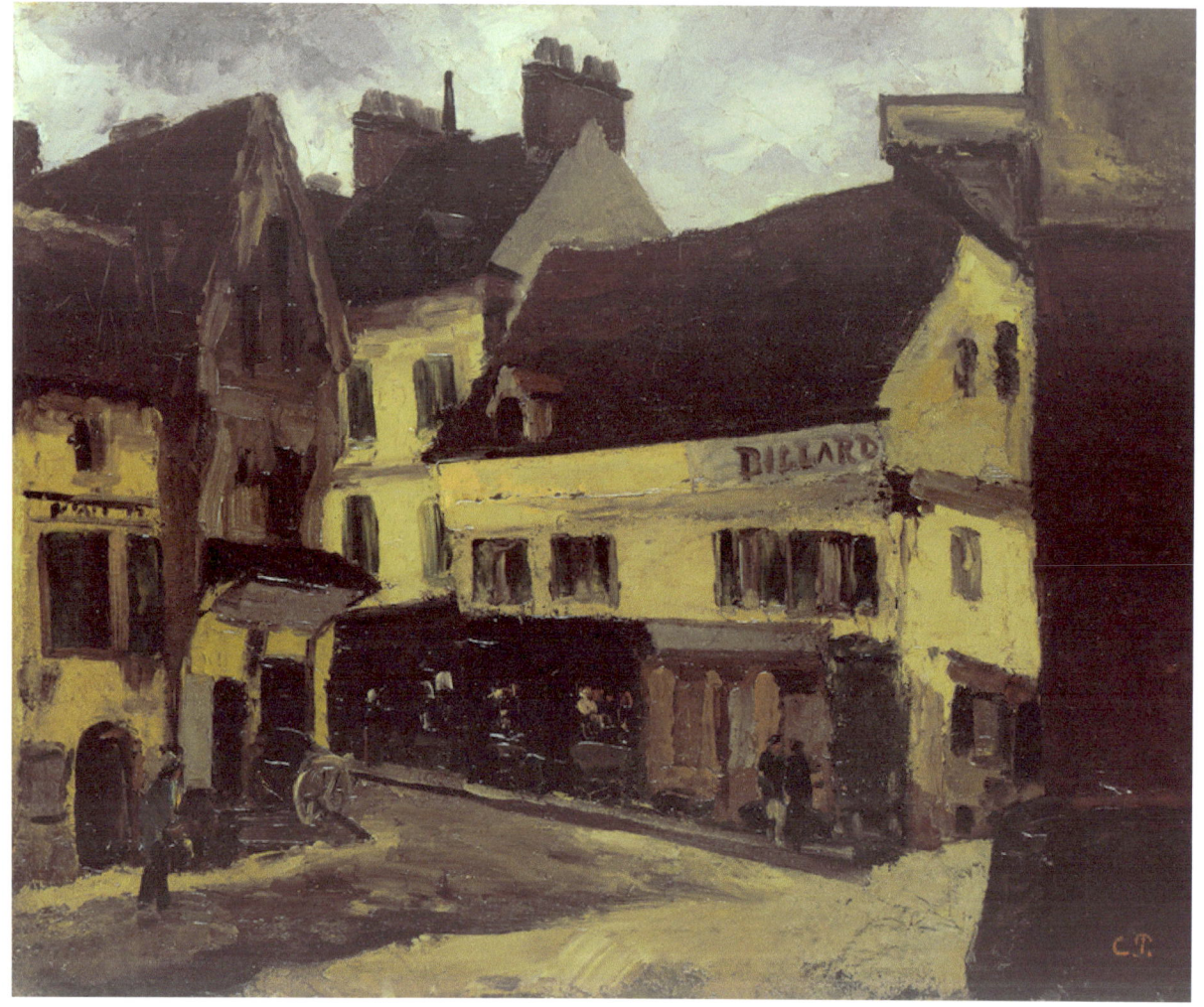

Fig. 39.
Square in La Roche-Guyon,
c. 1865, Staatliche Museen
zu Berlin, Nationalgalerie,
Berlin [PDRS 104]

the horizon, softening them at the lower edge with a band of trees. He added a cluster of houses, cast as simple cut-outs without volume, and a grid of walls enclosing terraces and trees. The two women on the path, almost hidden in the foliage, are hardly noticeable in view of this complex and engaging composition.

Pissarro was intrigued by Courbet's ability to use the palette knife, to create a range of different textures on the canvas, depicting smooth rock cliffs, rough tree trunks, or a cloudy sky. In *Square in La Roche-Guyon* (c. 1865), Pissarro demonstrated his facility with the palette knife. In reality, the actual corner of the village of La Roche-Guyon is spacious, but Pissarro overlapped the buildings to create a composition that is locked and solid. Because the horizon line is so high, the gray-white sky seems almost irrelevant, but it emphasizes the distinct angles and shapes of the roofs.

Pissarro loaded his palette knife with slabs of paint in shades of brown and tan to construct the buildings, including the decorative wood elements on the dormer roof and doorways.[62] The buildings interlock tightly, essentially closing the narrow street. The smaller building with the uneven roof and billiard-parlor sign pushes forward toward the dormer roof, creating "a visual tension and a quickened response in the viewer that surpass[es] mere representational art."[63] To the right, the edge of an unidentified building creates pressure, pushing toward the crowded site. The heavy impasto and marks of the palette knife make it impossible to focus on the street corner; the viewer is forced to consider the artist's hand on the canvas.

Other Influences on Young Pissarro

As a young artist, Pissarro carefully examined the work of artists in Paris and the surrounding areas and found much to admire. With artists of the Barbizon School, Théodore Rousseau, and Narcisse Diaz de la Peña, he shared an appreciation for working from nature and reinforcement of his preferred practice of painting

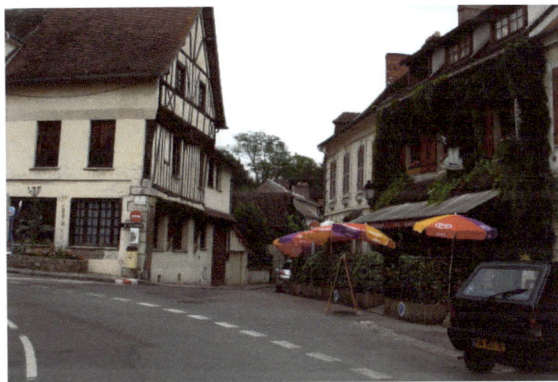

62. Pissarro used artistic license to move the dormer roof from the other side of the building.

63. Lloyd, *Pissarro*, 64.

en plein air, though he disregarded their predilection for details, such as carefully shaped individual leaves.

People frequently compared Pissarro's work to that of Jean-François Millet, but there is little similarity except for choice of motif. The depiction of ordinary people in work situations was not new to Pissarro; many of the drawings and paintings he made earlier in St. Thomas and in Venezuela were of workers engaging in everyday activities (in contrast to the "lofty" subjects favored by academic painters). When Pissarro painted French peasants in the fields, his depiction of them was strikingly different from that of Millet. Pissarro abhorred the sentimentality of Millet's paintings. After seeing a Millet exhibition in 1887, he wrote Lucien that some of the people viewing *The Angelus* (1857-59) were in tears: "This canvas, one of the painter's poorest, . . . has just this moral effect on the vulgarians who crowd around it; they trample one another before it! . . . idiotic sentimentality. . . . These people see only the trivial side in art."[64]

While Millet's paintings sensationalized the hard life of the peasant, Pissarro's paintings showed them as modern farmworkers who, on market day, sold what they had grown. The English painter Walter Sickert described the difference: "Pissarro no more pitied the peasant than the peasant pitied himself."[65]

During the Franco-Prussian War, while Pissarro was exiled in London, he saw the works of Turner, Constable, and other English landscapists. He later described their influence on him: "Turner and Constable, while they taught us something, showed us in their works that they had no understanding of the *analysis of shadow* [his emphasis], which in Turner's painting is simply used as an effect, a mere absence of light." He said that Turner proved the value of tone division but "did not apply it correctly and naturally."[66] Brettell suggested that Turner's major influence was on the artist's use of color: "Pissarro's palette of the early 1870s was very much affected by the pastel palette of Turner's late watercolors and oils."[67]

64. Rewald, ed., *Camille Pissarro: Letters to His Son Lucien*, 110.

65. Lloyd, *Pissarro*, 138.

66. Rewald, ed., *Camille Pissarro: Letters to His Son Lucien*, 356.

67. Brettell, *Pissarro and Pontoise*, 215 n. 26.

Throughout his life, Pissarro continued to look at other artists, even those of antiquity. He advised Lucien: "Look at the Persians, the Chinese, the Japanese. Derive your taste from those who are truly strong, for you must always go to the source: in painting to the primitives."[68] His enthusiasm for art of that period is reflected in an 1896 letter to Lucien, written from Rouen: "I have been looking at illuminated books. Flemish works of the thirteenth and Gothic French of the fourteenth and fifteenth centuries, admirable books, some in the bindings of the time and very beautiful. These are manuscripts that would fill you with joy."[69]

While Pissarro remained open to influence, he remained very much his own person. What he learned from others, he interpreted in his own unique manner and, in the process, he invented a totally new way of painting that points towards abstraction. Joachim Pissarro explained the phenomenon: "They [Pissarro's paintings] demonstrate how painting was being freed from its bondage to the supremacy of an accepted subject matter. . . .The gradual process of freeing pictorial elements (subject matter, line, color, form, etc.) from the necessity of following tradition-imposed conceptions would, only thirty years later, reach a climax in the **creation of abstraction** [emphasis mine] wherein painting rid itself of all possible meaning drawn from an external referent."[70]

For Pissarro, the direction was clear. "Work, see, and don't give way too much to other concerns, and it will come. But persistence, will and *free* [his emphasis] sensations are necessary, one must be undetermined by anything but one's own sensation."[71]

68. Rewald, ed., *Camille Pissarro: Letters to His Son Lucien*, 39.

69. Ibid., 285; Joachim Pissarro and Stephanie Rachum, *Camille Pissarro: Impressionist Innovator* (Jerusalem: The Israel Museum, 1994), 140-41.

71. Rewald, ed., *Camille Pissarro: Letters to His Son Lucien*, 202.

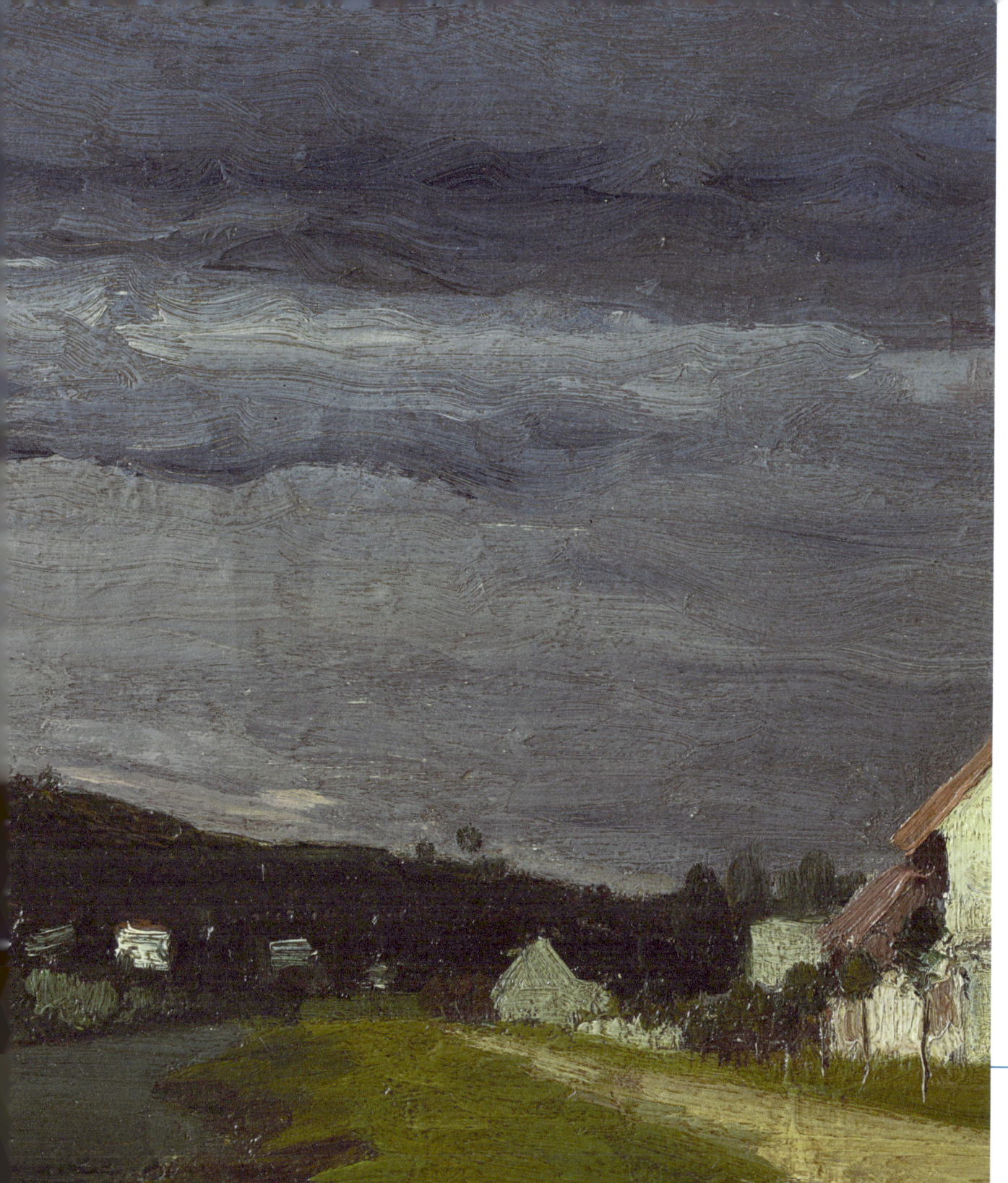

Fig. 41.
Landscape at La Varenne-Saint-Hilaire, detail, 1864,
Private collection [PDRS 95]

5 Impressionism Plus

One confronts, at this point, the remarkable abstractness and detachment of Pissarro's landscape vision. . . . a structural vision, one more concerned with balance and a deliberate blandness than with any forcefully associationist concepts of landscape.[1]

The raw visual impression so often considered to have been of paramount importance to the "Impressionist" painter was less important for Pissarro than ideas about art and the various ways of making it.[2]

— Richard Brettell

1. Brettell, *Pissarro and Pontoise*, 116-17.

2. Ibid., 145.

3. Anne Coffin Hanson, *Manet and the Modern Tradition* (New Haven, Conn.: Yale University Press, 1977), 7.

4. Tinterow and Loyrette, *Origins of Impressionism*, 55.

5. Hanson, *Manet and the Modern Tradition*, 10.

6. Ibid., 26.

The Académie des Beaux-Arts was already losing its control over French art when Pissarro arrived in Paris in 1855. As early as 1845, the art critic Théophile Thoré-Bürger noted the disorder, declaring French painting "without system, without direction, and abandoned to individual fantasy." This, he added, was not entirely bad because "originality is the first condition of art."[3] History painting in the classical style was declared to be dead,[4] and landscape paintings, formerly considered inferior, were appearing in increasing numbers in the Salons.[5] Formulaic methods of academic painting were being short-circuited or discarded entirely as painters presented as finished paintings what had previously been considered studies.[6]

While the 1855 Exposition Universelle revealed historic changes, the real turning point was the Salon of 1859, which art critics declared to be the end of French art as they had known it.[7] The following decade saw the emergence of Impressionist characteristics—commonplace motifs, visible brushstrokes, unconventional composition, lighter palettes—and the inception of modern art.[8]

Pissarro not only witnessed this transformation, he was in the thick of it. He was obliged to live up to the expectations of his father, whose measure of success was acceptance by the Salon, and Camille's first entry, *Donkey in Front of a Farm, Montmorency* (c. 1858), was exhibited at the Paris Salon of 1859. A number of his paintings were selected during the following years:

7. Tinterow and Loyrette, *Origins of Impressionism*, 7.

8. Ibid., 233.

9. Pissarro and Durand-Ruel Snollaerts, *Pissarro: Catalogue Critique des Peintures*, 1:361.

Year of Salon	Title	Date	PDRS
1859	*Donkey in Front of a Farm, Montmorency*	c. 1858	37
1864	*Banks of the Marne* (Fig. 33)	1864	90
	Route de Cachalas, à La Roche-Guyon		*
1865	*Banks of the Marne at Chennevières* (Fig. 35)	c. 1865	103
	Le Bord de l'eau		*
1866	*Banks of the Marne in Winter* (Fig. 9)	1866	107
1868	*The Jardin de Maubuisson, Pontoise*	c. 1867	115
	Côte des Jalais, Pontoise (Fig. 37)	1867	116
1869	*L'Ermitage* (possibly *The Hills at L'Hermitage, Pontoise*)	c. 1867	121
1870	*Houses at Bougival* (possibly)	1870	157
	Paysage		*

*Paintings without PDRS numbers are not included in the most recent catalogue raisonné (Joachim Pissarro and Claire Durand-Ruel Snollaerts, *Pissarro: Catalogue Critique des Peintures*, 2005) and may have been destroyed when Prussian soldiers occupied Pissarro's home during the Franco-Prussian War (1870-71). Their titles are from listings in Salon catalogues.[9]

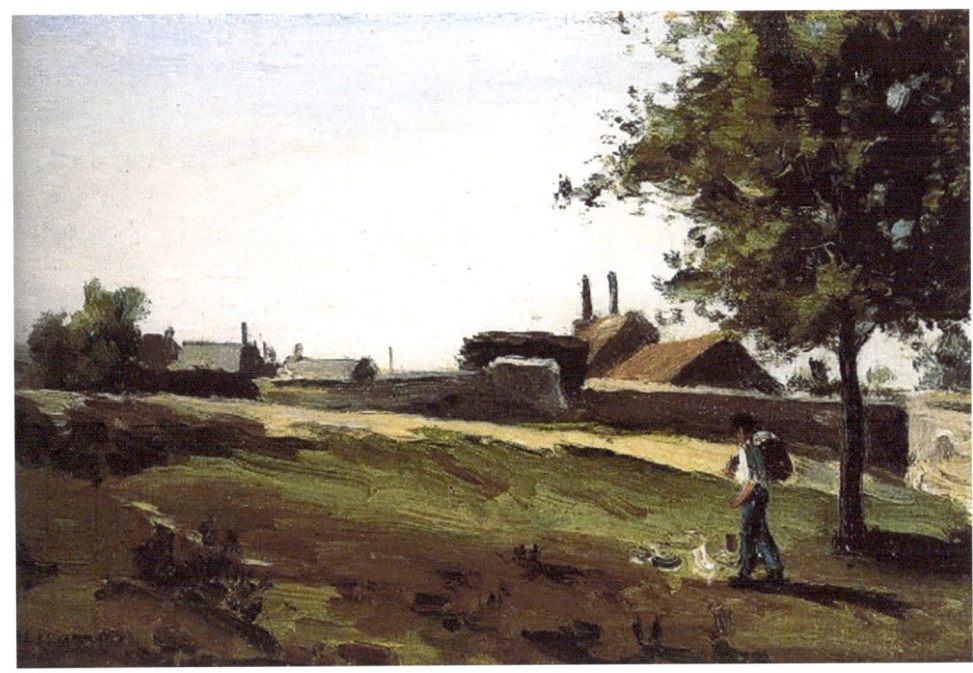

Fig. 42.
Walking Figure, Entering a Village, c. 1862, Private collection [PDRS 64]

The painting *Walking Figure, Entering a Village* (c. 1862) bears little resemblance to his earlier paintings, which reflect Corot's influence. The notion of "entering a village" is one that Pissarro explored time and again throughout his career. In this case, no specific location is indicated, and this commonplace motif has no distinguishing features. In the foreground, shades of brown and dark tan form the first diagonal stripe. Another olive-green stripe partially covers the lower layer, its loose brushstrokes revealing the brown underneath. This is topped by a bright creamy beige that widens on the right, focusing attention on the sketchily drawn man and tree. Above is a line of buildings without windows or doors, executed in broad, flat strokes. The only possible identifying feature is the pair of tall vertical strokes that might be smokestacks. The whole assemblage appears to be totally flat, like a cutout, functioning as just one more strip in a composition of layered colors. The hazy sky is light blue, brushed over with light-gray and white strokes. The large tree at the right provides a strong perpendicular that holds the layers together. Its foliage is

However, while he worked on Salon entries, Pissarro was also making paintings that can only be described as unconventional, testing the limits of brushstrokes, composition, paint application, and use of the palette knife. The fact that these are signed and dated indicates that Pissarro **intended** them to look as they do. These radical paintings were, in Pissarro's eyes, finished works.

defined with short "constructive" strokes, a form of the stroke that Cézanne adopted for his own use in later years.

In 1862, this painting would have been radical compared to those of other artists. Some would have called it unfinished, but Pissarro's signature in the lower-left corner indicates that he considered it complete. The extreme simplification of the subject, the abundant evidence of visible brush-strokes, and the flatness of the buildings are all techniques used by today's abstract artists. While this painting loosely represents a scene, it focuses more on the paint and the surface of the canvas. It was created in an abstract manner.

Another painting completed two years later, *Landscape at La Varenne-Saint-Hilaire* (1864), displays many of the same charac-teristics. Heavy brushstrokes loaded with paint depict the river and riverbank. The vanishing point, where the river and road intersect, is blocked by hills so dark they belie any sense of perspective. The white houses show no volume and look like flat

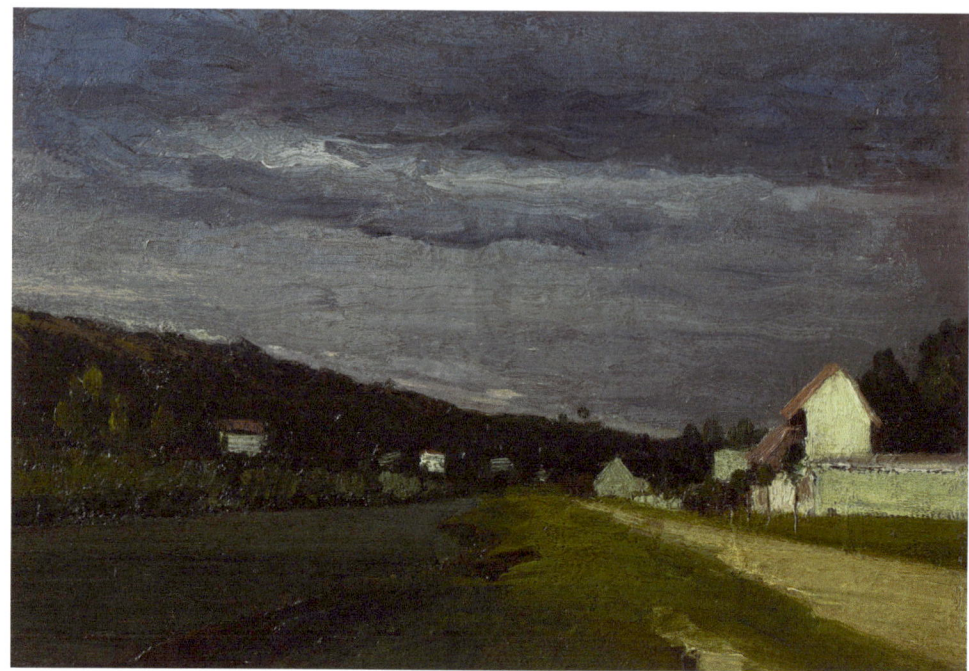

Fig. 43.
Landscape at La Varenne-Saint-Hilaire, 1864, Private collection [PDRS 95]

cutouts. The brushstrokes in the sky can only be described as "juicy," with their heavy impasto swirls. The motif itself is totally unimportant, and Pissarro stripped the scene bare of any picturesque elements.

During the mid-1860s, other Impressionists were still using predictable painting tech-niques. Pissarro was already utilizing tech-niques that would nearly one hundred years later be called abstract art.

Modernity

If the Salon of 1859 opened the curtains on modern art, then the Salon des Refusés provided the platform for artists of the future. After a particularly brutal rejection of three thousand paintings by the Salon jury of 1863, Napoleon III declared that the rejected paintings should be displayed in an adjoining hall.[10] Three of Pissarro's paintings in the Salon des Refusés won favorable attention of art critics.[11]

The greatest excitement in the Salon des Refusés was created by a painting that was originally entitled *Le Bain* but is now known as *Le Déjeuner sur l'herbe* (1863), by Édouard Manet. While the public and many writers criticized the painting, Zachary Astruc praised the artist's talent: "Manet! One of the greatest artistic characters of the time!"[12] Because of the impact of his work and especially this painting, Manet became known as the leader of the new artistic movement.[13] Even today, many art historians consider him to be the father of modernism.[14]

It was not so much the subject matter of Manet's paintings that was exciting to artists but the execution. Instead of the highly finished manner he had been taught in the studio of Thomas Couture,[15] he developed a looser brushstroke and paid scant attention to details in the background. Instead of drawing forms, he shaped them with brushstrokes and set colors side-by-side with few or no transitional tones.[16] These characteristics are also evident in an earlier painting by Manet, *Music in the Tuileries* (1862), which was exhibited at Galerie Martinet in Paris. The subject matter is certainly modern—fashionable people enjoying a leisurely afternoon in the Tuileries Garden near the Louvre. Many of the figures are actually portraits of real people, some of whom have been identified.[17] What is more interesting is just how far Manet had moved from the academic training of Couture's studio when he made this painting. The looser brushstrokes are evident in the stylish dresses of the women. Manet used bright yellow with little shadow to mold the voluminous garments worn by the women at the lower left. The blue of their bonnets against

10. Rewald, *The History of Impressionism*, 79-80.

11. Pissarro and Durand-Ruel Snollaerts, *Pissarro, Catalogue Critique des Peintures,* 1:115. The paintings, entitled *Landscape, Study,* and *Village,* are not identified in Pissarro's catalogue raisonné.

12. Rewald, *The History of Impressionism*, 85.

13. Ibid., 86.

14. Rebecca Rabinow, "Édouard Manet (1832-1883)," The Metropolitan Museum of Art, http://www.metmuseum.org/toah/hd/mane/hd_mane.htm.

15. Tinterow and Loyrette, *Origins of Impressionism*, 393.

16. Rewald, *The History of Impressionism*, 86.

17. Françoise Cachin and Charles S. Moffett, *Manet: 1832-1883* (New York: Harry N. Abrams, 1983), 122.

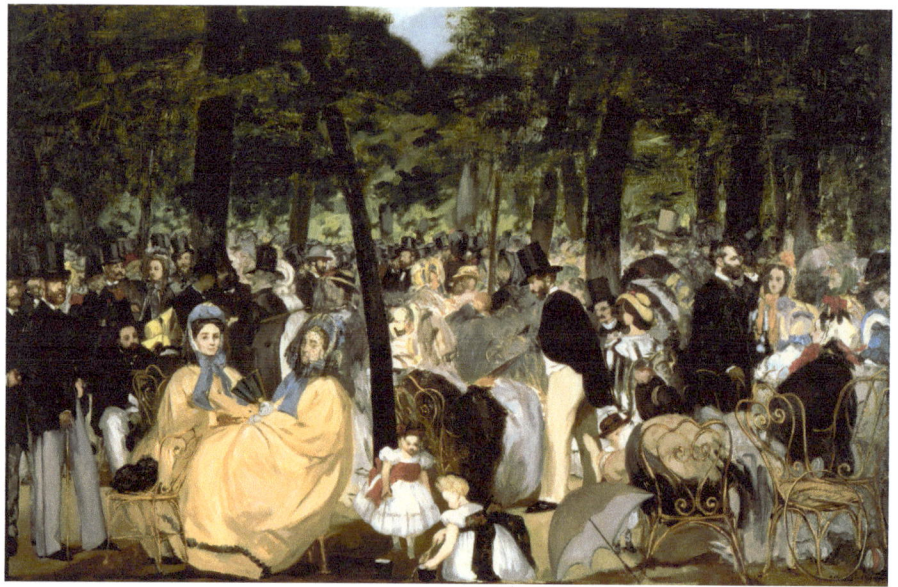

Fig. 44.
Édouard Manet, *Music in the Tuileries*, 1862, National Gallery, London,
Sir Hugh Lane Bequest, 1917

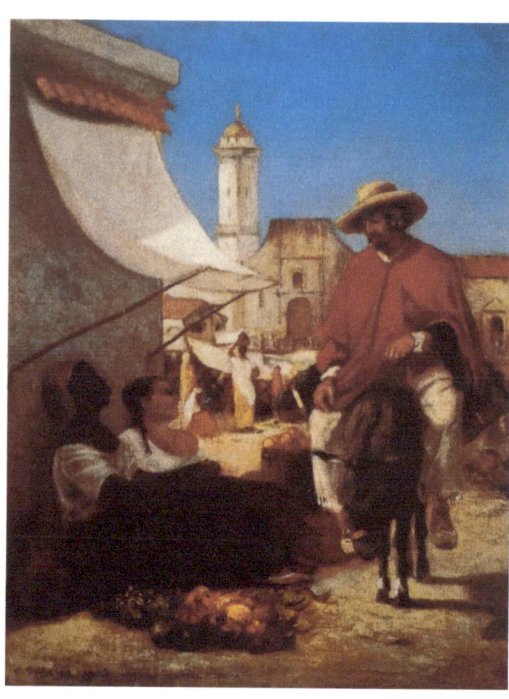

Fig. 45.
Market Scene on the Plaza Mayor, Caracas, 1852-54, Presidential Residence, La Casone, Caracas, Venezuela [PDRS 1]

the yellow is abrupt, without transitional tones. These painting techniques must have seemed jarring to people accustomed to highly finished Salon paintings. Even today, this painting is considered to be "the earliest true example of modern painting, in both subject matter and technique."[18]

These techniques were not new to Pissarro because he had already used them in paintings made ten years earlier in Venezuela.

The comparison of a painting depicting a market place in Caracas, Venezuela, with one of fashionable Parisians is not such a long reach. Both are thoroughly modern scenes: the Pissarro depicts an everyday market scene in the city center; the Manet portrays a commonplace leisure activity in the center of Paris. The most obvious difference—the wide horizontal format of the Manet versus the vertical of the Pissarro—is of little importance in the discussion of characteristics.

18. Ibid., 126.

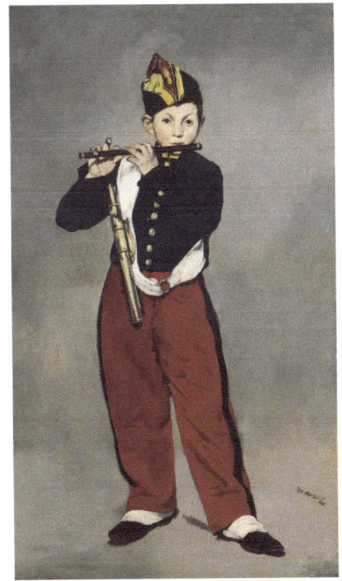

Fig. 46.
Édouard Manet, *The Fifer*,
1866, Musée d'Orsay, Paris

19. Pissarro and Durand-Ruel Snollaerts, *Pissarro: Catalogue Critique des Peintures*, 2:41.

What is important is that Pissarro's painting is a composition of shapes made of paint while Manet's painting (even with its loose brushstrokes) places emphasis on the many recognizable people in the scene. This Pissarro painting, argurably the more modern of the two, was made in 1852-54, nearly **a decade earlier** than Manet's painting.

Throughout the Caracas painting, brushstrokes are evident. Since Pissarro was not trained in French academic methods, he never used the highly finished brushstrokes that Manet had learned from Couture. The looseness of his brushwork is especially evident in the depiction of the donkey and the man's trousers. Pissarro used color to define shapes, such as the red coat of the rider and the white tent shading the women. His depiction of light and shadow over the stretched cloth foreshadows the transient effects of light explored later by Monet and Renoir. Since Pissarro did not use transitional tones between colors, he boldly set the red coat and white shade bluntly against the brilliant blue sky. He used brushstrokes to carefully mold the figures of the two women under the shade.[19] It is interesting to note that Pissarro included a small still life of vegetables, depicted in loose brushstrokes of green, red, and yellow in the foreground. Manet used a similar device ten years later in his painting *Le Déjeuner sur l'herbe*, although his overturned basket of fruit is depicted much more realistically.

Another comparison between Manet and Pissarro is also quite revealing. *The Fifer* was painted by Manet in 1866, three years after his scandalous painting *Olympia*. While it is certainly reminiscent of Velázquez, the Spanish artist whom Manet so admired, it has its own presence. This young boy looks directly out from the painting with an expressionless face, holding his fife to his lips. Though one of his fingers is raised, there is no sense of motion in his hands. He wears a black jacket and baggy red pants with a stripe down each leg. Around his neck is a white sash with a case for his instrument. Only hints of shadows from his left leg and under the toes of his black shoes are indicated. There is no frame of reference, and he appears almost suspended in space.

The most radical characteristics of this painting, however, are the large blocks of red and black. His jacket is so solidly black that it is impossible to see the curve of his left arm as he reaches for the keys. His left hand, extending out of the cuff of the sleeve, is the only clue that the left arm is folded across his chest. The bright red pants, delineated by black stripes on each side, are described with only the barest shadows to indicate volume. Manet placed the white sash directly over the black coat and red pants with little or no transitioning values, setting the whole figure on a stark, gray background. It is no wonder that people thought the figure looked like a signboard. Émile Zola, who praised the painting, wrote, "the young musician's outfit was handled with a sign painter's simplicity: yellow braid, blue-black tunic, red trousers, all have become broad patches of color."[20]

More than a decade before Manet's painting, Pissarro made a similar painting. *Woman with a Jug on Her Head* (1854-55), painted while he was still in the

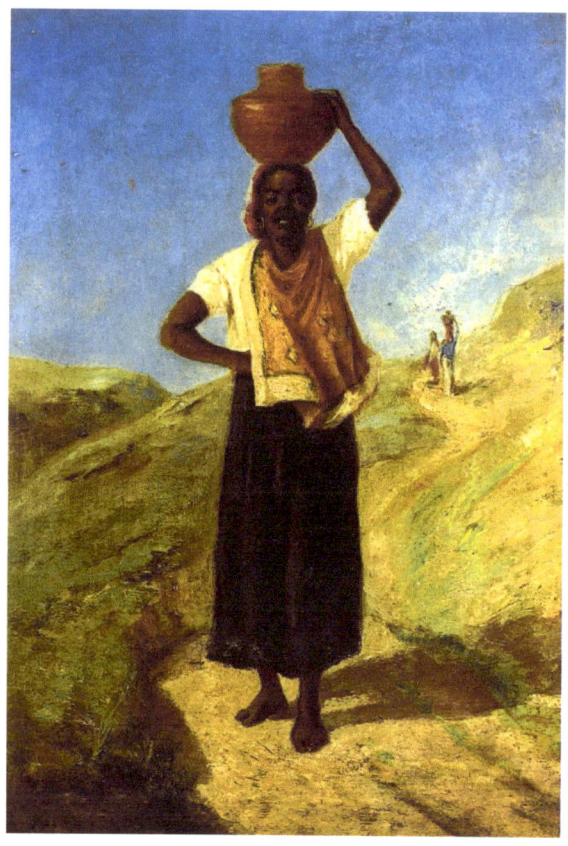

Fig. 47.
Woman with a Jug on Her Head, 1854-55, Private collection [PDRS 15]

Caribbean, is every bit as bold in its use of color as the Manet painting. The native woman, with dark skin, stands barefoot on the dusty road in brilliant sunlight. Her skirt is one, single, dark, color block and her white blouse another; there is virtually no modeling. The only volume is indicated in her bright orange scarf that appears

20. Cachin and Moffett, *Manet,* 246.

to be blowing in the breeze. The bright orange of the pot on her head is outlined boldly against the blue sky with no transitional values, as are her dark arms and white blouse. Her dark skirt and bare feet are sharply defined against the sandy road. While the background provides a slight frame of reference, there are minimal details to take away from the striking figure herself.

Courbet once referred to Manet's *Olympia* saying that it looked as flat as a playing card.[21] That description might also be said about this figure by Pissarro, which looks so flat she could almost be a sign board or a cut-out. In both instances, the paintings by Pissarro were made well before those by Manet. Pissarro was aware that he was not being acknowledged for his radical innovations and that Manet and others were getting credit for techniques he initiated. In 1891, he wrote Lucien: "There are, of course, certain young intriguers who claim that I spent much of my life being influenced by Manet (the height of absurdity), Monet, Renoir, Sisley (astonishing to say

the least), and even the pointillists."[22] It is interesting to consider what might have happened if these Pissarro paintings had been exhibited beside Manet's paintings. Would critics have recognized that Pissarro was the real innovator?

Japonisme

Even while the world of French art was being shaken by the changes of modernity, outside influences were making themselves felt. In Japanese prints artists found new ways of representing nature and space. The appearance of Japanese art in Europe is thought to have occurred after the expedition of Commodore Matthew Perry in 1853-54, which brought a flood of Japanese art, lacquerware, and porcelain into France.[23] For some two hundred years before that, trade between Europe and Japan was dormant, except for some commerce conducted with Holland, which included Japanese prints. However, a collection of Japanese prints from Holland had been auctioned in Paris in 1818, and color lithographs of Japanese prints were available in France, Austria, and Britain.

21. Ibid., 247.

22. Rewald, ed., *Camille Pissarro: Letters to His Son Lucien*, 166.

23. Widar Halén, "Japan Revealed: Collecting of Japanese Art around the Opening of Japan," in *Perspectives on Japan and Korea: 2nd Nordic Symposium on Japanese and Korean Studies* (Copenhagen, 1991).

Reproductions of Japanese prints exhibited at the Exposition Universelle in 1855 were said to have caused a "great sensation."[24] Pissarro is known to have attended that Exposition Universelle, and he may have seen Japanese prints then. However, his paintings of that period do not reveal the dramatic influence as seen in the paintings of Monet and Whistler.

The biggest impact of Japanese prints came during the 1867 Exposition Universelle, where one hundred Japanese works were exhibited, creating "a great Japanese explosion."[25] Many artists collected Japanese prints, fans, and porcelain, and featured them in their paintings. The art critic Émile Zola wrote about the "strange elegance" and "beautiful touches" of Japanese prints.[26] More important, artists looked closely at the prints and began to see new ways of painting: they were attracted by the flatness, the asymmetrical compositions, and the simplification of background.[27]

Japanese art was also exhibited in Paris at the 1872 Exposition Universelle during the formative years of Impressionism and also at other exhibitions in 1883 and 1884. The introduction of Japanese art made definitive impact on many artists, most notably James Abbott McNeill Whistler, who not only used Japanese artifacts in many of his paintings but also adopted many of its techniques. The influence on other artists was more subtle, expressed more in freedom of the use of color, the choice of commonplace motifs, and unusual compositions.

While Pissarro may have felt the influence of Japanese prints, it is not very evident in his work, because by 1855 he had already incorporated many of its characteristics—flat blocks of clear color set side-by-side, asymmetrical compositions, and scenes of everyday life. In 1893, Pissarro saw an exhibition of Japanese art at Durand-Ruel's gallery in Paris and wrote his son Lucien: "Damn it all, if this show doesn't justify us! There are grey sunsets that are the most striking instances of Impressionism."[28]

24. Ibid.

25. Michael Sullivan, *The Meeting of Eastern and Western Art*, rev. ed. (Berkeley: University of California Press, 1989), 212.

26. Ibid.

27. Gabriel P. Weisberg et al., *Japonisme: Japanese Influence on French Art, 1854-1910* (Cleveland, Oh.: The Cleveland Museum of Art, 1975), 120.

28. Rewald, ed., *Camille Pissarro: Letters to His Son Lucien*, 206.

Impressionism

In 1857, Pissarro enrolled at the Académie Suisse,[29] where he, Claude Monet, and Paul Cézanne met. He was ten years older than Monet and eight years older than Cézanne, and, because of his experience as a working artist, the younger men looked up to him. In 1862, Monet introduced Pissarro to Frédéric Bazille, Alfred Sisley, and Auguste Renoir. While they became friends at that time, it was the 1867 Exposition Universelle that made them comrades in their struggle for independence from the Salon. That year, the Salon rejected all the paintings submitted by Pissarro, Cézanne, Monet, Renoir, Sisley, and Bazille.[30] Disappointed and impatient with the dictates of the Salon, the artists attempted to stage their own exhibition. Even though they were unable to raise sufficient funds to rent space, they held fast to the notion of an independent exhibition of their paintings.[31]

In the spring of 1869, Pissarro and his family moved from Pontoise to Louveciennes, a small town near the river Seine, where they rented a large house on the route de Versailles near the Marly aqueduct.[32] In Louveciennes, Renoir frequently visited his mother and grandmother, and Monet was situated nearby in Saint-Michel, a small hamlet near Bougival. In the autumn of 1870, Sisley moved to Voisins, a neighboring village.[33] The group of artists discussed art, looked at each other's works, and painted together. Pissarro had brought with him from the Caribbean a large portfolio of "highly competent drawings and paintings."[34] Richard Brettell believes that "Monet, Renoir, Cézanne, and Sisley had all seen Pissarro's early oil paintings from the years before 1855 and that this material played a considerable role in the development of Impressionist picture-making."[35]

Over time, the main characteristics of Impressionism have been defined—painting *en plein air*, a light palette of pure or mixed colors, ordinary subject matter (not historical or mythological), loose and visible brushstrokes, and transient effects of light. Many of these characteristics are clearly evident in paintings Pissarro brought with

29. The Académie Suisse provided an alternative to the École des Beaux-Arts in Paris. For a small fee, artists could draw from living models, and there were no instructors or examinations.

30. Rewald, *The History of Impressionism*, 594-95.

31. Ibid., 172.

32. Pissarro and Durand-Ruel Snollaerts, *Pissarro: Catalogue Critique des Peintures*, 1:125-26.

33. Tinterow and Loyrette, *Origins of Impressionism*, 447.

34. Pissarro and Durand-Ruel Snollaerts, *Pissarro: Catalogue Critique des Peintures*, 1:6.

35. Ibid, 1:8.

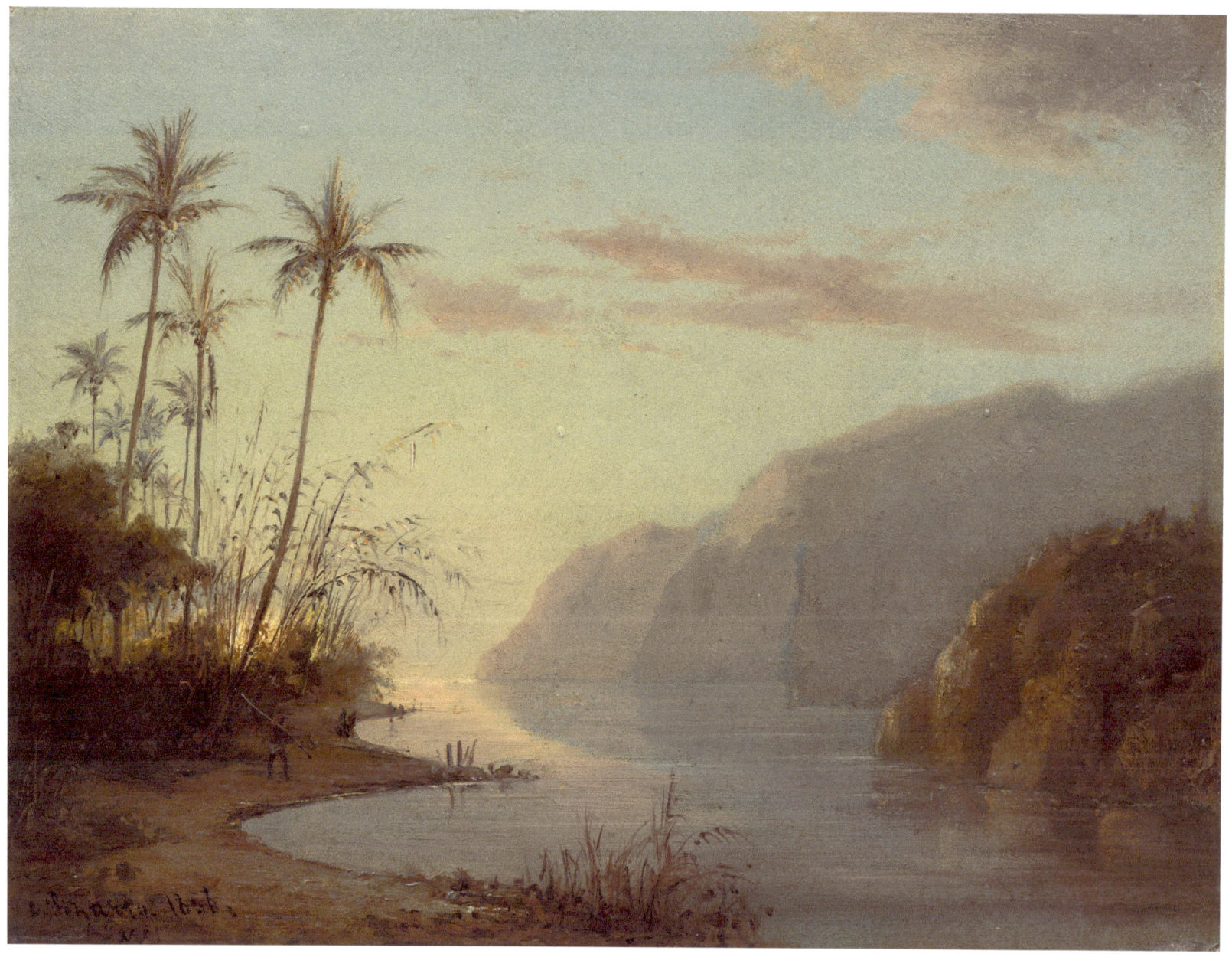

Fig. 48. (left)
A Creek with Palm Trees, 1856, National Gallery of Art, Washington, D.C., Collection of Mr. and Mrs. Paul Mellon [PDRS 16]

36. Tinterow and Loyrette, *Origins of Impressionism,* 440.

37. Cachin et al., *Pissarro,* 20.

38. Tinterow and Loyrette, *Origins of Impressionism,* 440.

39. Richard R. Brettell, "Cat. 3 Snow at Louveciennes, c. 1870: Curatorial Entry. In *"Pissarro Paintings and Works on Paper at the Art Institute of Chicago* (Chicago: The Art Institute of Chicago, 2015), https://publications.artic.edu/pissarro/reader/paintingsandpaper/section/12.

him from the Caribbean and in some of his early paintings in France. The three younger artists must have seen a group of nine paintings Pissarro made in 1856 based on his memories of the Caribbean. One of these paintings, *A Creek with Palm Trees* (1856), displays strong Impressionist characteristics. While Pissarro probably made this painting in his Paris studio, he undoubtedly took inspiration from the many drawings and watercolors he had made *en plein air* in St. Thomas.

This site, typical of the Caribbean, where numerous inlets and bays fringe coastal areas, has no particular significance and suggests no narrative. The palette is light, blending pinks, blues, and lavenders with dull greens. This painting was made nine years before 1865, when Pissarro is said to have removed all black and the umbers from his palette. Even so, light colors in the depiction of air, clouds, and water dominate the painting. Brushstrokes are evident in the rocky cliff and the smooth water, especially in the reflections. The depiction of light and atmosphere is eloquent in the haziness of the setting sun. The impressionistic qualities of this painting are astounding, considering it was made some **fourteen years** before Monet, Renoir, Sisley, and Pissarro all converged on the area around Louveciennes.

The evidence is clear that Pissarro was painting in an impressionist manner long before other artists, and what they learned from him became known as Impressionism. In the winter of 1869-70, when heavy snows blanketed the region, Monet and Pissarro set out to capture the glistening scenes near Pissarro's home on the route de Versailles in Louveciennes. While Monet had painted snow scenes before, in 1867,[36] painting in the snow was a new experience for Pissarro.[37] During his visit with Pissarro, Monet made six small paintings in and around Louveciennes.[38] Pissarro made at least eight paintings of the snow that year, six of them on the route de Versailles and two others in nearby wooded areas.[39] They painted the same motif, but each artist interpreted it differently.

While the scenes in these two paintings are almost identical, they must have been made on different days, since there is less snow in the Monet. The house where Pissarro lived is the first one on the left in both paintings,[40] so Monet's position was farther back on the street. In his symmetrical composition, the road, bordered by tall trees, dominates the foreground as it recedes to the vanishing point, drawing the eye to the center of the canvas. The treetops assist by forming an "X" with the sides of the road. This painting of Monet's seems more realistic than impressionistic, with its depiction of gray and yellow tracks on the snow and the dark-green grass beside the road. There seems to be little, if any, reflection of light from the partly cloudy sky. The light on the yellow houses fades their facades to a nearly neutral color, leaving the pink roof in the distance the only spot of bright color. This may have been an artistic addition by Monet, as the Pissarro painting shows no pink roof.

In contrast, Pissarro put the road at an acute angle, creating two diagonal lines to the center of the low horizon line. These diagonals are intensified by perpendicular trees and horizontal shadows crossing the road. The pale orange of the houses complements the blue shadows on the road and the bright blue sky. The shadow cast in the lower-right corner of the canvas from an unseen tree or building is created with a mélange of colors—blue, green, and light yellow—that contrasts with the whiteness of the snow.

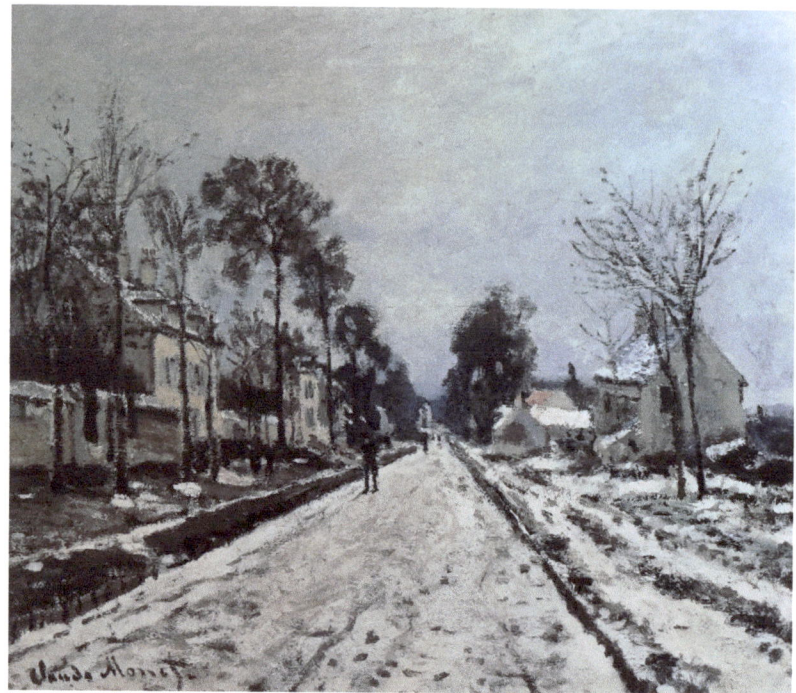

Fig. 49.
Claude Monet, *Route de Versailles*, 1869-70, Private collection

40. Pissarro and Durand-Ruel Snollaerts, *Pissarro: Catalogue Critique des Peintures*, 2:130.

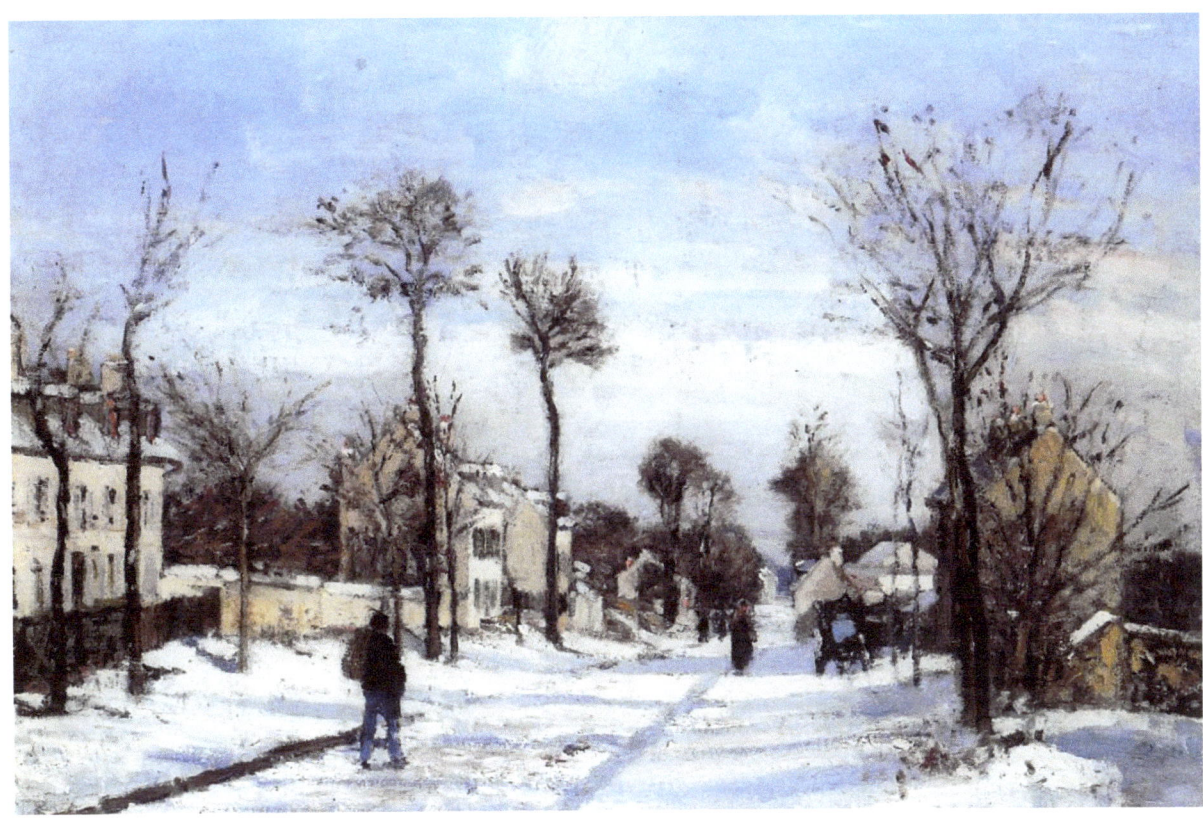

Fig. 50.
*Route de Versailles,
Louveciennes, Snow*, c.1870,
Stiftung Sammlung E. G.
Bührle, Zurich [PDRS 142]

41. Joachim Gasquet, *Joachim Gasquet's Cézanne: A Memoir with Conversations*, trans. Christopher Pemberton (London: Thames and Hudson, 1991), 164.

During the formative years of Impressionism, and especially during those years in Louveciennes, Pissarro shared his ideas and techniques freely with other artists. Because he was older than the others and had much more experience, his influence on them was profound. According to Cézanne, "It's he who was really the first Impressionist." [41]

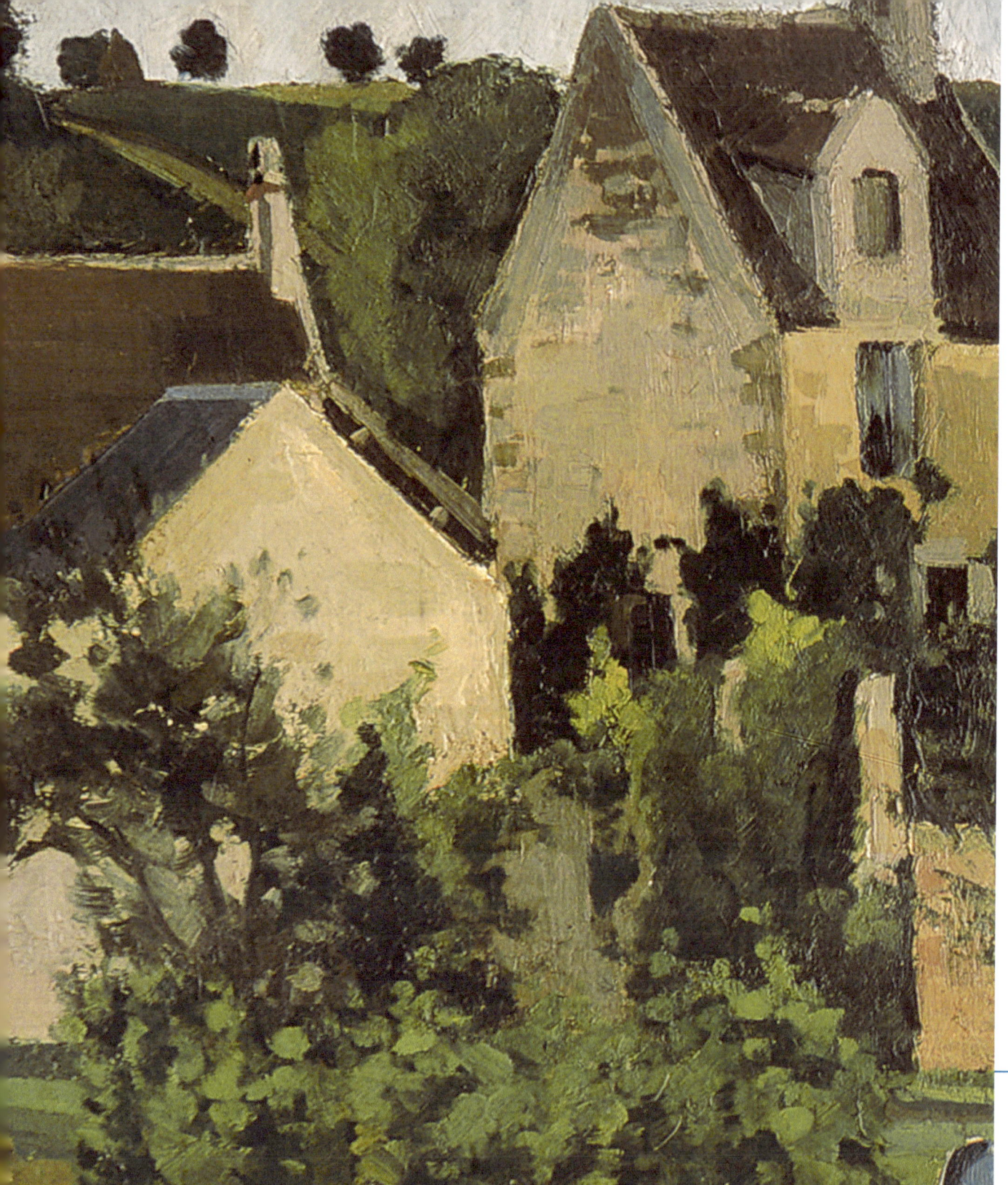

Fig. 51.
L'Hermitage à *Pontoise*, detail, 1867, Wallraf–Richartz-Museum, Fondation Corboud, Cologne, Germany [PDRS 119]

From Pissarro to Cézanne

The twenty-year period of their interaction had long-lasting repercussions on their lives and careers. One of the most moving testimonies of this is the fact that the aging Cézanne, after Pissarro's death, sent watercolors to a local exhibition under the name: "Paul Cézanne, pupil of Pissarro."[1]

—Joachim Pissarro

1. Pissarro, *Pioneering Modern Painting—Cézanne and Pissarro, 1865-1885*, 70.

2. Ibid.

3. Pissarro and Durand-Ruel Snollaerts, *Pissarro: Catalogue Critique des Peintures*, 1:110.

4. Brettell and Lloyd, *Catalogue of Drawings by Camille Pissarro in the Ashmolean Museum, Oxford*, 5.

The friendship between Camille Pissarro and Paul Cézanne is legendary in art history. Though Pissarro (born 1830) was nine years older than Cézanne (born 1839), the two artists became close friends and worked together on and off for nearly two decades.[2] By the time they met in April of 1861, Pissarro was already an experienced artist. Two years earlier, one of his landscapes had been accepted by the Salon and noted in reviews of the art critics.[3] However, Pissarro was more interested in experimenting with paint on canvas than in pleasing the Salon jury. In many of his paintings, he used what were then considered radical techniques. He simplified motifs down to bare elements and reduced figures to sketches. He flattened structures so that the geometric design of the composition took precedence. He accentuated brushstrokes, focusing on texture rather than representation. And he had already experimented with the same short, parallel strokes that he used in drawing, constructing shapes and forms with them rather than using them for shadows or modeling.[4] Although he borrowed from Corot and Courbet, he used what he learned from them to express his own individuality—his "sensation."

The twenty-two-year-old Cézanne had just arrived in Paris when he first met Pissarro in 1861 at the Académie Suisse.[5] He was from Aix-en-Provence, where he had been studying law to please his father. At the same time, he was a student at the École Gratuite de Dessin (Free School of Drawing) for three years (1857 to 1861). His father finally gave him an allowance of 125 francs per month and allowed him to move to Paris to pursue an artistic career.[6]

Things did not go well for Cézanne in Paris. In both 1861 and 1862, his applications to the École des Beaux-Arts were rejected. Frustrated, he returned home to work in his father's bank.[7] In 1863, Cézanne returned to Paris, where he worked at the Académie Suisse, and this is when the artistic dialogue between Pissarro and Cézanne began.[8] Years later, Pissarro remembered their first meeting: "Was I seeing right in 1861 when Oller and I went to see that peculiar Provençal at the Académie Suisse, where Cézanne was doing life studies that provoked roars of laughter from all the impotents of the school . . . ."[9] Cézanne's drawings of nude models were anything but ideal—all sharp angles carved with dark, determined lines and modeled with deep shadows. Pissarro must have focused on the vigorous strokes, radical attitude, and independent spirit displayed in Cézanne's drawings. He saw in Cézanne a kindred spirit—someone intent on defying generally accepted standards and eager to explore new ways of making art.

Though they met in 1861, the friendship between Pissarro and Cézanne did not become close until a few years later. An 1865 letter opens with the formal salutation "Monsieur Pissarro." A year later, Cézanne wrote to Pissarro as "Mon cher ami [my dear friend],"[10] suggesting the development of the relationship between them.

Pissarro's advice was an essential influence on Cézanne. They shared ideas and

5. Pissarro and Durand-Ruel Snollaerts, *Pissarro: Catalogue Critique des Peintures*, 1:113.

6. Françoise Cachin et al., *Cézanne* (Philadelphia: Philadelphia Museum of Art, 1996), 530-31.

7. Maloon, *Paths To Abstractions, 1867-1917*, 9.

8. Joachim Pissarro made a comprehensive study of the close friendship and artistic dialogue between Pissarro and Cézanne, resulting in a 2005 exhibition, "Cézanne and Pissarro: Pioneering Modern Painting," at the Museum of Modern Art (MoMA), New York; Los Angeles County Museum of Art; and the Musée d'Orsay, Paris. The catalogue published by MoMA is an invaluable resource on the two artists.

9. Pissarro, *Pioneering Modern Painting—Cézanne and Pissarro, 1865-1885*, 17-18.

10. Ibid., 40.

techniques, and "Pissarro opened his eyes to Courbet."[11] Together, they explored the use of the palette knife for applying paint to canvas. Pissarro took Cézanne into the countryside to paint *en plein air* and encouraged him to lighten his palette. English art critic Roger Fry said that Cézanne became apprentice to Pissarro, "who was already master of his method and in full possession of his personal style. It was, one may say, his first and his only apprenticeship."[12]

In July 1872, Cézanne took up residence in a hotel near Pontoise, where Pissarro was living with his family. In December, Cézanne moved his family to Auvers-sur-Oise to be near Pissarro. For almost two years, Cézanne walked 1.8 miles (about 3 kilometers) to Pontoise, and the two artists worked side-by-side on a daily basis.[13]

During this time, Cézanne had opportunity to look at all of Pissarro's paintings. One in particular caught his interest, and he asked Pissarro for permission to copy it. Lucien Pissarro wrote later about this incident:

"All I can say is that Cézanne borrowed one of father's pictures in 1870 to make a copy, probably to study how it was painted. Cézanne's copy still exists. . . . It is good to say this because one day it might be said that father copied Cézanne."[14]

Though Cézanne's version turned out somewhat different from Pissarro's original painting, the younger artist learned from the experience. According to art historian Theodore Reff: "The rendering of forms by small juxtaposed touches was itself no innovation [by Cézanne], of course, but derived from Pissarro, whose view of Louveciennes Cézanne copied carefully soon after arriving in Pontoise in 1872."[15]

Before he began working directly from nature with Pissarro, Cézanne had chosen imaginary subjects for his paintings—subjects based on religion, fantasy, and even violence. As Cézanne worked with Pissarro, his subject choices changed dramatically. "Pissarro is justly credited with having transformed Cézanne's style and, to some degree, his temperament, by encouraging

11. Gasquet, *Joachim Gasquet's Cézanne: A Memoir with Conversations*, 68.

12. Pissarro, *Pioneering Modern Painting—Cézanne and Pissarro, 1865-1885*, 72.

13. Pissarro and Durand-Ruel Snollaerts, *Pissarro: Catalogue Critique des Peintures*, 1:138.

14. Pissarro, *Pioneering Modern Painting—Cézanne and Pissarro, 1865-1885*, 103.

15. Theodore Reff, "Cézanne's Constructive Stroke," *The Art Quarterly* 24, no. 5 (1962): 222.

him to interact more fully with nature and by initiating him into a more deliberate, less subjective approach to his craft," explained Joseph Rishel, curator and specialist in the art of Cézanne.[16] Pissarro showed the younger artist that a subject portraying an image that is dramatic, horrific, sentimental, or even pretty will draw attention to itself and overpower the artist's "sensations." A simple, ordinary scene, like a landscape, provides a much better space for one's "sensations."[17]

By observing Pissarro's paintings, Cézanne also learned how to use the geometric lines and shapes he found in nature to structure his compositions. Pissarro's geometric compositions were complicated, as shown in his painting *View of the Côte des Mathurins, Pontoise* (1873). The diagonals of the garden lots in the foreground are emphasized by the sharp angles of the cottage roofs. These are set against the contrasting curves of fields on nearby hills. The geometric structuring he learned from Pissarro may have inspired Cézanne to seek motifs with similar geometric possibilities.

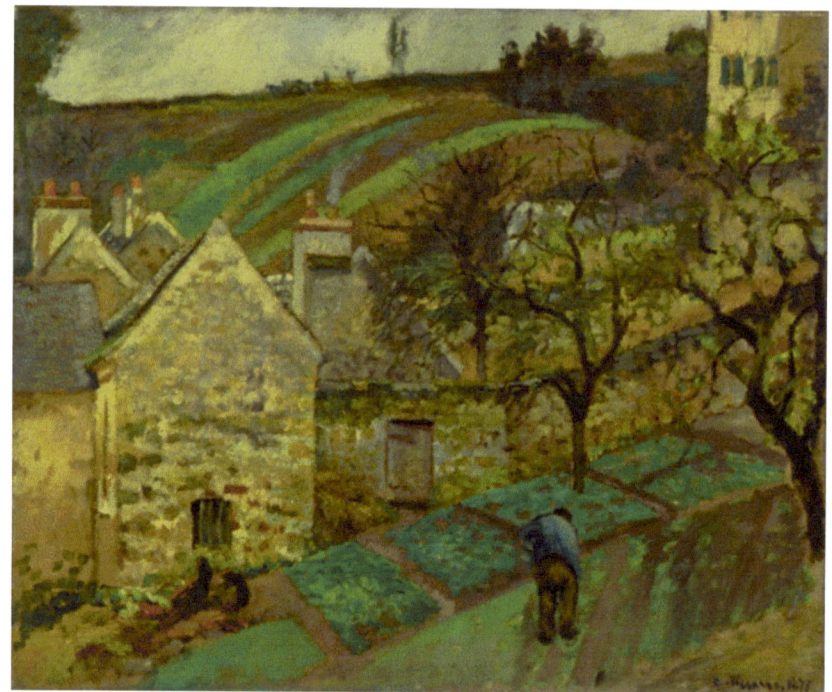

The Hanged Man's House, Auvers-sur-Oise (1873) is replete with opposing diagonals set against the strong perpendiculars of two tree trunks and the right edge of the house. A strong curve on the right indicates the steep descent of the path.

In 1872, Pissarro wrote to Paul Guillemet: "We have high hopes for our friend Cézanne . . . he will astonish a lot of artists who were too quick to condemn him."[18]

Fig. 52.
View of the Côte des Mathurins, Pontoise, 1873, Musée d'Orsay, Paris [PDRS 291]

16. Cachin et al., *Cézanne*, 229.

17. Pissarro, *Pioneering Modern Painting—Cézanne and Pissarro, 1865-1885*, 39-40.

18. Pissarro and Durand-Ruel Snollaerts, *Pissarro: Catalogue Critique des Peintures*, 1:18.

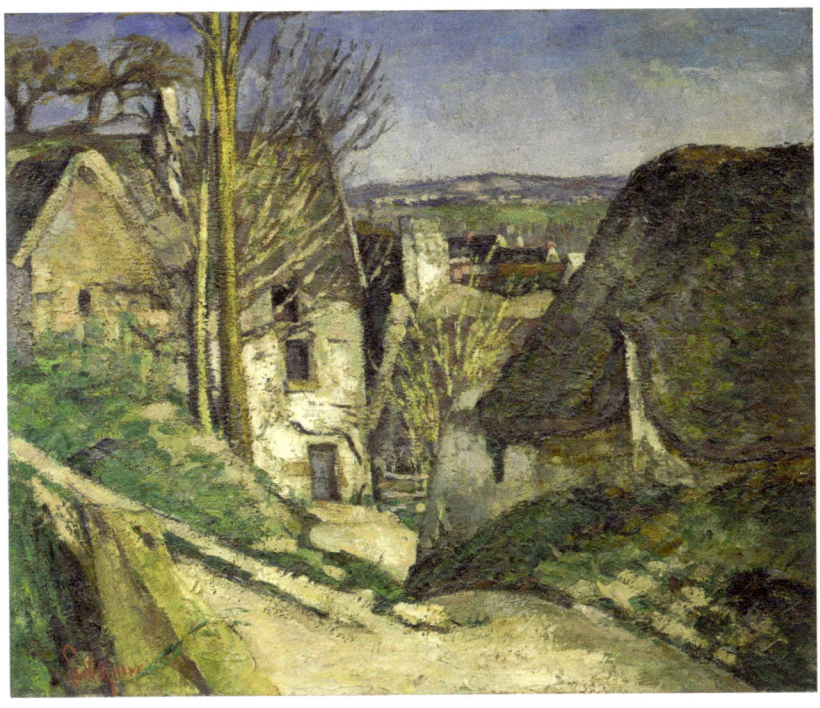

Fig. 53. Paul Cézanne, *The Hanged Man's House, Auvers-sur-Oise,* 1873, Musée d'Orsay, Paris

19. Rewald, ed., *Camille Pissarro: Letters to His Son Lucien,* 276.

20. Gasquet, *Joachim Gasquet's Cézanne: A Memoir with Conversations,* 164.

21. Cachin et al., *Cézanne,* 48.

As he painted with Pissarro, Cézanne began to lighten his color palette. He later recalled Pissarro's advice to him: "Never paint with anything but the three primary colours and their derivatives, he used to say to me."[20] Julius Meier-Graefe, the first non-French critic of Cézanne explained: "He followed Pissarro in that development to high tones, which Monet enjoined. . . . Without Pissarro, he would probably have gone on quietly painting his blacks."[21]

Cézanne also observed how Pissarro used color to create shapes and forms on the canvas instead of drawing them with outlines. In the painting *L'Hermitage à Pontoise* (1867), Pissarro painted patches of color with no shadows or modeling, so they seem to be flat on the canvas. The houses appear to have no volume at all; the curving fields on the hillside look like trapezoidal color blocks. Increasing that sense of flatness, the colors at the top of the hill are just as intense as those in the fore-ground, causing the background to push forward. Pissarro created a slight sense of recession by overlapping houses of slightly

There were frequent comments on the similarity of paintings by the two artists. This did not seem odd to Pissarro. Years later, in 1895, he wrote Lucien: "Curiously enough, in Cézanne's show at Vollard's there are certain landscapes of Auvers and Pontoise [painted in 1871-74] that are similar to mine. Naturally, we were always together! But what cannot be denied is that each of us kept the only thing that counts, the unique 'sensation!'—This could easily be shown."[19]

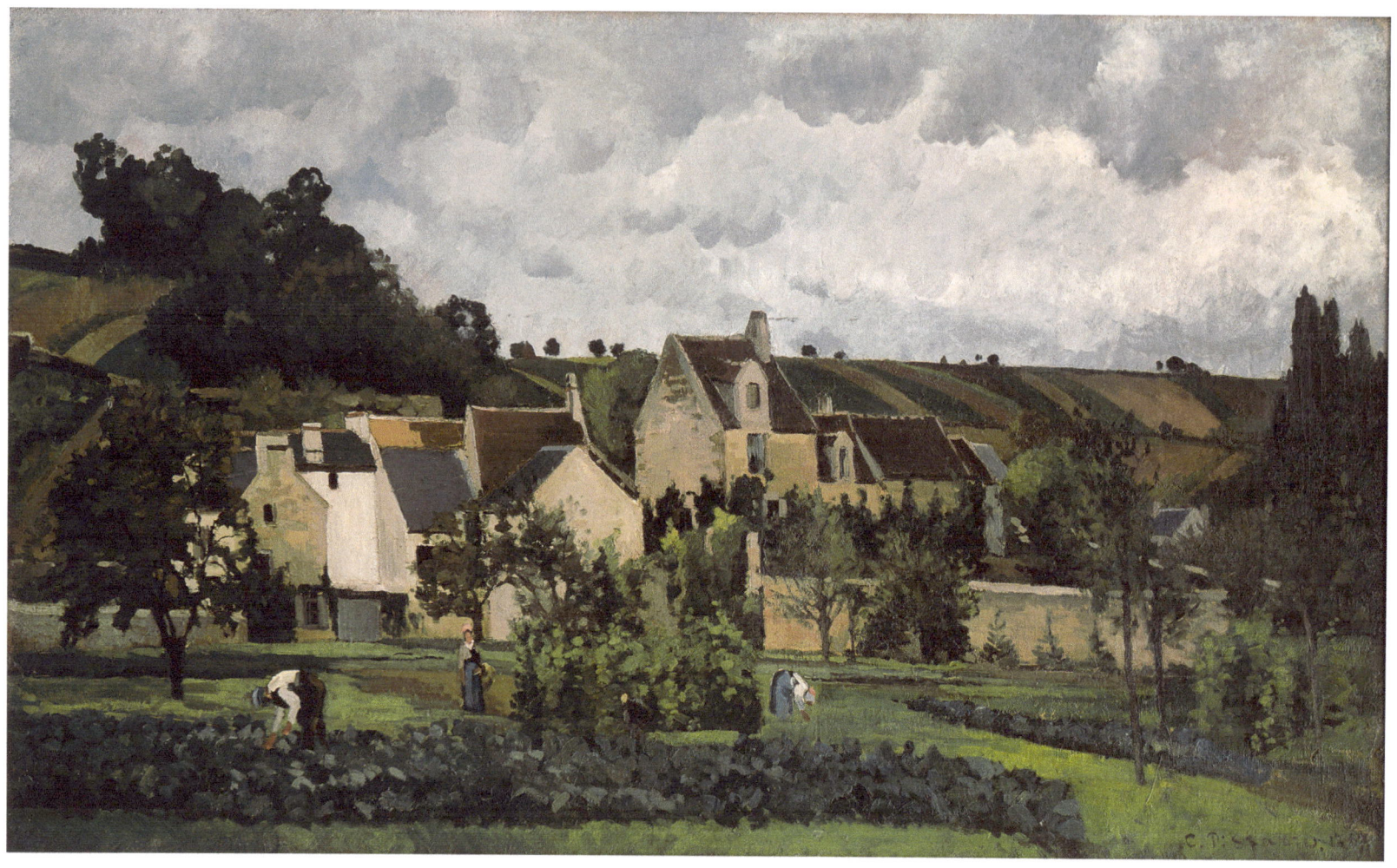

different colors. Only in the foreground is there indication of perspective. The houses and hillside are flat as theatrical scenery.

He was creating a new way of painting—one which called attention to the shapes of paint on the canvas rather than the picture.

Fig. 54.
L'Hermitage à *Pontoise*, 1867, Wallraf-Richartz-Museum, Fondation Corboud, Cologne, Germany [PDRS 119]

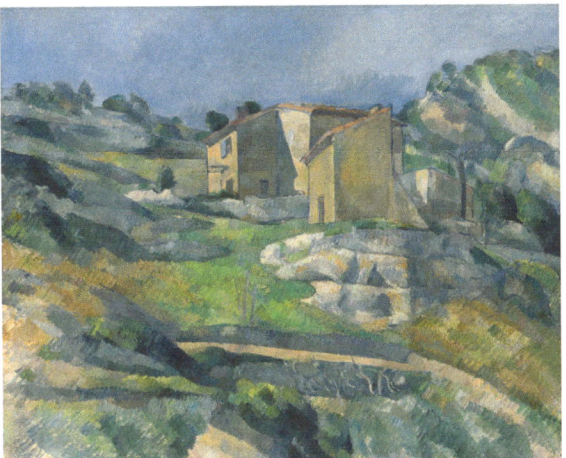

Fig. 55.

Paul Cézanne, *Houses in Provence: The Riaux Valley near L'Estaque*, c. 1873, National Gallery of Art, Washington, D.C., Collection of Mr. and Mrs. Paul Mellon

Cézanne's painting *Houses in Provence: The Riaux Valley near L'Estaque* (c. 1883) clearly indicates that he followed Pissarro's lead in painting blocks of color. However, his houses have more volume than Pissarro's, and the lighter colors in the distance suggest perspective. But, as he learned from Pissarro, he used the patches of color to formulate the composition without drawing contours and created a sense of depth by placing contrasting colors next to each other.[22]

Many of the things Cézanne learned from Pissarro have been attributed to Cézanne himself. Even during his lifetime, art critics and writers such as Félix Fénéon and Émile Bernard described Cézanne as having invented a new way of painting by himself.[23] For example, while Cézanne's exaggerated use of the "constructive" stroke gave it unusual importance, this was not something he invented entirely on his own.

The roots of the "constructive" stroke and its use in creating forms and shapes can be found throughout the works of Pissarro as early as the 1850s. In *Catalogue of Drawings by Camille Pissarro in the Ashmolean Museum, Oxford*, Richard Brettell and Christopher Lloyd examine the diagonal hatching in Pissarro's early drawings. Rather than using hatching to represent shadows or to create modeling, Pissarro used it to create forms and shapes within the drawing. "[It] has a remarkable affinity with Cézanne's so called "constructive stroke" of the 1870s."[24] Lloyd reiterated his point more recently, "the hatching in the foliage ANTICIPATES [emphasis his] Cézanne's 'constructive' stroke."[25]

22. Pissarro, *Pioneering Modern Painting—Cézanne and Pissarro, 1865-1885*, 59.

23. Ibid., 66.

24. Brettell and Lloyd, *Catalogue of Drawings by Camille Pissarro in the Ashmolean Museum, Oxford*, 5-6.

25. Christopher Lloyd, personal correspondence to author, April 25, 2017.

In his drawing *Route de Bussy*, Pissarro used small groups of parallel lines to represent clumps of leaves. When observing casually, the eye perceives the impression of foliage as it really looks. The space between each of the parallel lines serves to let in light, just as if sunlight were shining through the foliage. A closer inspection, however, reveals that the parallel lines are organized into shapes and oriented in various directions that also suggest leaves growing on different limbs rather than depictions of the actual leaves.

Pissarro carried this technique into many of his early paintings as well. While he did not use it consistently or exclusively, he used it along with other techniques.

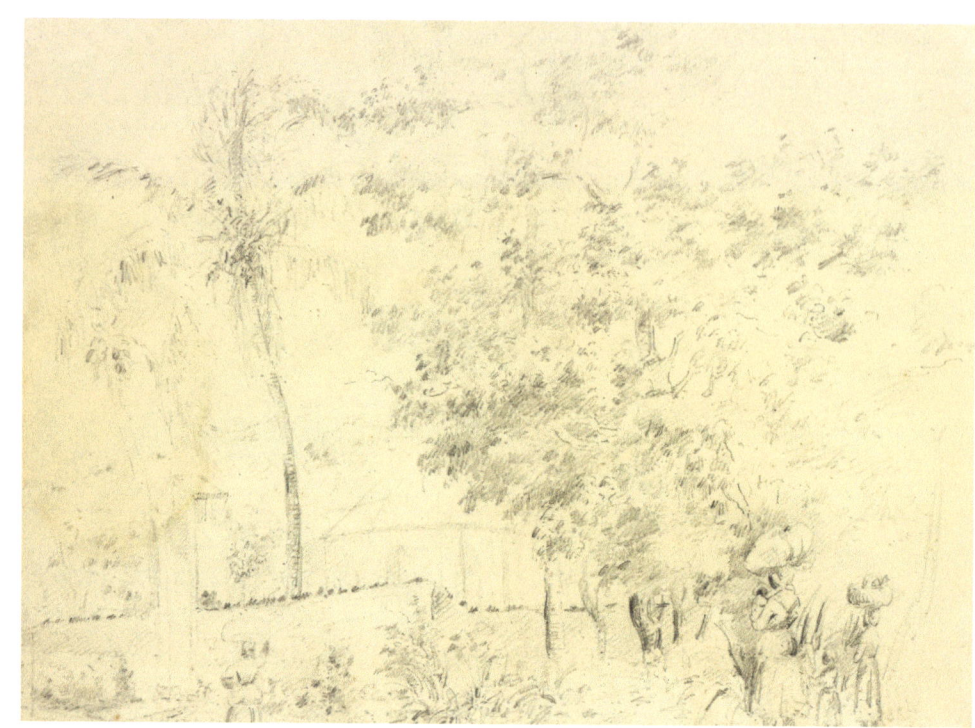

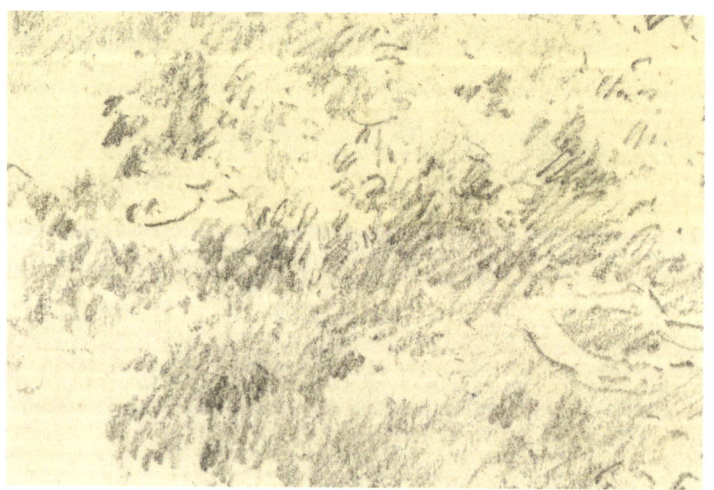

Fig. 56. (top)
Route de Bussy, No. 4, recto, Ashmolean Museum, Oxford

Fig. 57. (right)
Route de Bussy, detail, No. 4, recto, Ashmolean Museum, Oxford

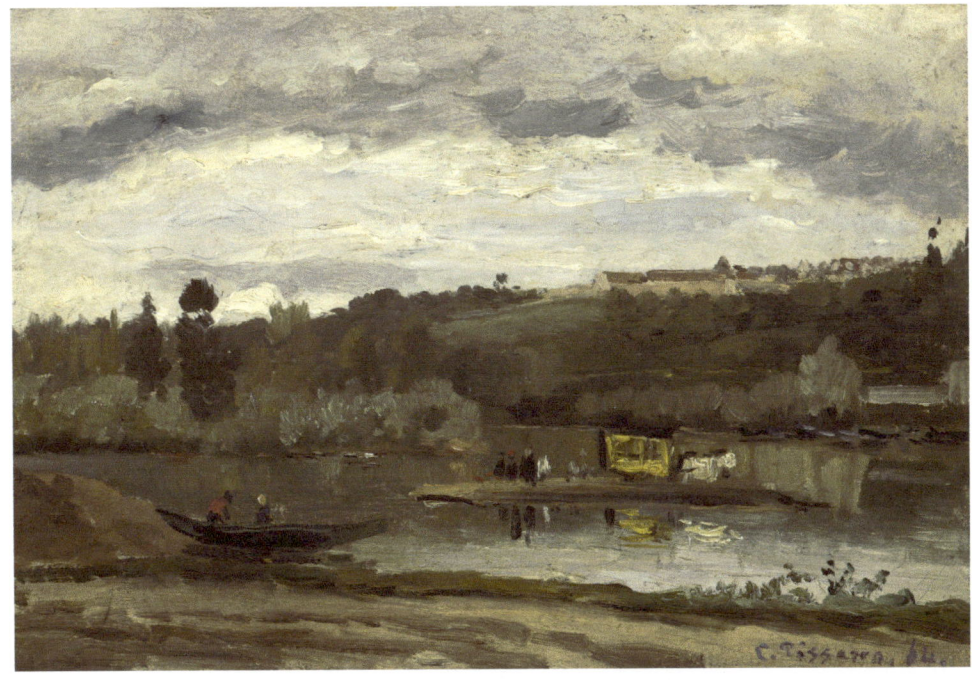

In his painting *Bac à La Varenne-Saint-Hilaire* (1864), Pissarro used the parallel strokes extensively in the foliage, again orienting them in different directions. This is clearly visible in the detail of the painting. He also used vertical parallel strokes for the segment behind the horse, which extends to the right, and in the trees. This was in 1864, before he and Cézanne had begun painting together on a regular basis.

The same kind of parallel strokes also appear in Pissarro's painting *Harvesting Potatoes, Pontoise*, (1874). This painting was made during a time when he and Cézanne were frequently together and often painted the same motifs.

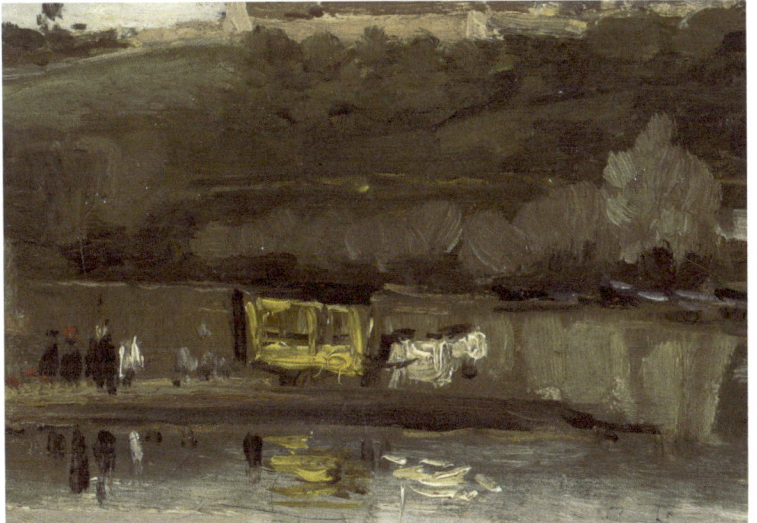

Fig. 58. (top)
Bac à La Varenne Saint Hilaire, 1864, Musée d'Orsay, Paris [PDRS 81]

Fig. 59. (left)
Bac à La Varenne-Saint-Hilaire, detail, 1864, Musée d'Orsay, Paris [PDRS 81]

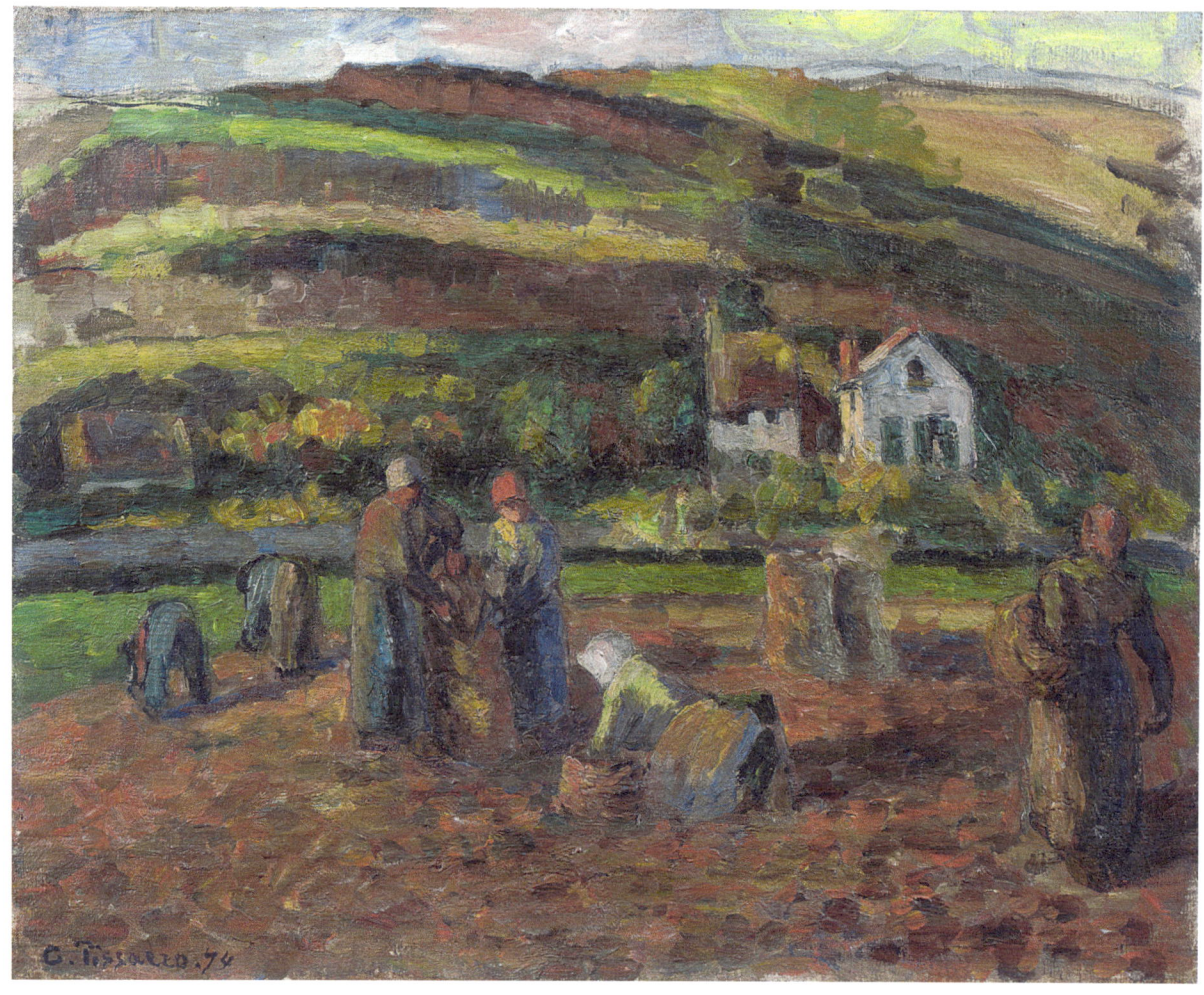

Fig. 60.
Harvesting Potatoes,
Pontoise, 1874, Private
collection [PDRS 360]

The parallel strokes are most evident in the colorful ridges on the hill, especially the dark-red one near the top of the canvas. Cézanne would certainly have seen this painting and noted Pissarro's use of the parallel strokes. It seems logical that he might have experimented with this device in his own paintings.

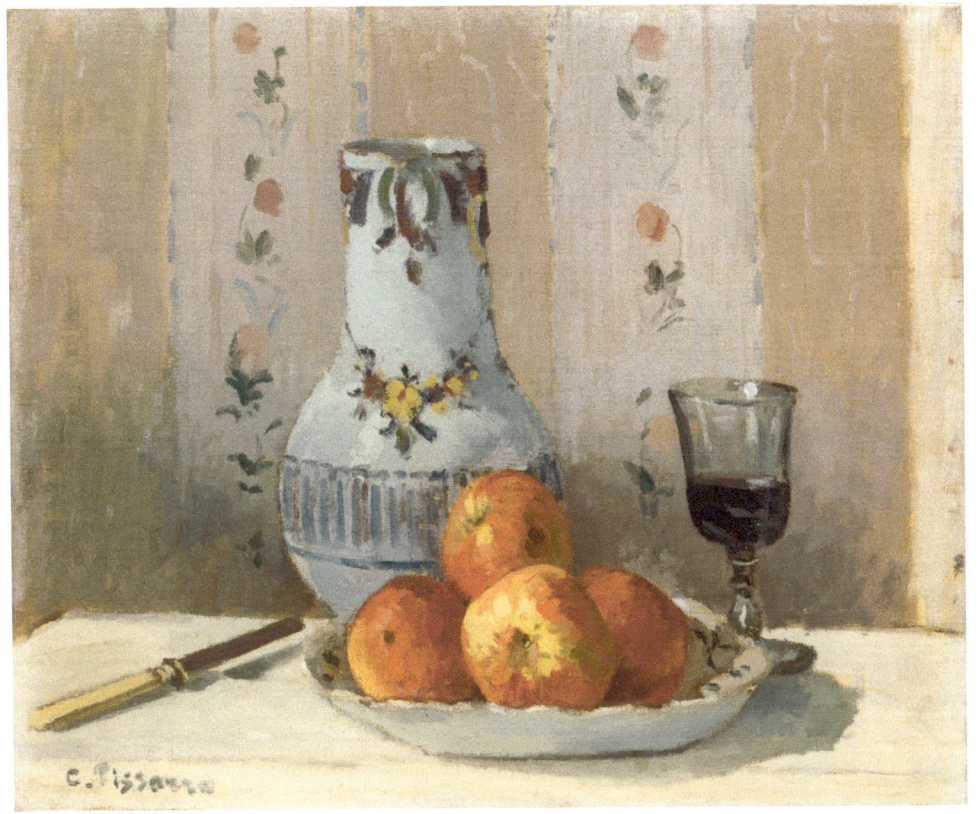

To determine when Cézanne began to use the "constructive" stroke, it is useful to compare his paintings with Pissarro's during those early years (1872 to 1874), when they painted together almost daily.[26]

A still life by Pissarro, *Apples and Glazed Earthenware* (c. 1872), provides an interesting example. A close-up reveals parallel, directional brushstrokes, especially on the foremost apple, in the light-red diagonal stripes pointed up, and the darker red diagonal stripes to the right pointed down.

Fig. 61.
Apples and Glazed Earthenware, c. 1872, The Metropolitan Museum of Art, New York, Purchase, Mr. and Mrs. Richard J. Bernhard Gift, by exchange, 1983

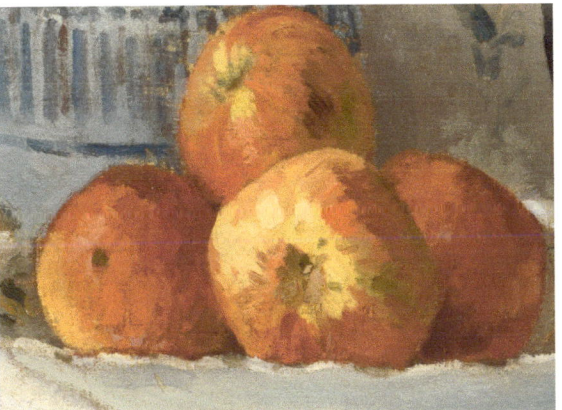

26. Pissarro and Durand-Ruel Snollaerts, *Pissarro: Catalogue Critique des Peintures*, 1:138.

Fig. 62.
Apples and Glazed Earthenware, detail, c. 1872, The Metropolitan Museum of Art, New York, Purchase, Mr. and Mrs. Richard J. Bernhard Gift, by exchange, 1983

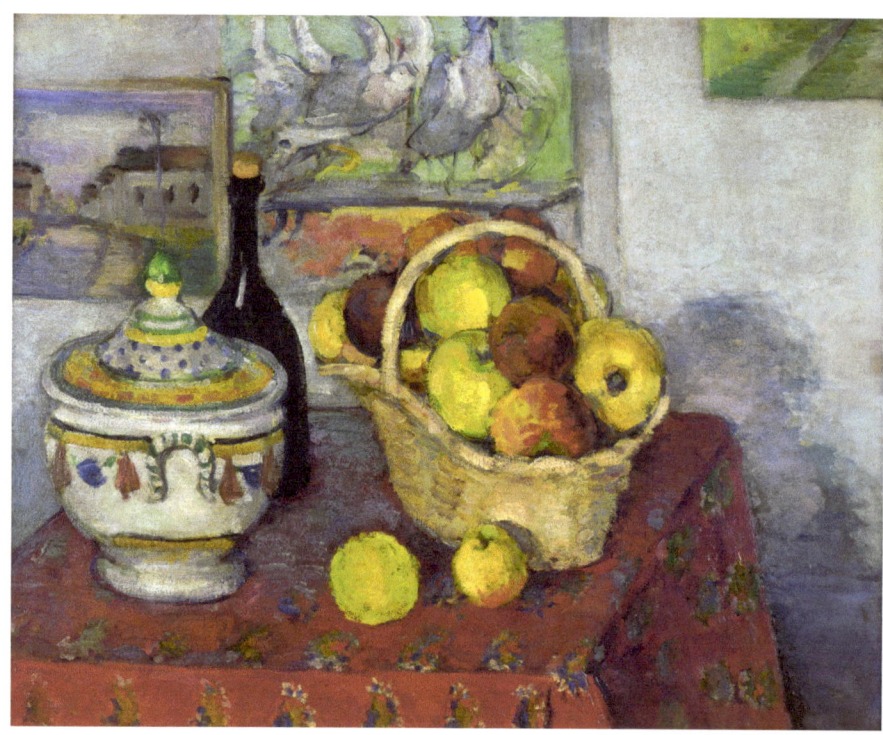

Fig. 63.
Paul Cézanne, *Still Life with Soup Tureen*, c. 1873-74, Musée d'Orsay, Paris

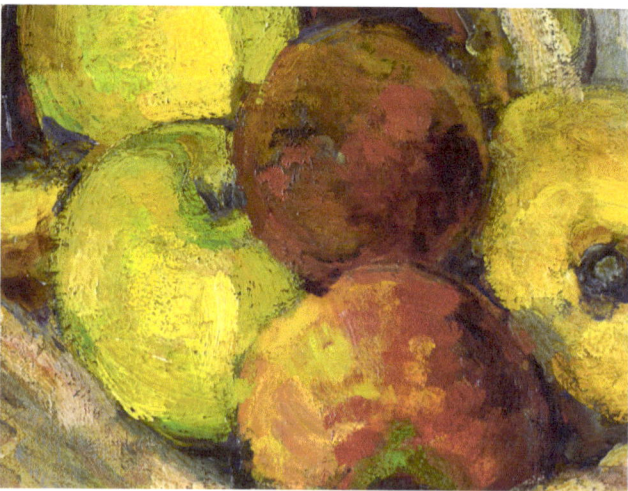

Fig. 64.
Paul Cézanne, *Still Life with Soup Tureen*, detail, c. 1873-74, Musée d'Orsay, Paris

The painting *Still Life with Soup Tureen* (c. 1873-74) by Cézanne was actually painted in the Pissarro home and was first owned by Pissarro. It depicts two of Pissarro's paintings in the background.[27] A close look at the apples shows that Cézanne's brushstrokes are smooth and connected, unlike the parallel strokes seen in Pissarro's apples.

27. Cachin et al., *Cézanne*, 143; ibid. The date of this painting is problematic, and art historians have previously put it at 1877. However, recent scholarship places it at c. 1873-74, because of its solid, continuous brush-strokes, which are different from the parallel strokes Cézanne began using around 1877.

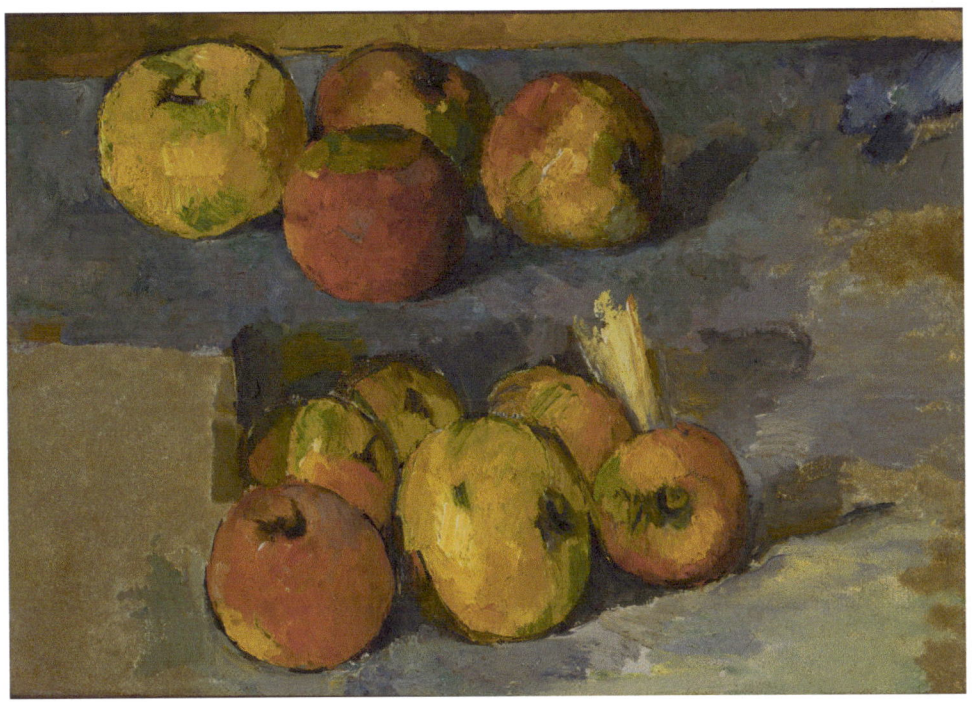

Fig. 65.
Paul Cézanne, *Apples*, 1878-79, The Metropolitan Museum of Art, New York, The Mr. and Mrs. Henry Ittleson, Jr., Purchase Fund, 1961

This method would change in a few years, and Cézanne's apples would look very different. In the Cézanne painting *Apples*, made in 1878-79, the parallel lines are evident, especially in the yellow apple in the upper-left corner. Above the yellow parallel lines in the center are green lines. This is about the time when art historians believe that Cézanne was beginning to use the "constructive" stroke in a variety of ways.[28]

Fig. 66.
Paul Cézanne, *Apples*, detail, 1878-79, The Metropolitan Museum of Art, New York, The Mr. and Mrs. Henry Ittleson, Jr., Purchase Fund, 1961

28. Reff, "Cézanne's Constructive Stroke" (1962), 222.

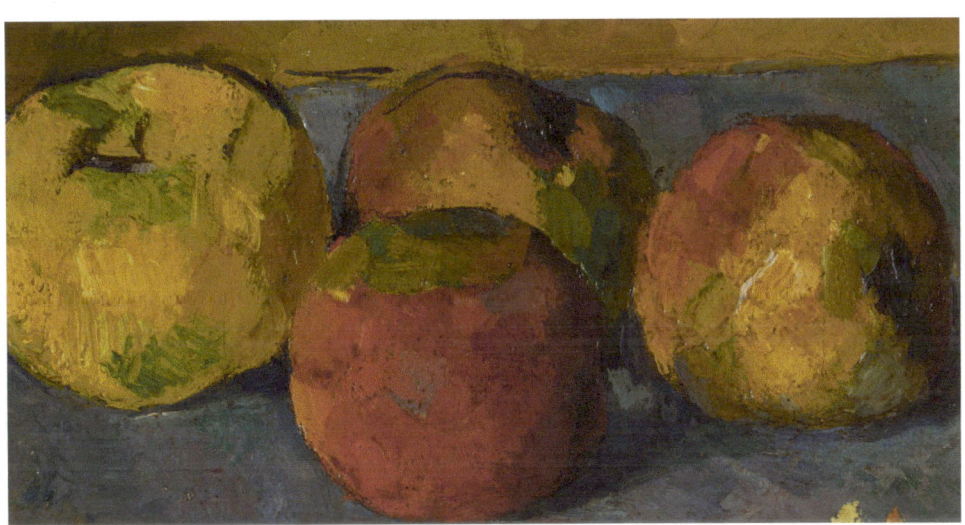

Cézanne's use of the parallel strokes is also evident his landscapes such as *The Gulf of Marseilles, Seen from L'Estaque* (c. 1885). He used them in different shades of green to depict foliage. The same strokes can be found in blue on the distant mountain and in yellow and blue in the sky. He used strokes like Pissarro used patches of color to create forms and shapes, eliminating drawing and outlines.[29]

At this point, the differences in the two artists' use of the parallel strokes is clear. Pissarro used them as one of many different techniques he might employ in a single painting. Unlike him, Cézanne began to emphasize the parallel strokes, and, by 1880, he was using them to construct entire paintings, building up shapes and forms of all kinds with parallel lines.

Later in his life, Cézanne described what he was trying to do in developing what became known as the "constructive" stroke: "I too was an Impressionist, I don't conceal the fact. Pissarro had an enormous influence on me. But I wanted to make

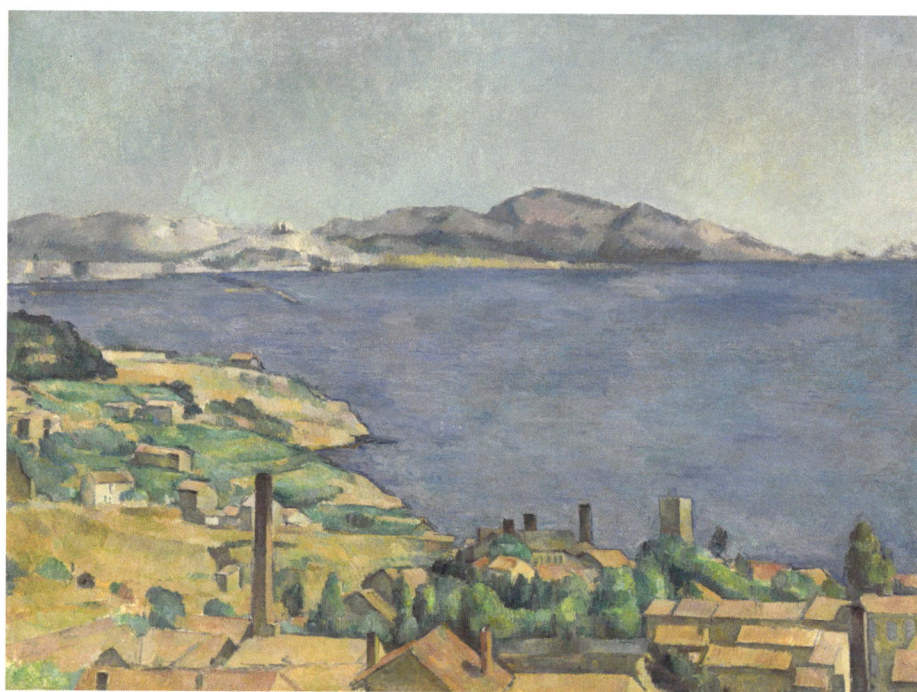

out of Impressionism something solid and lasting like the art of the museums."[30] How he achieved his goal is best described by Rishel: "The key to this breakthrough was a novel approach to facture, the way pigment was applied to canvas. In this new technique, pictorial space is constructed through repeated parallel brushstrokes that produce a patterned, woven effect. The effect produced is extremely sensuous and very subtle."[31]

29. Pissarro, *Pioneering Modern Painting—Cézanne and Pissarro, 1865-1885*, 54.

30. Gasquet, *Joachim Gasquet's Cézanne: A Memoir with Conversations*, 164.

31. Cachin et al., *Cézanne*, 193.

Pissarro experimented with Cézanne's reductionist version of Pissarro's own technique in the early 1880s, but he never adopted it. He was more interested in the innovations of Georges Seurat and would ultimately join in the explorations of Pointillism. Cézanne and Pissarro may have painted together one last time in 1882.[32] Though Cézanne visited Paris and stayed for a while at Vernon, a village across the river Seine from Monet's home in Giverny, he left without saying goodbye to Pissarro.[33] The close relationship of almost twenty years had ended.

This did not keep Pissarro from promoting Cézanne's work. In 1883, he wrote art critic Joris-Karl Huysmans: "How is it that you have not said a word about Cézanne? There is not a single one of us who doesn't regard him as one of the most astonishing and curious personalities of our era and he has had an enormous influence on modern art."[34]

Cézanne did not return the favor, however. In an 1896 letter to his son Lucien, Pissarro wrote that art critic Georges Lecomte told him that Cézanne "started to run me into the ground. . . . How nice: I, who for thirty years defended him with so much energy and conviction. . . . Oh, Bah! Let's work hard and try to make splendid grays! That would be better than running others into the ground."[35]

After Pissarro's death, Cézanne said, "As for the old Pissarro, he was a father to me. He was a man you could turn to for advice; he was something like God."[36] Describing the interactions between the two artists, Rishel wrote: "Pissarro's influence on Cézanne cannot be overestimated."[37]

Pissarro's influence had been discounted in 1921 in an editorial in the *Burlington Magazine*: "All have come to an agreement about Cézanne. . . . [He] is universally recognized as the father of the whole movement."[38] That conclusion was accepted by art-history textbooks and is the reason Cézanne is known today as the father of modern art. Even though Pissarro's influence is barely recognized, it is reasonable to say that without Pissarro, there would have been no Cézanne.

32. Pissarro, *Pioneering Modern Painting—Cézanne and Pissarro, 1865-1885*, 242.

33. Ibid.

34. Ibid.

35. Ibid., 243.

36. Ibid.

37. Cachin et al., *Cézanne*, 378.

38. Robert R. Tatlock, "Cézanne and the Nation," *The Burlington Magazine for Connoisseurs* 38, no. 218 (1921), 209.

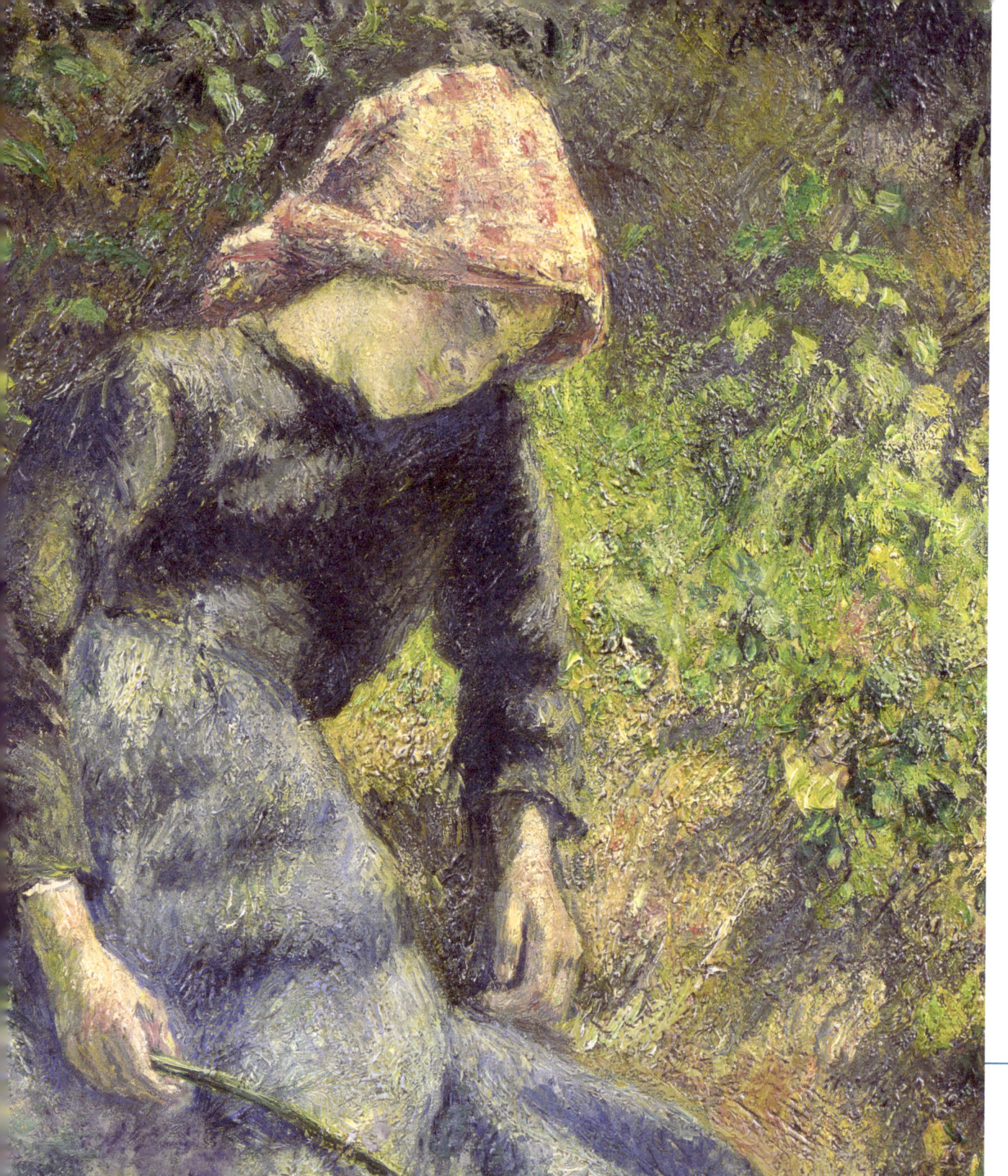

Fig. 68.
Peasant Girl with a Stick,
detail, 1881, Musée d'Orsay
[PDRS 653]

7 Pissarro's Pointillism

The painter was won over by Seurat's revolution, immediately recognizing it as the radicalization of his own attempts to renew Impressionism. Seurat himself admitted that he had been influenced by Pissarro's work of the early 1880s.[1]

—Christophe Duvivier

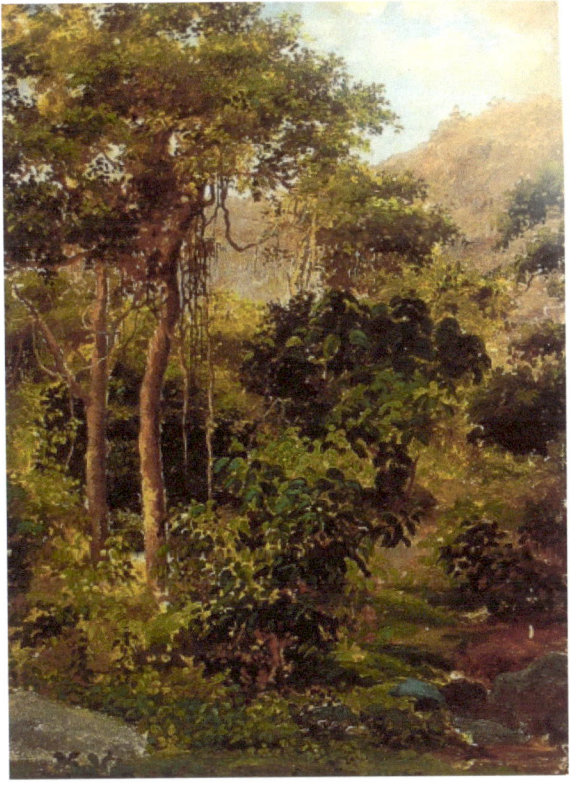

Fig. 69.
Tropical Forest, Galipan,
c. 1854, Private collection
[PDRS 6]

1. Claire Durand-Ruel Snollaerts and Christophe Duvivier, *Camille Pissarro: The First among the Impressionists* (Vanves, France: Éditions Hazan, 2017), 102.

2. Pissarro and Durand-Ruel Snollaerts, *Pissarro: Catalogue Critique des Peintures*, 1:99.

Pissarro had attended the Salon during his time as a schoolboy in Passy (1842-48),[2] and he may have seen Eugène Delacroix's bold use of color at a young age. He could have heard about Delacroix's notorious painting *The Barque of Dante*, also known as *Dante and Virgil in Hell* (1822), and the artist's interest in the color theories of Michel-Eugène Chevreul. Even as a young artist in the Caribbean, Pissarro had applied the notion of broken color to many of his paintings.

In *Tropical Forest, Galipan* (c. 1854), he used tiny brushstrokes in many separate, unblended shades of yellow and green—pale bluish green, light yellow-green, lush green, dark bluish green, dark forest-green—to capture sunlight and to define the foliage.

When Pissarro discarded black, bitumen, raw sienna, and the ochers in 1865,[3] his palette became even lighter and brighter, and his use of complementary colors became more dramatic. In 1881, Ogden Rood's *Modern Chromatics: Students' Text-Book of Color with Applications to Art and Industry* was translated into French. Its influence, along with the theories of Chevreul, is evident in Pissarro's work of that period. Richard Bretell explains: "Any careful examination of Pissarro's work will reveal that many, if not all, the major stylistic traits of the neo-impressionist movement were already present by 1883 . . . . It seems that Pissarro was familiar with optical theories of colour well before his discussions with Seurat in 1885."[4]

His painting *Young Peasant Girl Having Café au Lait* (1881) is a study in the optical mixing of colors and reflections. The blue-green on the wall behind her is reflected on the shoulder and sleeve of her pink blouse.

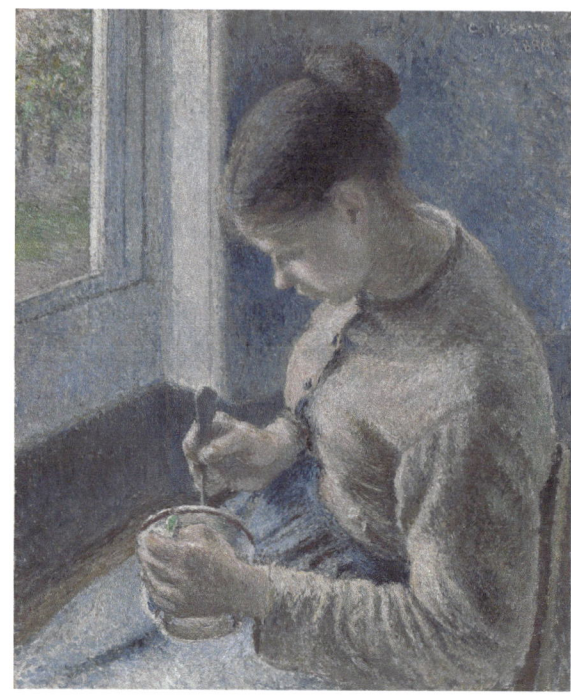

Fig. 70.
Young Peasant Girl Having Café au Lait, 1881, Art Institute of Chicago, Potter Palmer Collection [PDRS 662]

Her dark-blue skirt is reflected on the front of her blouse, and the pink of her long sleeve is reflected in the skirt at the bottom of the canvas. The brushstrokes are tiny and, for the most part, crisscrossed. This painting clearly foreshadows what the young Georges Seurat would be doing a few years later.

Seurat must have grown up knowing Pissarro's work. At the age of twenty,

3. Gasquet, *Joachim Gasquet's Cézanne: A Memoir with Conversations*, 164.

4. Cachin et al., *Pissarro*, 30.

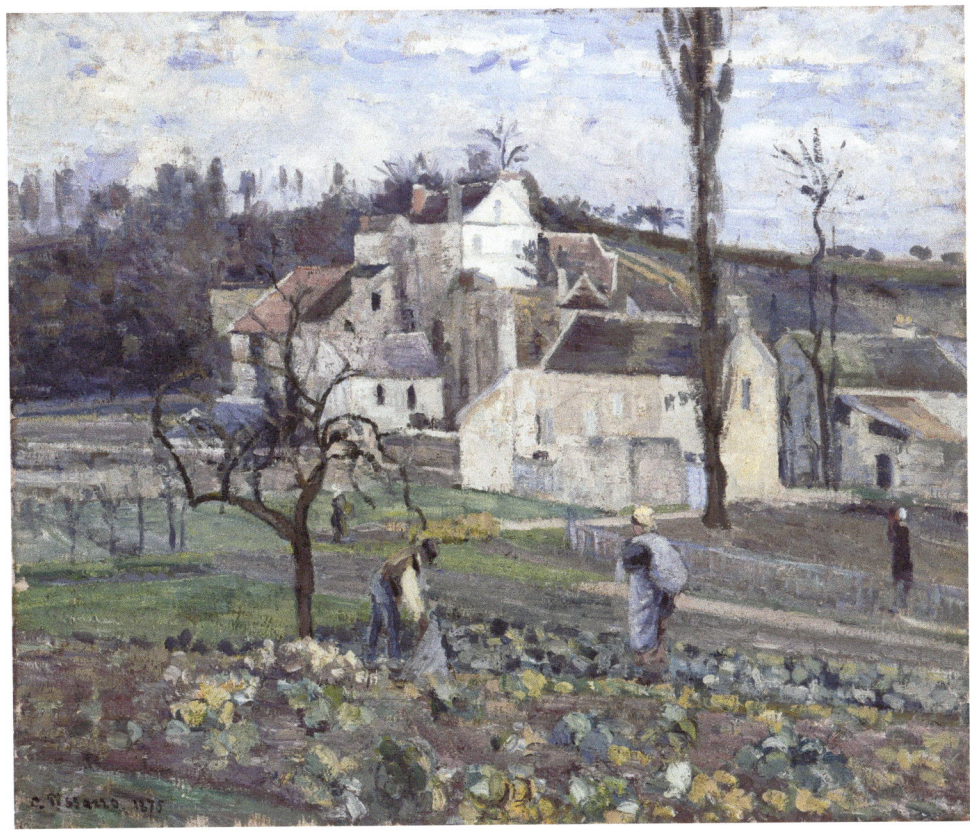

Fig. 71.
The Cabbage Harvest, L'Hermitage, Pontoise, 1875, Cincinnati Art Museum, Ohio, Gift of Albert P. Strietmann [PDRS 399]

5. Robert L. Herbert et al., *Georges Seurat: 1859-1891* (New York: Harry N. Abrams, 1991), 104.

he visited the Fourth Impressionist Exhibition (1879) with a friend who made note of the event.[5] He could also have attended the Second (1876) and the Third Impressionist Exhibitions (1877), since he was living in Paris and studying art at the time. In the 1879 exhibition, Seurat would have seen some twenty paintings by

Pissarro, including *The Cabbage Harvest, L'Hermitage, Pointoise* (1875). The scene of an unimportant farm is no more than a series of horizontal panels, beginning in the foreground, with cabbages described in circular brushstrokes. Pissarro displayed his facility in color division, using a wide range of greens— yellow green, light green, grass green, blue green, and dark green. Just above that layer is a complicated panel, including longer brushstrokes of slate blue, grass green, tawny yellow, and pale pink. The largest panel consists of an assemblage of houses stacked one upon the other, flattened against a dark hill. The structures are formed solely with colors—white, pale pink, slate blue, and coral. The walls are solid blocks, with only a few dark brushstrokes to suggest windows. At the top, the brushstrokes make no effort to form clouds. The blue-gray brushstrokes are tied to the lower panels only by one very tall poplar tree that dwarfs the two-story houses. The three (maybe four) people are simply elements, as unimportant as the scraggly tree to the left.

At the Sixth (1881) and Seventh (1882) Impressionist Exhibitions, Seurat would have seen even more radical paintings by Pissarro, including *Young Peasant Girl Having Café au Lait* (1881). Pissarro's influence on the young Seurat seemed evident to Robert L. Herbert, Seurat expert: "He must have seen Impressionist pictures by this time, but only Pissarro—significantly the most 'Barbizon' of the Impressionists—had any effect on him."[6]

Seurat's early paintings reflect the Barbizon traditions with landscapes and peasant scenes similar to those of Pissarro. In *White Houses, Ville d'Avray* (1882-83), Seurat used composition as in many of Pissarro's paintings. By this time, however, he is beginning to experiment with divided color, which will lead to the dots of his Neo-Impressionist period. The lower panel appears to be light orange, but closer inspection reveals dashes of light reds and yellows with just enough pale green to increase the brilliance. Above that is a green panel, spiked with just a bit of red. Clearly, he did not want this green to be more brilliant than

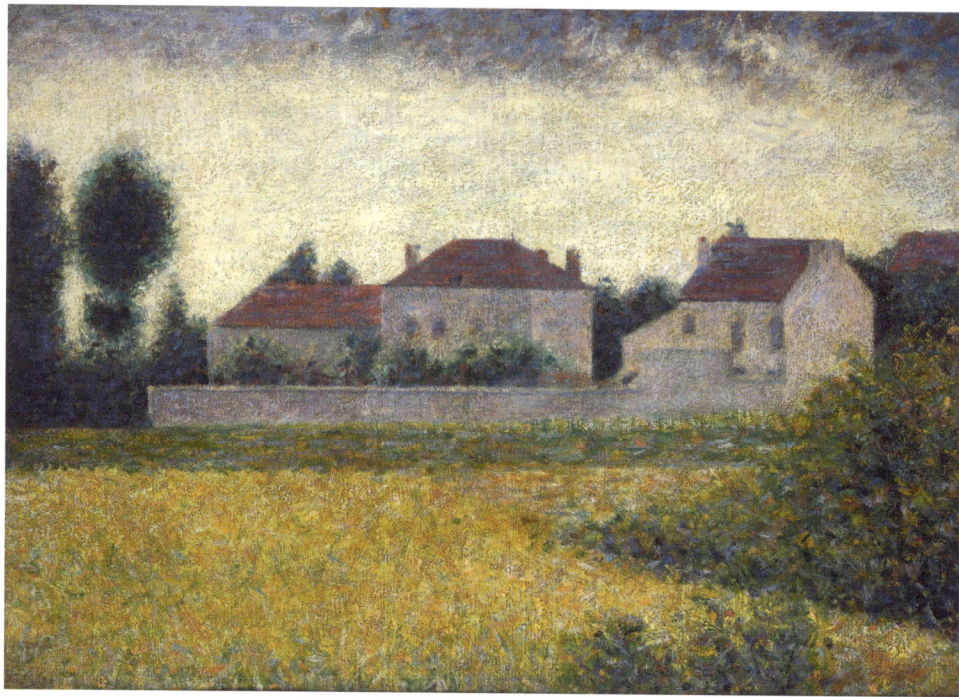

Fig. 72.
Georges Seurat, *White Houses, Ville d'Avray*, 1882-83, Walker Art Gallery, Liverpool

the wide strip at the bottom. Just above the center of the canvas are three white houses with dark roofs. The buildings, similar to those in Pissarro's painting, are simply flattened colored panels, with few windows to define them. The sky is a mélange of white and gray and disappears into dark slate blue at the top.

Seurat may have taken note of Pissarro's figure paintings, several of which were

6. Ibid., 9.

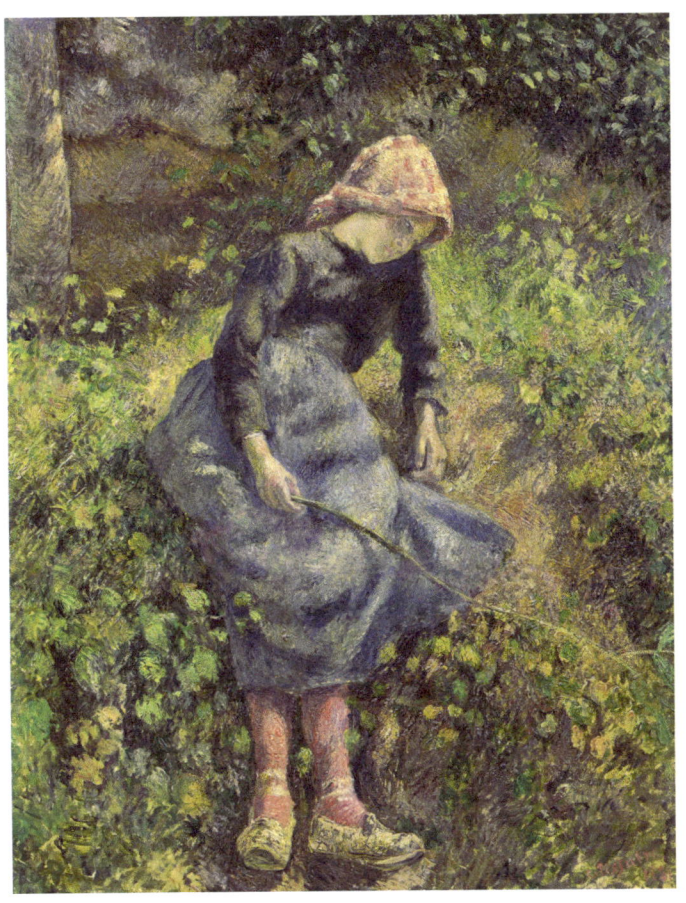

Fig. 73.
Peasant Girl with a Stick, 1881, Musée d'Orsay
[PDRS 653]

7. Pissarro and Durand-Ruel Snollaerts, *Pissarro: Catalogue Critique des Peintures*, 1:175.

as well as part of her blue skirt. To the right, bright green overlaps yellow, highlighted by deep green, with small patches of orangish red brushed thinly over the green. On the left her blue skirt disappears into the foliage, reflecting the bright green of the leaves. The pale yellow of her hand is highlighted with orangish red, providing a complement (according to Rood's color chart) to the blue brushstrokes surrounding it. Pissarro used large white checks to soften the pale red color of her kerchief (a solid red would have produced too harsh a contrast with the surrounding green grasses). The girl's striped stockings are the same pale red, mellowed by white streaks reflecting the sunlight.

shown in the Seventh Impressionist Exhibition (1882).[7] *Peasant Girl with a Stick* (1881) pictures a girl against background foliage with no horizon line. Pissarro used tiny brushstrokes, which are both directional and crisscrossed, to portray the grasses behind the girl

In 1883, Seurat made a similar painting, *Peasant Woman Seated in the Grass*, that suggests the influence of Pissarro's figure paintings. His painting shows a woman seated in lush foliage, with no horizon line and no sky. The younger artist also used tiny directional strokes of yellow, green, and pale orange to suggest a grassy area.

Though the woman's face is barely visible, her pose suggests a pensive mood, like some figures painted by Pissarro.

However, much in this painting reveals Seurat's unique sensibilities. The background contains no recognizable foliage nor tree trunks to define the space. Instead of integrating the figure into the background, Seurat clearly outlined her shape with deep color. He seated her on a reddish brown blanket and extended her profile with reddish purple shadow. The strong contrast of sunlight and shadow on her body gives her the appearance of a sculpture. He used complementary colors, as defined by Rood, placing the orangish red tint on her back against deep greenish blue. The background of complementary blue and orangish yellow provides a bright, clear contrast to the dark figure.

Though Seurat is certain to have seen Pissarro's paintings at Impressionist exhibitions, the two did not meet until October 1885, when Paul Signac introduced them at Durand-Ruel's gallery in Paris. At this

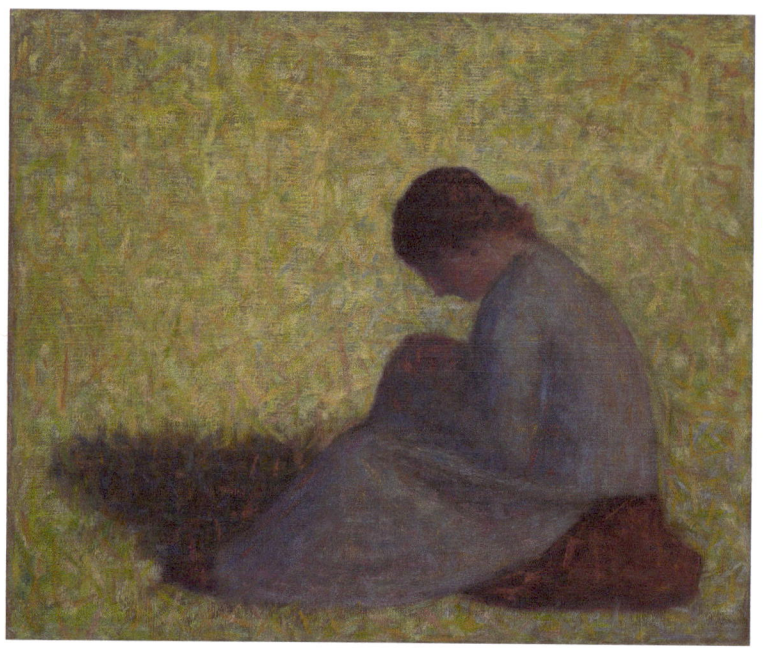

time, Pissarro was already fifty-five years old and Seurat was only twenty-six, just four years older than Pissarro's oldest son Lucien.[8] Age was never an issue with Pissarro, who was always eager to share his ideas and experience with other artists.

Later, in a letter to Félix Fénéon, Seurat himself described his development as a young artist: He claimed that he had been looking for an "optical formula" since he first held a brush in 1876. He read about

Fig. 74.
Georges Seurat, *Peasant Woman Seated in the Grass*, 1883, Solomon R. Guggenheim Museum, New York, Solomon R. Guggenheim Founding Collection, By gift

8. Ibid., 1:189.

Delacroix's use of color in his journal and studied the color theories described in Charles Blanc's *Grammar of Painting and Engraving* (published 1867) and Michel-Eugène Chevreul's *Principles of Harmony and Contrast of Colors* (published 1839). After reading a review of Ogden Rood's *Modern Chromatics: Students' Text-Book of Color with Applications to Art and Industry* (French edition published, 1881), he immediately obtained a copy and began studying it. Even though he had seen paintings of the Impressionists, most of whom no longer used earth colors, it took him two years (1882-84) to completely eliminate them from his palette.[9]

In keeping with technological advances of the Industrial Revolution, Seurat was taking a scientific approach to painting. His experiments led him to invent a new technique in which his brushstrokes were smaller and more regular in order to achieve the optical mixing described by Rood.[10] Since his paintings resembled the regular stitches of tapestries, critics referred to his technique as "Pointillism" (French for "stitch").

Robert L. Herbert explained how Pissarro's technique of the early 1880s influenced the young artist: "The elder artist interlaced fine touches to form nearly abstract tapestries of paint. However, he varied his facture in direction and size to create a 'natural' look, and he avoided the strong contrasts between areas that give *La Grand Jatte* its striking patterns."[11]

It was very important to Seurat to be known as the inventor of this new technique. In fact, he once said that he did not want to be known as the "pupil of Pissarro."[12] Pissarro, who was legendary for his generosity to friends, was pleased to give Seurat the credit for Pointillism. When he wrote a letter to Durand-Ruel explaining the new technique, he said definitively that it was Seurat "who was the first to have the idea of applying the scientific theory after thorough study."[13] When he wrote Fénéon in 1886, he was especially sensitive to Seurat's need for recognition: "I think we need to . . . be specific when it comes to Seurat who first had the good sense to conscientiously practice the theories of Chevreul."[14]

9. Herbert et al., *Georges Seurat: 1859-1891*, 383.

10. Ogden N. Rood, *Modern Chromatics: Students' Text-Book of Color with Applications to Art and Industry* (London: C. Kegan Paul, 1879), 279-80.

11. Herbert et al., *Georges Seurat: 1859-1891*, 114-16.

12. Ibid., 408.

13. Janine Bailly-Herzberg, *Correspondance de Camille Pissarro*, 5 vols. (Paris: Valhermeil, 1986), 2:75.

14. Ibid., 2:73.

By 1888, Pissarro's patience with Seurat must have been wearing thin. In a letter to Paul Signac, he recalled how they had "taken the greatest precautions," pointing out to Fénéon, Durand-Ruel, and others who wrote about Neo-Impressionism that they should give "Seurat all the glory of having been the first in France who had the idea of applying science to painting. He would like to be the only owner of it today! It's absurd!" He suggested to Signac that maybe it would be necessary to give Seurat a patent for his idea if it would flatter his pride.[15]

Pissarro was concerned that under Seurat's leadership Neo-Impressionism would revert back to the classicism of the French academy. He warned Signac that they should "remain outside the influence of the School of Seurat . . . . Seurat belongs to the École des Beaux-Arts; he is saturated with it."[16] Pissarro was also beginning to lose patience with Pointillism—the amount of time required to complete a painting, its lack of spontaneity, and the disapproval of collectors.

The previous summer (1887), he had complained to Lucien that one of his paintings was "hardly advancing, yet I work there every day; it is decidedly too long . . . . Maybe I will be forced to come back to my old way? It is embarrassing."[17] In September 1888, he again shared his concerns with Lucien: "How is one to combine the purity and simplicity of the dot with the full-bodiedness, suppleness, freedom, spontaneity and freshness of sensation of our Impressionist art? That is the question, it preoccupies me a lot, for the dot is meagre, lacking in body, diaphanous, more monotonous than simple."[18]

His break with the dot was finally complete in the summer of 1891, when he wrote Lucien: "It's no longer the dot, which I've entirely abandoned, returning instead to the division of pure colours, without waiting for the paint to dry, which had the drawback of cooling the sensation. I'm much happier that way, and I can assure you that the colours are every bit as delicate, and freer in sensation, more personal."[19]

15. Ibid., 2:247.

16. Ibid.

17. Ibid., 2:194.

18. Pissarro and Durand-Ruel Snollaerts, *Pissarro: Catalogue Critique des Peintures*, 1:211.

19. Ibid., 1:229.

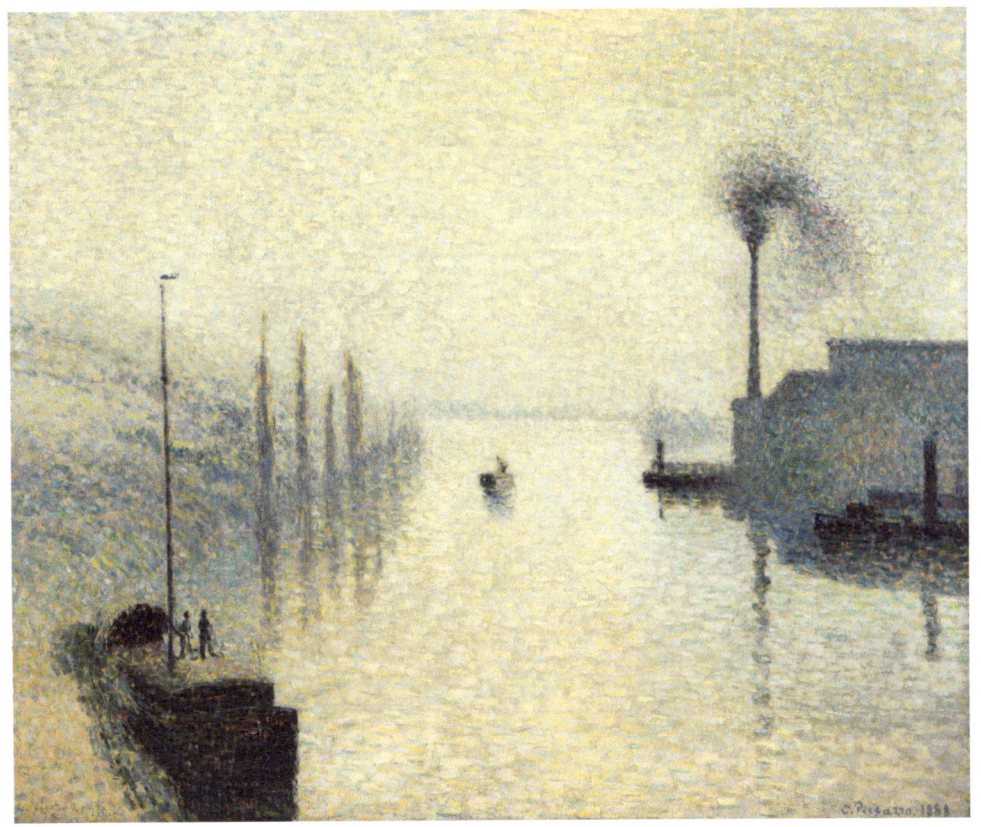

Fig. 75.
The Seine at Rouen, The Île Lacroix, Effect of Fog, 1888, Philadelphia Museum of Art, John G. Johnson Collection, 1917 [PDRS 855]

While his great experiment with Pointillism was not to be satisfying in the long run, Pissarro made many extraordinary paintings in this manner. One painting, *The Seine at Rouen, The Île Lacroix, Effect of Fog* (1888), is sublime in its delicacy of color and close interweaving of tiny brushstrokes. As in his other Pointillist works, there is a real sense of optical mixing in this painting, which creates a smooth, pearlescent surface to portray the stillness of the water. The dark outlines of the barge on one side and the mill on the other are stark reminders of reality in what would otherwise be an abstract painting. The shimmering water is made up of tiny strokes of pale violet, pale yellow, and white with dark blue added for shadows. The same colors are slightly more intense in the sky, and only the barest shadow marks the horizon line. The tranquility is disturbed only by the dark smoke spilling forth in Pointillist dots into the sky. In paintings like this, Pointillism was not a fruitless experiment for Pissarro.

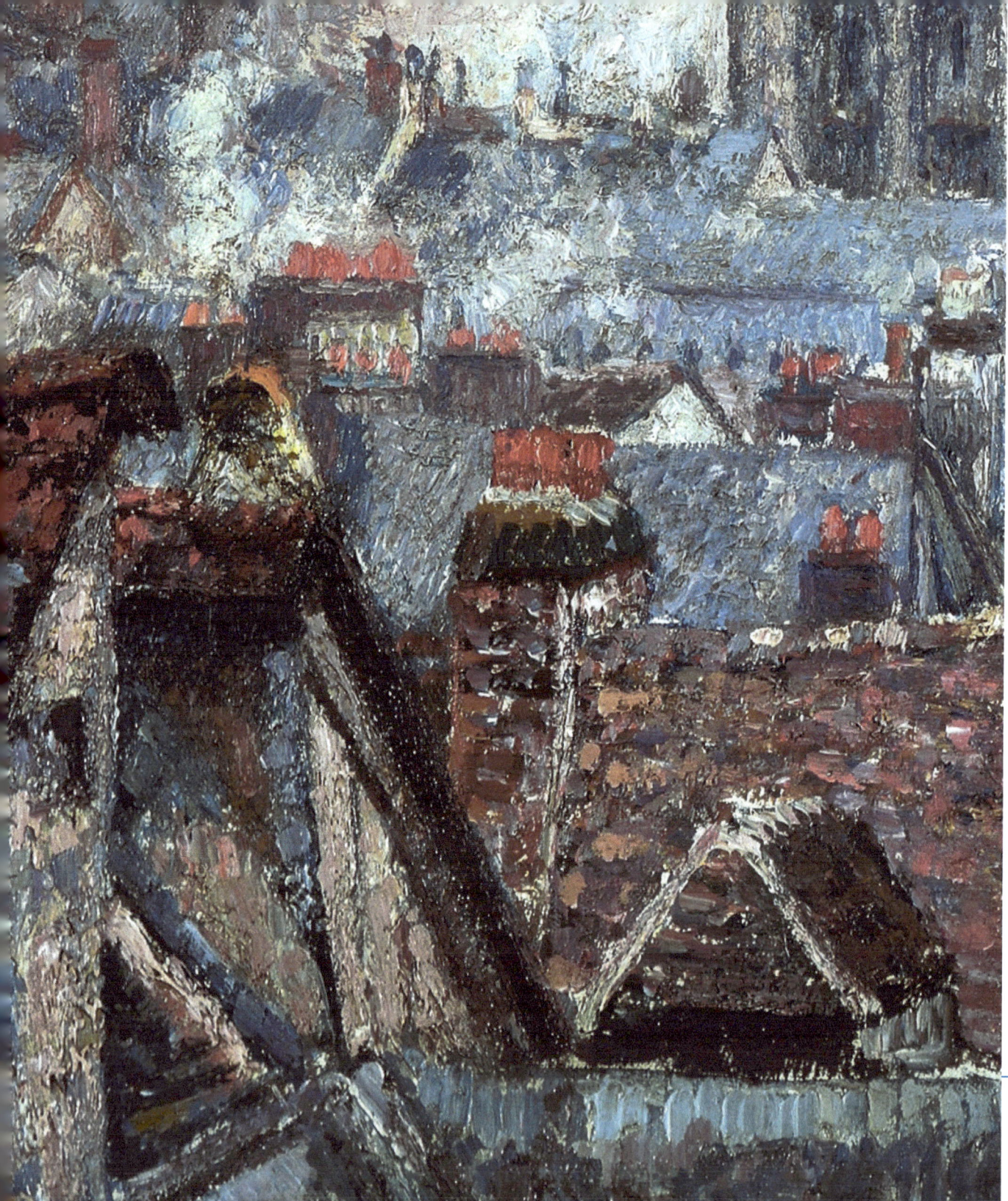

Fig. 76.
*The Roofs of Old Rouen,
Notre-Dame Cathedral,
Overcast Sky*, detail. 1896,
Toledo Museum of Art,
Ohio [PDRS 1114]

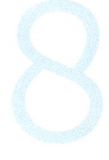

Pissarro—Post-Impressionism and Beyond

All the young painters who, at the turn of the century, looked back on the Impressionist movement which was already part of history . . . were struck by [Pissarro's] vision of nature. This was not so immediate as it appeared, but was rather a pretext for pure painting.[1]

— Françoise Cachin

1. Cachin et al., *Pissarro*, 55.

2. Rewald, ed., *Camille Pissarro: Letters to His Son Lucien*, 297.

Pissarro never visited Venice, but he must have seen the city as portrayed in paintings by Canaletto and J.M.W. Turner in London. He would also have seen paintings of Venice made in 1881 by Auguste Renoir at Durand-Ruel in Paris. See http://www. mfa.org/collections/object/ grand-canal-venice-31792.

Pissarro found new and interesting challenges in 1883 during his first painting expedition to Rouen. He made multiple visits to Rouen, Dieppe, London, and Paris over the next twenty years and painted many series of city streets, rivers, and bridges. Of the bridge Boïeldieu, he proclaimed, "You should see all this in the morning when the light is misty and delicate . . . . It is as beautiful as Venice."[2] The urban scenes provided him with new compositional possibilities. He treated buildings and bridges less like discrete structures and more like architectural stripes that run horizontally or diagonally and intersect with perpendicular boat masts or smokestacks. He cast structures in the city as pure shapes on the canvas.

In *Pont Boïeldieu, Rouen, Morning, Rainy Weather* (1896), Pissarro formed a horizontal line in the middle of the canvas by tightly weaving together the flattened buildings. Against it, he set three diagonals: the bridge, the bank in the foreground emphasized by the sleek steamboat, and the black arm of a crane loading cargo. He balanced the fat smokestack of the boat with the extremely tall, skinny smokestack on the other bank, connecting the tops of them in another invisible diagonal. This painting was bought by his dealer Durand-Ruel along with ten others of the fifteen paintings he made during this expedition.[3]

The following year, Pissarro made three painting expeditions to Paris. From February until late April 1897, he stayed at the Grand Hôtel de Russie, where he painted fourteen views of boulevard Montmarte and boulevard des Italiens.[4] At Durand-Ruel's gallery in Paris, the young Henri Matisse, then twenty-eight years old and working as an artist only for a few years, met Pissarro for the first time.[5] Matisse would probably have seen Pissarro's previous paintings of Rouen at Durand-Ruel's gallery.[6]

The two artists became good friends and together, in February 1897, they visited the galleries of the Musée du Luxembourg to see the exhibition of Impressionist paintings bequeathed to France by Gustave Caillebotte.[7] The bequest included seventeen paintings by Pissarro, seven of which were chosen by the State for the Luxembourg exhibition.[8] With Pissarro at his side to comment, the young Matisse would have seen the following paintings by the older artist:

The Red Roofs, Côte Saint-Denis at Pontoise, Winter Effect, 1877 [PDRS 489][9]

Harvest at Montfoucault, 1876 [PDRS 465][10]

The Chemin des Mathurins, Climbing through Fields, Pontoise, 1879 [PDRS 602][11]

The Jardin de Maubuisson, Pontoise, Spring, 1877 [PDRS 494][12]

The Wheelbarrow in the Orchard, Le Valhermeil, Auvers-sur-Oise, c. 1879 [PDRS 608][13]

Path through the Woods, Summer, 1877 [PDRS 520][14]

The Seine at Port-Marley, the Wash-House, 1872 [PDRS 229][15]

3. Pissarro and Durand-Ruel Snollaerts, *Pissarro: Catalogue Critique des Peintures*, 3:717.

4. Ibid., 1:273.

5. Ibid., 1:274.

6. Ibid., 3:640.

7. Hilary Spurling, *The Unknown Matisse* (New York: Alfred A. Knopf, 1998), 134.

8. Kirk Varnedoe, *Gustave Caillebotte* (New Haven, Connecticut: Yale University Press, 1987), 204.

9. Pissarro and Durand-Ruel Snollaerts, *Pissarro: Catalogue Critique des Peintures*, 2:346.

10. Ibid., 2:333.

11. Ibid., 2:405.

12. Ibid., 2:349.

13. Ibid., 2:409.

14. Ibid., 2:363.

15. Ibid., 2:188.

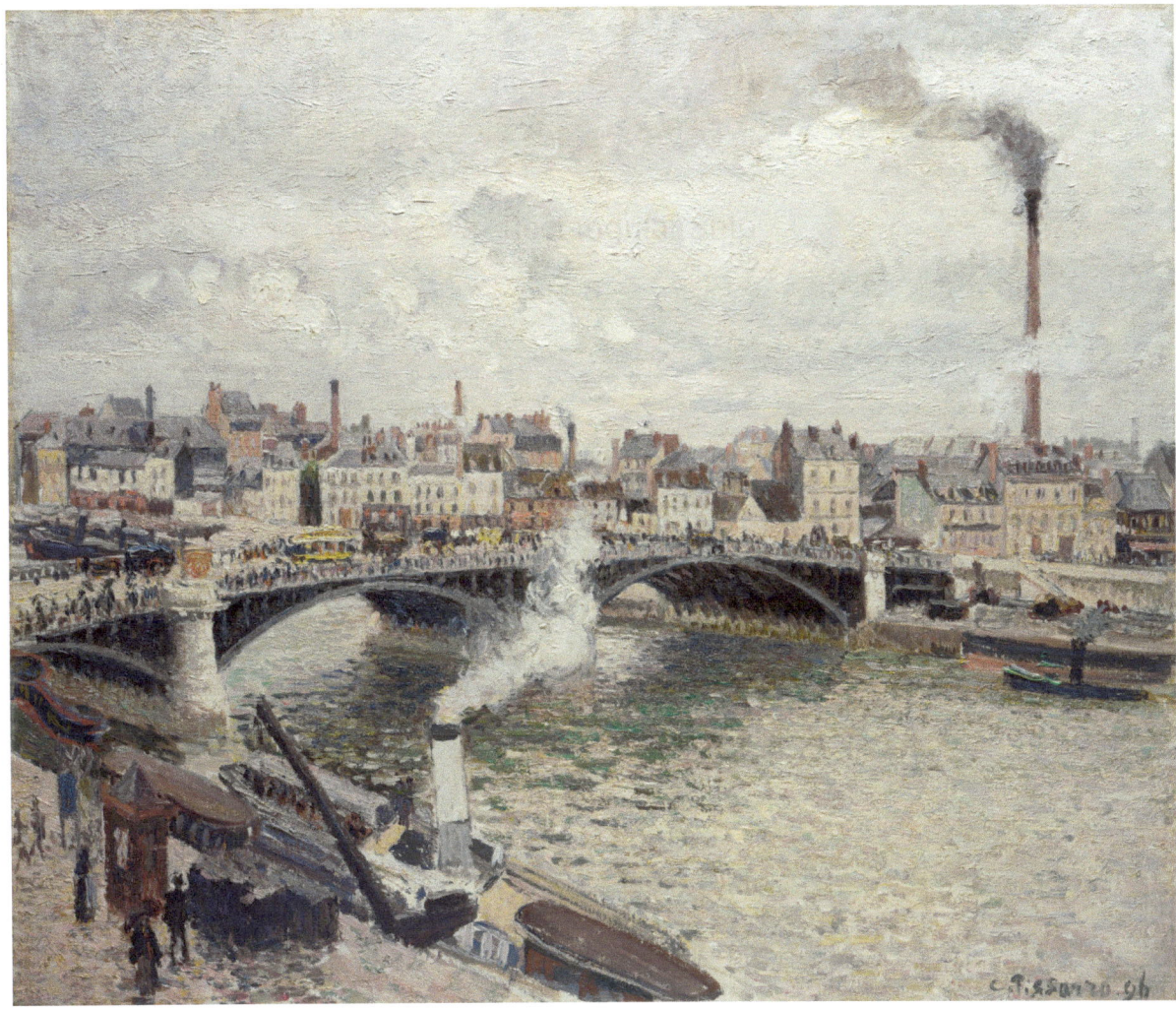

Fig. 77.
Pont Boïeldieu, Rouen, Morning, Rainy Weather, 1896, The Metropolitan Museum of Art, New York, Bequest of Grégoire Tarnopol, 1979, and gift of Alexander Tarnopol, 1980 [PDRS 1140]

It is also likely that Matisse visited the older artist at the Grand Hôtel de Russie and saw his current paintings in progress. Pissarro made fourteen paintings of the boulevard Montmarte from his hotel window, all of them picturing the wide street on a diagonal toward the vanishing point. In every case, the buildings are flattened to wedge-like strips, creating a large "X."

Pissarro's spectacular painting of the boulevard Montmarte at night depicts streetlights, cab lights, and lighted storefronts reflected in the rain-slicked streets.

The buildings are flattened to ribbons; the intense orange reflections contrast with blue streets; and flickering brushstrokes give the painting a decidedly abstract

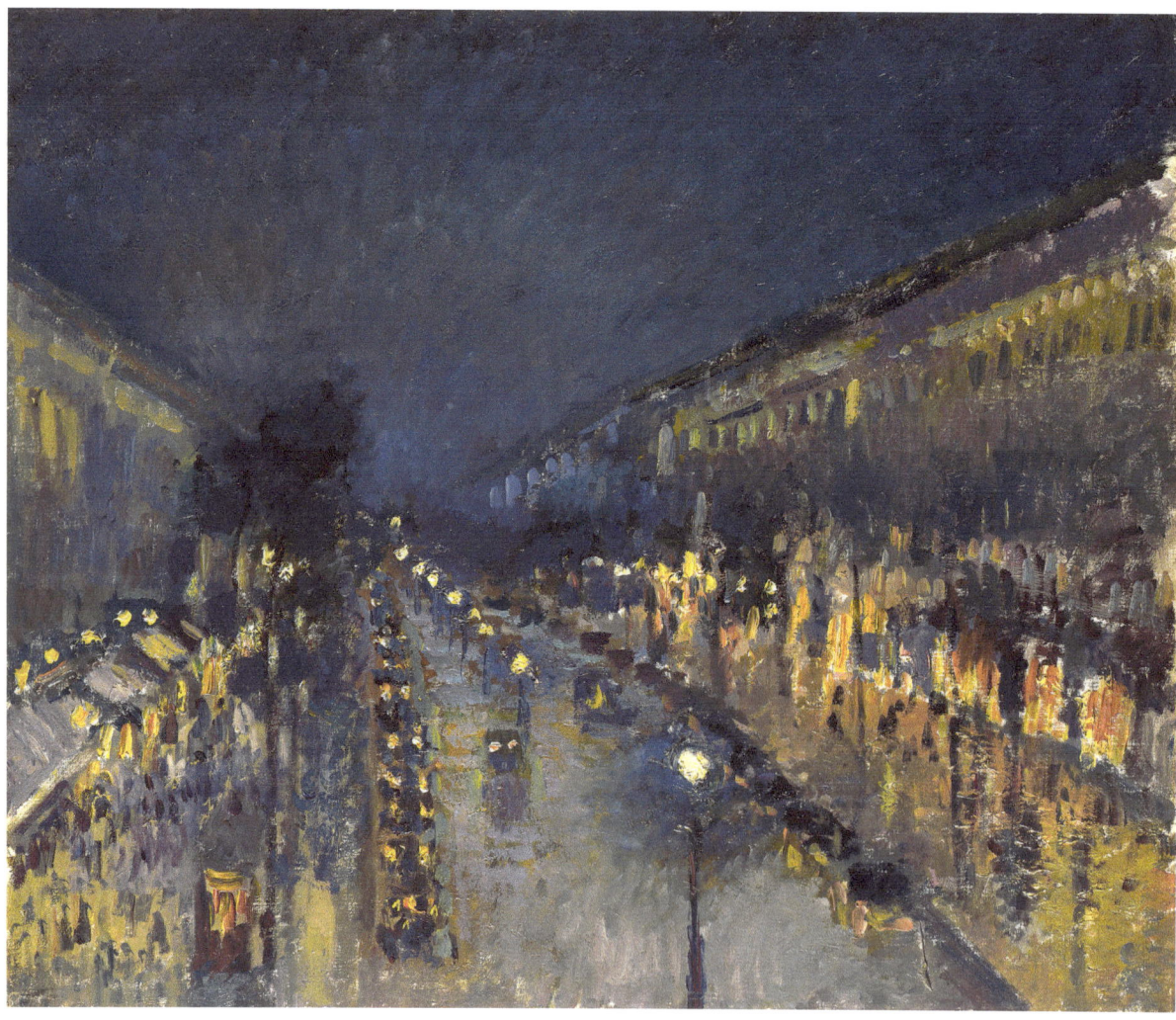

Fig. 78.
Boulevard Montmarte, Night Effect, c. 1897, The National Gallery, London [PDRS 1168]

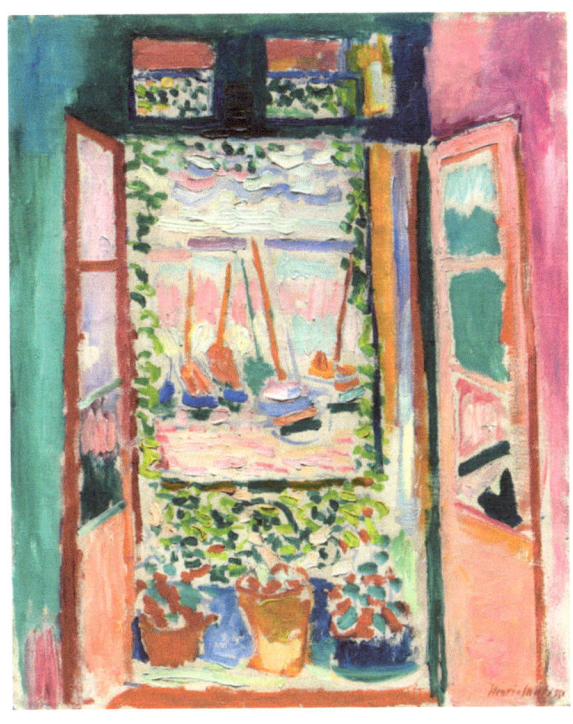

Fig. 79.
Henri Matisse,
Open Window, Collioure,
1905, National Gallery
of Art, Washington, D.C.,
Collection of Mr. and
Mrs. John Hay Whitney

16. Jeffrey Weiss, "Art for the Nation," National Gallery of Art, Washington, D.C. See https://www.nga.gov/collection/art-object-page.106384.

17. Pissarro and Durand-Ruel Snollaerts, *Pissarro: Catalogue Critique des Peintures,* 1:287-90.

18. Spurling, *The Unknown Matisse,* 178.

19. Ibid., 190.

the painting. The saturated colors with intense complementary contrasts of green and red are typical of paintings of that period by Matisse and his colleagues André Derain, Maurice de Vlaminck, and Georges Braque and demonstrate why these artists came to be known as Les Fauves ("the Wild Beasts").[16]

Pissarro and his family spent the winter of 1899 in Paris, on the rue de Rivoli, where he painted fourteen views of the Tuileries from his third-floor window.[17] Matisse visited Pissarro regularly, "conducting an increasingly companionable dialogue with the older artist,"[18] during this expedition and the following winter of 1899-1900, when Pissarro returned to the rue de Rivoli to paint another series of the Tuileries.[19]

By this time, Pissarro's use of abstract elements had become common among other artists, and what was acceptable in art was changing very quickly. This can be seen in the work of Matisse and the Fauves as well as in Cézanne's "constructive"

sensation. The abstract composition of the painting is such that it is equally pleasing when viewed upside down or sideways.

Perhaps the young Matisse was remembering the paintings Pissarro made from his hotel window when, seven years later, he made the painting *Open Window, Collioure* (1905). The obvious difference is that Pissarro never showed the window frame, and Matisse made it a feature of

stroke and its subsequent morphing into analytic Cubism. The foreshadowing of Cubism can be detected in the flat planes and overlapping roofs of Pissarro's *The Roofs of Old Rouen, Notre-Dame Cathedral, Overcast Sky* (1896).

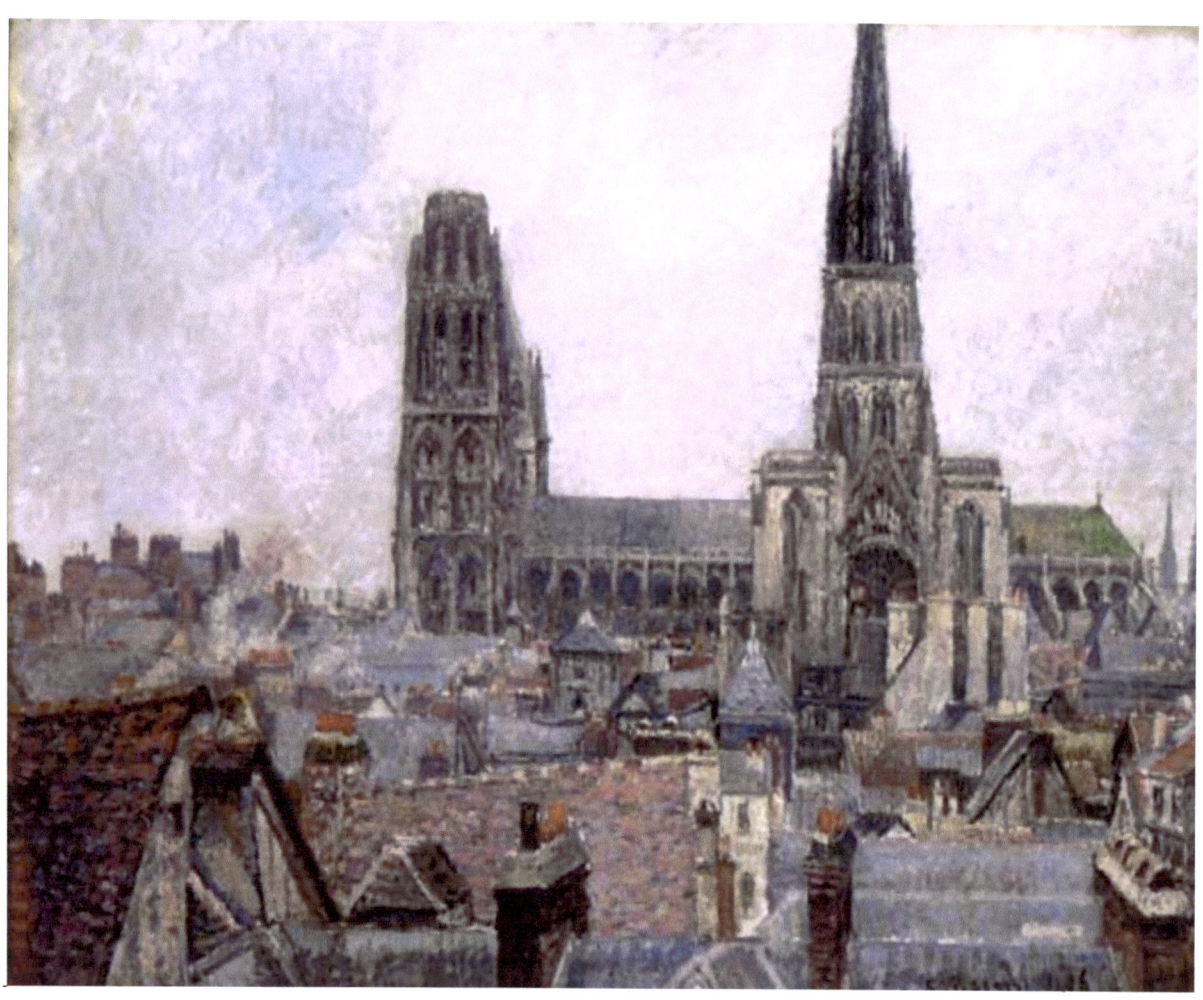

Fig. 80.
The Roofs of Old Rouen, Notre-Dame Cathedral, Overcast Sky, 1896, Toledo Museum of Art, Ohio [PDRS 1114]

On his second trip to Rouen in 1896, Pissarro found a "really uncommon motif" and imagined a canvas "filled with old, grey, worm-eaten roofs? It is extraordinary!"[20] Clearly, what intrigued Pissarro was not the "prettiness" of the view; in general, he did not choose motifs for the sake of beauty. He was, no doubt, interested in the historical aspect; he spent time in Rouen, drawing many of the "old streets which are being destroyed."[21] However, this painting does not document historical buildings since only the roofs are seen. What seems to have drawn his eye are the geometric shapes suggested by the roofs and turrets. The large roof on the left offers a very slight sense of depth, but the remainder of the roofs seem jammed together, layered so that their roof lines are flattened out and seem to be connected and absent of shadows under the cloudy sky. Pissarro's colors also provide few clues as to perspective—the blue-grays and rosy oranges in the foreground are of the same intensity as the houses in the background. The result is a panoply of horizontal and vertical shapes that appear to advance and recede in turn, dipping and weaving, almost dancing around the old cathedral. "These cubist roofs can be found in Pissarro's paintings as far back as the 1860s," wrote Dana Gordon, abstract artist: "Indeed, they were seen so often for so long that they could well have had a strong effect on the appearance of Cubism (both analytic and synthetic)."[22]

It was painted only thirteen years before Pablo Picasso painted *Houses on the Hill* (1909), an early example of block-like structures, absence of depth, and uncertain picture planes that characterize Cubism. The roofs and houses are layered geometrically, almost denying their own

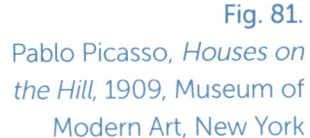

Fig. 81.
Pablo Picasso, *Houses on the Hill*, 1909, Museum of Modern Art, New York

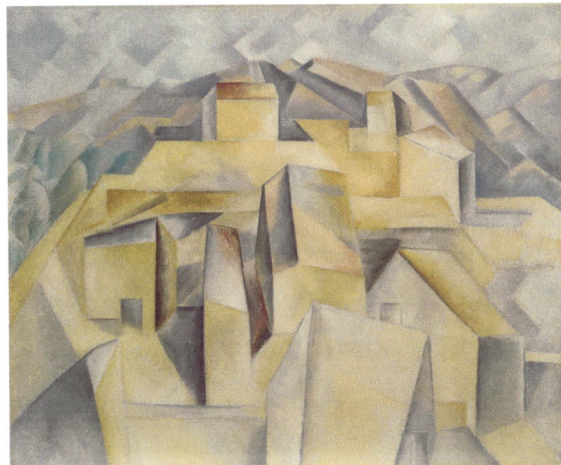

20. Rewald, ed., *Camille Pissarro: Letters to His Son Lucien*, 238.

21. Ibid., 282.

22. Author's correspondence with Dana Gordon, May 3, 2018.

volume. The more intense colors in the background advance boldly, forcing the light colors in the foreground to smash together. The forms are interconnected, so that the eye moves rhythmically from one spot to another. Picasso's sky is filled with white Cubist clouds with only a small hint of sunlight or shadow. His colors are even the same as Pissarro's—slate-blue-gray and rosy orange.

The major difference between the two paintings is the presence of the cathedral in Pissarro's painting. He obviously did not intend the cathedral, per se, as the focal point, since he cropped the top of the spire on the right and hid the lower part of the building behind rooftops. The side of the cathedral that he chose to include depicts the lovely Gothic arches of the windows as well as some flying buttresses at the right. The solidity of the cathedral's architectural features provides a dramatic contrast to the color and movement of the roofs below. Pissarro added contrast by deepening the gray of the cathedral and giving it a tinge of yellowish tone.

Pissarro's painting was supposed to have been purchased by François Depeaux, whom Pissarro called "one of my collectors."[23] Depeaux, a wealthy philanthropist of Rouen, was highly involved in the industrial development of the city, including the unique transporter bridge built in 1899. A few days after he promised to buy it, Pissarro wrote Lucien that Depeaux "doesn't care for the sky! I shall keep the picture for us."[24] Perhaps Depeaux considered the sky too drab. However, changing that aspect to suit the collector's tastes would have divested the painting of its character. Fewer clouds and more sunlight would have created shadows to solidify the aspect of the rooflines. The painting would have lost much of its movement, and the colors would have been bleached to lighter tones.

Pissarro reveals how very close his landscapes are to nonrepresentational art in his painting *Landscape with Haystacks, Osny* (1883). Only one haystack, the second from the right, can be identified by its form, and its light color dramatically diminishes

23. Rewald, ed., *Camille Pissarro: Letters to His Son Lucien*, 281.

24. Ibid., 285.

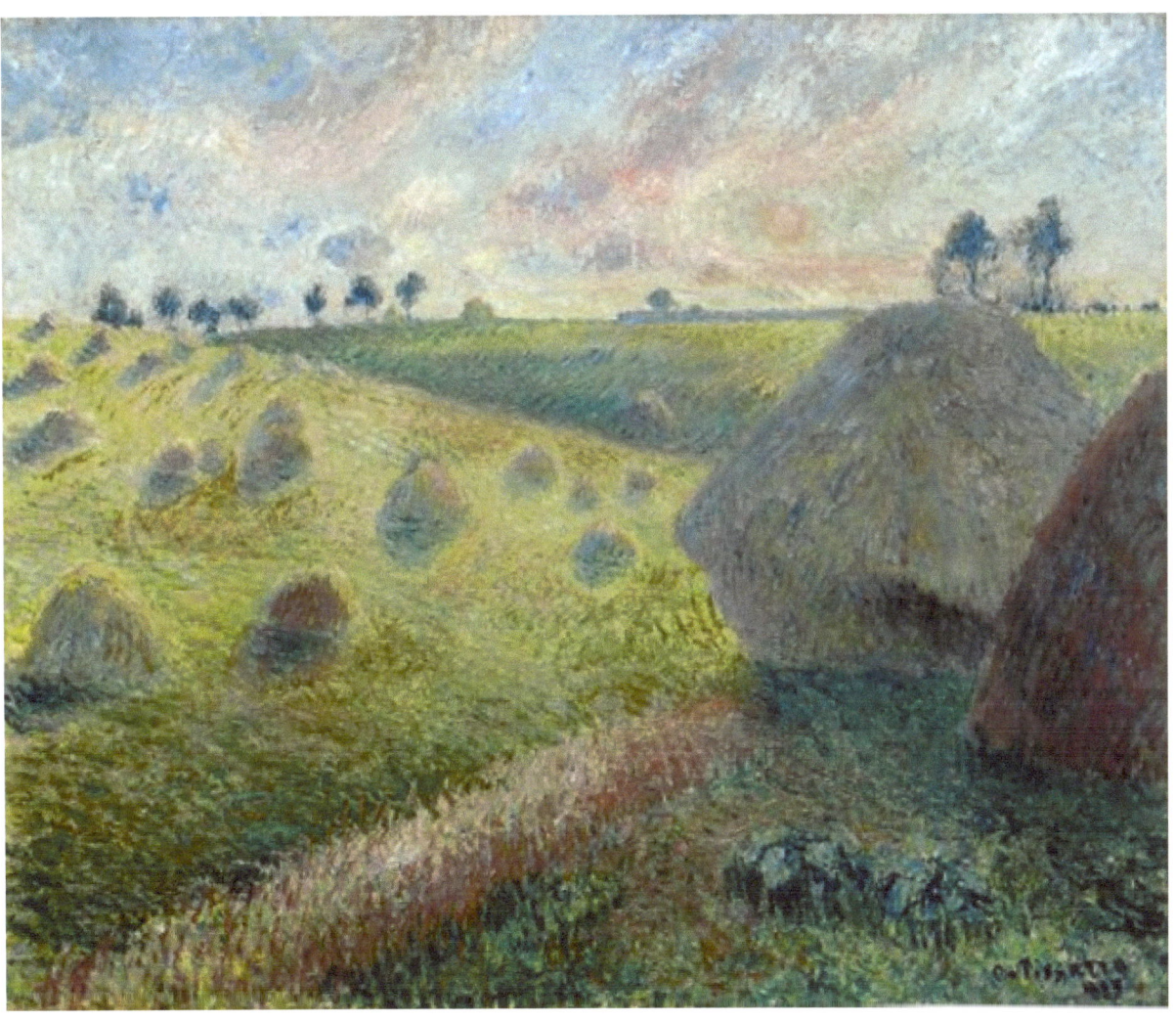

its importance. Even the brushstrokes are tightly woven marks of complementary yellow and lavender. The form is identifiable only by a small shadow. Most of the haystack on the far right is composed of dark orange and blue strokes and is cropped out of the picture. The other stacks on the far left are tight knots of orange and blue. Even the

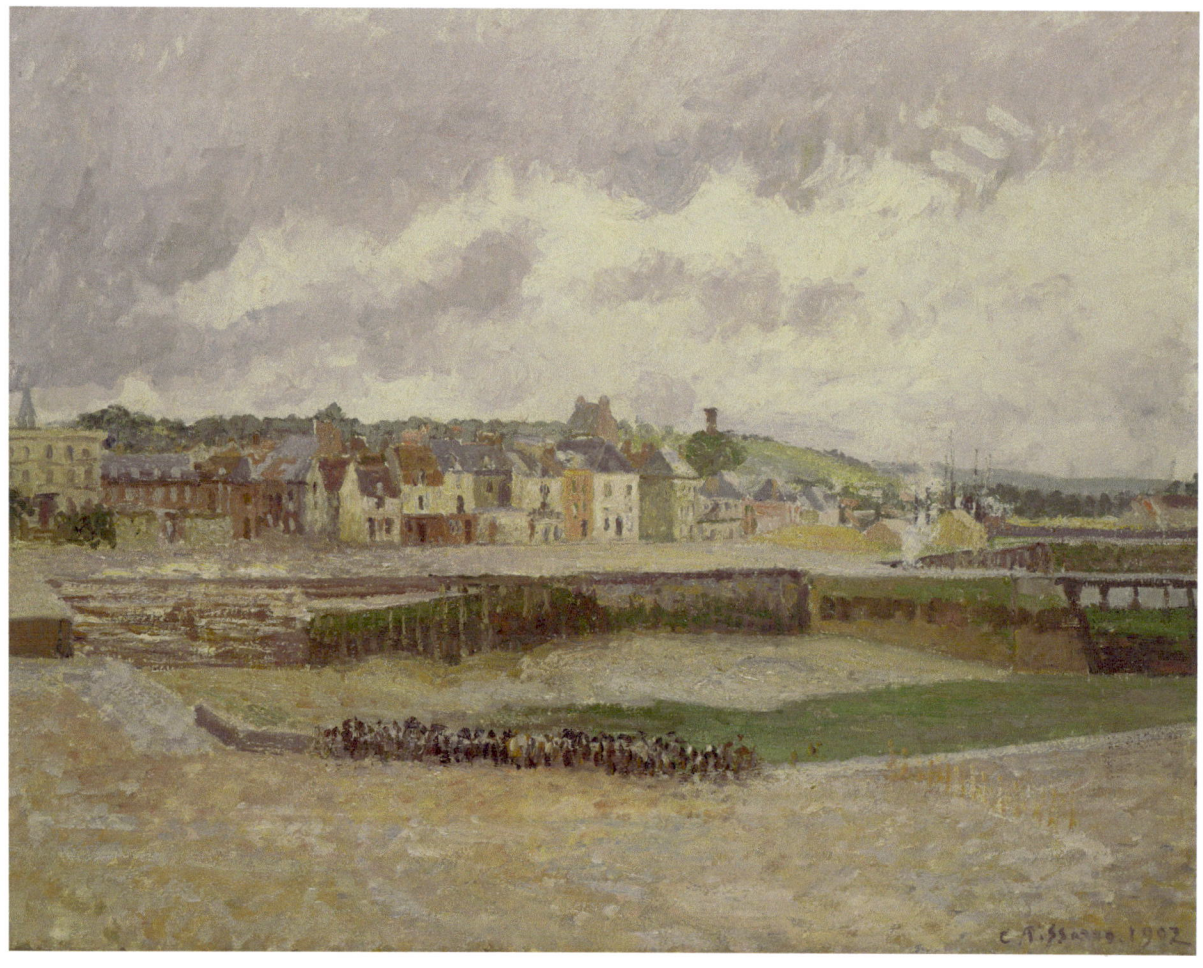

Fig. 83.
The Fishing Port, Dieppe, Low Tide, 1902, Montreal Museum of Fine Arts, Canada, Gift of Mr. and Mrs. Paul Ivanier [PDRS 1452]

treetops on the horizon are merely squiggles of dark greenish blue beneath clouds of orange and pink. The painting is basically composed of patches of color separated by light and dark diagonals. It is only the organization of the color patches above and below the horizon line that firmly identifies this as a landscape. Without the top third of the canvas picturing the sky, the work could easily be interpreted as totally abstract.

Throughout his career, Pissarro continued to make paintings that emphasized abstraction. *The Fishing Port, Dieppe, Low Tide* (1902), painted on his last visit to Dieppe, is an excellent example. The bottom half of the canvas is covered in large stripes of pink and green. On the top, shapes in multiple shades of gray are set against pale blue-white, which can be read as negative space creating its own shapes. The only suggestion of representation is the line of tiny houses, painted as flattened blocks set side-by-side. This painting, so nearly abstract, was painted by Pissarro in 1902, just ten years before Wassily Kandinsky's nonrepresentational paintings. Yet, until now, the abstract elements in Pissarro's paintings have not been fully explored and identified as abstract.

To accept the obvious in Pissarro's paintings is to miss the point of his work. In his quest to create new effects, Pissarro constantly experimented with techniques and raised new questions. From the early 1860s, one of the ways Pissarro's paintings approached abstraction was by eliminating a focal point or narrative. This is a major characteristic of early abstraction—images that represent nothing recognizable. And, it is only when close scrutiny is devoted to these unusual abstract elements in his paintings that the full extent of his genius is recognized. If Pissarro's paintings seem familiar and comfortable today, perhaps it is because his abstract elements had become fully developed by Picasso, Kandinsky, and the Abstract Expressionists.

Fig. 84
Fog, detail, 1874, Private collection [PDRS 331]

Pissarro in Pollock and Others

The degree of sophistication in the variety and application of colour by Pissarro during this final stage of his working life . . . finds a distant echo in, for example, the canvases of Jackson Pollock.[1]

—Christopher Lloyd

Old art offers just as good a criticism of new art as new art offers of old.[2]

— Jasper Johns

1. Lloyd, *Pissarro*, 110.

2. Riva Castleman, *Jasper Johns: A Print Retrospective* (New York: Little, Brown, 1986), 44.

3. The author has heard this and similar negative comments from some curators, art dealers, and others who would prefer that all Pissarro paintings fit into an Impressionist mold.

As early as the 1850s, Camille Pissarro was using artistic techniques that explicitly diverged from the generally accepted standards of French academic painting. And to make his point perfectly clear, he signed his name to these unconventional paintings, indicating that they were finished. With the current perspective of the twenty-first century and the experience of the Abstract Expressionists nearly seven decades in the past, it is easier to identify these elements as "abstract." But in his time, Pissarro's paintings were radical. Even today, some of his paintings are considered less interesting, even "boring,"[3] because they do not convey a storyline or portray an easily understood picture. Thus, these paintings are often misunderstood because they contain abstract elements that are not recognized or appreciated as such. Many of the abstract elements used by Pissarro are now the building blocks of contemporary art:

- Absence of narrative or storyline
- Ordinary sites lacking importance and stripped to bare elements
- Lack of focal point; allover painting
- Accentuation of visible brushstrokes and paint texture
- Structures without volume, pressed into flattened planes
- Figures reduced to mere sketches
- Forms created from patches of color
- Blocks of color juxtaposed without transitional tones
- Nontraditional composition based on geometric or other non-narrative framework
- Lack of depth, chiaroscuro, or shading; recession created by overlapping planes
- Focus on the materiality of the paint

Beginning in the mid-1940s, the Abstract Expressionists used these elements unreservedly and without hindrance from constraining academic standards. Some of the most difficult and least understood of Pissarro's paintings make perfect sense when compared with abstract art from the 1940s to the 1960s.

Jackson Pollock

The progression from Pissarro to Pollock was first observed by Christopher Lloyd, who described Pissarro's *Autumn, Morning, Overcast Sky, Éragny* (1900) as " 'pure' painting . . . ultimately leading to artists such as Jackson Pollock."[4] Unlike Pissarro, Jackson Pollock began with the academic painting of his day. A student of Thomas Hart Benton,[5] he learned the rules of representational painting. However, a new spirit was brewing in New York, one that would discard realism and retain only its essence. When abstract techniques did not yield the latitude he sought, Pollock spread his canvas on the studio floor, layered it with color, and dribbled it with paint.[6] Though the careers of the two artists were separated by several decades and a gulf of cultural change, a comparison of their paintings provides evidence that both artists were pushing the boundaries of contemporary painting in ways that are surprisingly similar.

4. Christopher Lloyd, *Camille Pissarro (1830-1903): St. Thomas to Paris* (London: Stern Pissarro Gallery, 2003), 44.

5. Kirk Varnedoe, *Jackson Pollock* (New York: The Museum of Modern Art, 2009), 23.

6. Ibid., 47.

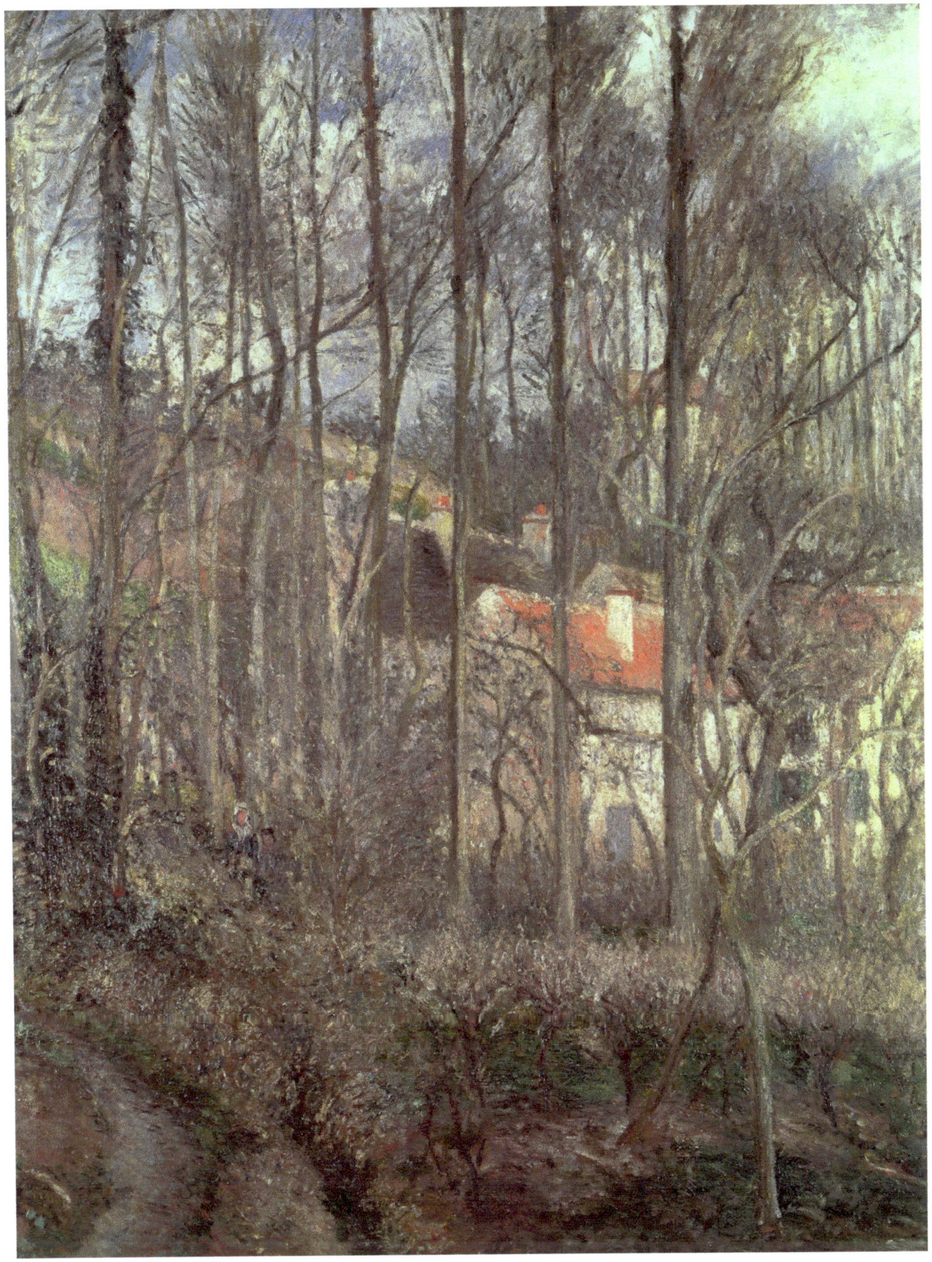

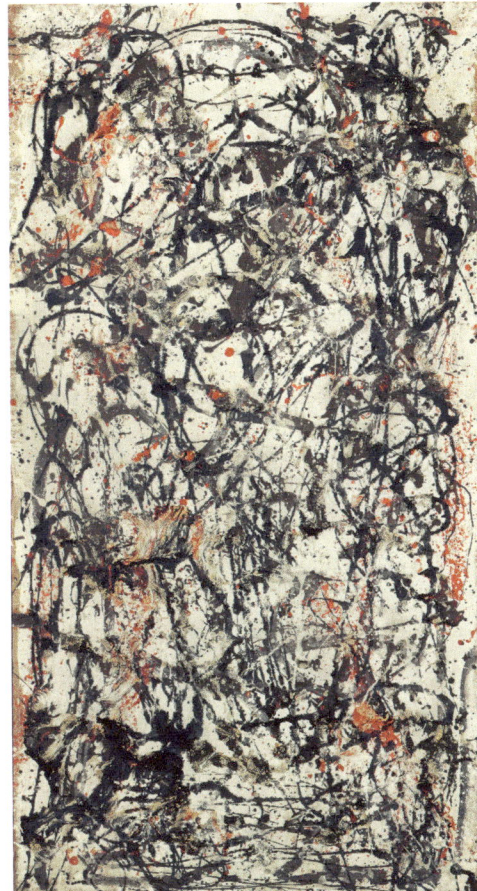

Fig. 86.
Jackson Pollock, *Enchanted Forest*, 1947,
Peggy Guggenheim Foundation, Venice

Fig. 85.
The Côte des Bœufs, Pontoise, 1877, The National
Gallery, London [PDRS 488]

A study of Pissarro's *The Côte des Bœufs, Pontoise* (1877) and Pollock's *Enchanted Forest* (1947) reveal many striking similarities. The most obvious comparison is the verticality of both paintings. The upright format of the Pissarro is in itself unusual because at that time most landscapes, both Impressionist and academic, had a horizontal format. Pollock's painting is also vertical (unusual for him as well) and even more slender relative to its height.

Like many of Pissarro's works, *The Côte des Bœufs, Pontoise* has no central focal point—no church, no bridge, nor bank of flowers. The background is blocked by a hill, creating a high horizon line and allowing little room for blue sky and clouds. The houses, set on the hill at various levels, are not the focus; they are virtually hidden by a screen of tall trees, forcing the eye to work through a maze to glimpse their red roofs. The trees, as trees, are obviously not the focal point because all the viewer sees is their cropped middle portion. Most of the treetops are cut off by the upper edge of the canvas. The tree roots are hidden by

scrubby bushes, which are bland in color, indicating they clearly are not a focal point. Across the left runs a small brook, but it is so insignificant in size, placement, and color that it often goes unnoticed. Peering out of the bushes are two small faces that, if they are seen at all, challenge the viewer to ponder their presence. Indeed, there is no clear focal point at all. The obvious conclusion is that Pissarro meant the viewer to see the overall painting—together as one unit made up of linear, abstract elements—forcing the eye to wander without guidance in and out of the trees, through the houses, and up the hill to the sky. In *History of Art*, Janson called this a "surprisingly abstract composition."[7]

In Pollock's *Enchanted Forest*, thin painted swirls resemble Pissarro's curvaceous tree branches and scrubby bushes. The underlying layers are spread with warm earthy tones from bottom to top and dotted with small, thin splashes of rusty red similar to Pissarro's red roofs. The upper layers are a tangle of green, beige, and black arches and curves, which forms an effective screen for

7. H. W. Janson, *History of Art*, 5th ed. (New York: Harry N. Abrams, 1995), 706.

the colors below. As with the Pissarro, there is no focal point. The eye wanders restlessly in and out of the swirls and beneath the various layers to locate the painting, which can only really be seen in its totality.

In 1955, Clement Greenberg gave this phenomenon the name "allover" painting,[8] and Abstract Expressionists used the technique to banish representational painting. Eighty years earlier, Pissarro was already using allover painting with no focal point. Even though the elements in his painting—trees, houses, hill, and sky—are recognizable, they dissolve into the painting's unity. In fact, allover painting became a feature of many of Pissarro's landscapes and cityscapes.

Though the Pissarro motif suggests depth, the intensity of the colors pushes the background forward, flattening the perspective and making the view appear shallower than one would imagine. In the Pollock painting, the multiple layers suggest that the painting has depth; yet the swirls and splatters contain the eye within the shallow view.

Pissarro and Pollock also used color in similar ways. In Pissarro's landscape, the earth-tone colors are nearly the same value, low-keyed to suggest the shade of the trees and perhaps late afternoon shadows. Even the blue sky is hazy, with grayish white clouds and no obvious sun. Similarly, Pollock used earth tones of close values, low-keyed and shadowy, along with black. The hints of red are muted brick. The green of the drippings is low-key, fitting into the earth-tone palette.

Both paintings use color and thickly applied texture to define layers. Pissarro used brushes to build thick masses of pigment on the canvas. Pollock used heavy coats of paint topped with swirls and splatters. While the two paintings are decidedly different in appearance, the effect each achieves is amazingly similar. Even though Pissarro pushed his innovative layering and allover painting to the limit in the 1870s, such innovations had no name because the concepts were not defined until eight decades later.

8. Clement Greenberg, "'American-Type' Painting," *Partisan Review* 22, no. 2 (1955): 179-96.

Mark Rothko

As Pissarro reached for the unknown, so did Mark Rothko, whose color-field paintings replicate Pissarro's experimental techniques in the extreme, as demonstrated by a comparison of Rothko's *Untitled* (*Gray and Mauve*) (1969) with Pissarro's *Fog* (1874). Color-field paintings were unimaginable in the Impressionistic vocabulary; however, a study of these two paintings from a twenty-first century perspective reveals their similarities. The simple reading of the Pissarro painting is that of a common landscape, depicting some condition of weather. Impressionists often portrayed various types of weather, painting fog or mist in their scenes. However, most of these artists provided a recognizable narrative focal point to draw the eye. In this painting, the eye searches for a central focal point but, finding none, settles instead on the complementary contrast of sky and land as two distinct color fields. The composition of the Pissarro is stunningly similar to the two well-defined sections of the Rothko. While the Pissarro does not have solid color fields like the Rothko, the overall effect is similar.

What sets the Pissarro apart from the Rothko are the three odd-shaped elements near the center of the canvas that look vaguely like a curved tree trunk and two people. On the right are shadowy outlines of trees. The pinkish gray forms in the foreground suggest an undefined texture.

Fig. 87.
Fog, 1874, Private collection [PDRS 331]

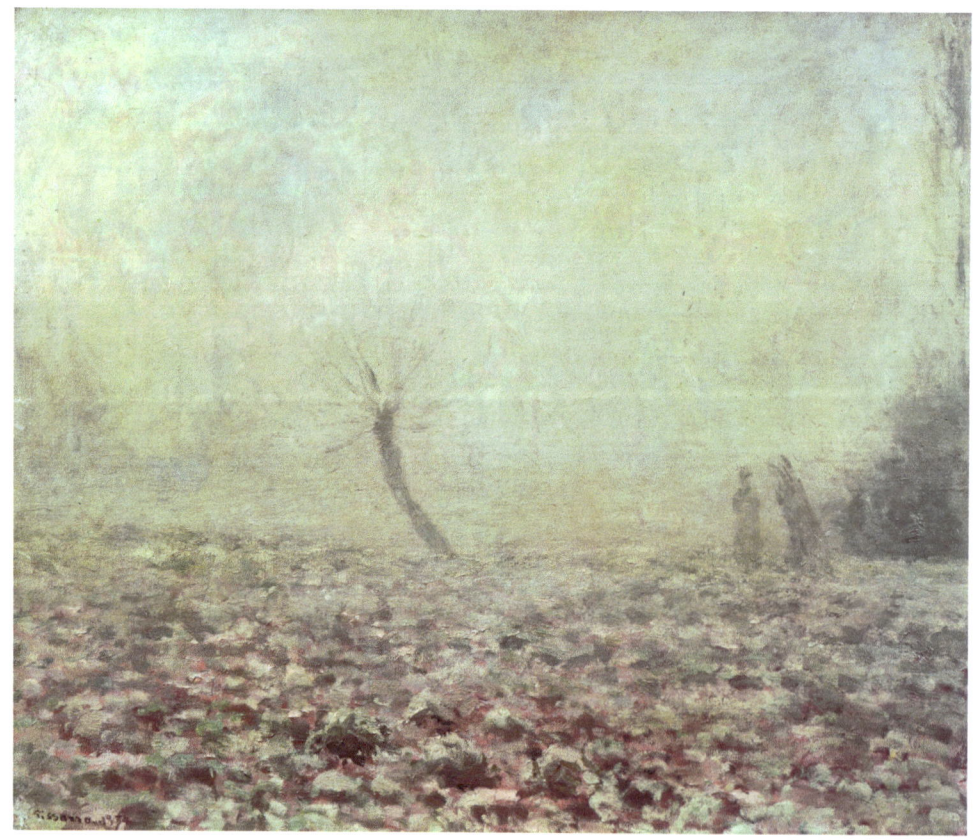

Unlike the Rothko, there is no definite horizon line dividing the two color fields. The lower portion simply fades into the upper portion.

Ordinarily, in a painting human figures create a focal point; but, in this case, Pissarro minimized their importance by dissolving both their shapes and the tree trunk into the background. Instead, the apparent point of interest becomes the complementary contrast between the sky and the ground, two color fields only slightly more complicated than those depicted in the Rothko painting.

One might argue that Pissarro just painted the scene as he saw it, and that he did not intentionally paint something that today resembles a color-field painting. However, such an explanation fails to appreciate the intellectual energy Pissarro constantly devoted to his original experimentations with technique.

Barnett Newman

Barnett Newman is perhaps the only abstract artist to have a direct connection with Pissarro. They had much in common intellectually, politically, and artistically. Joachim Pissarro recounted a conversation he had with Newman's wife, Annalee, after Newman's death, in which she said that

133

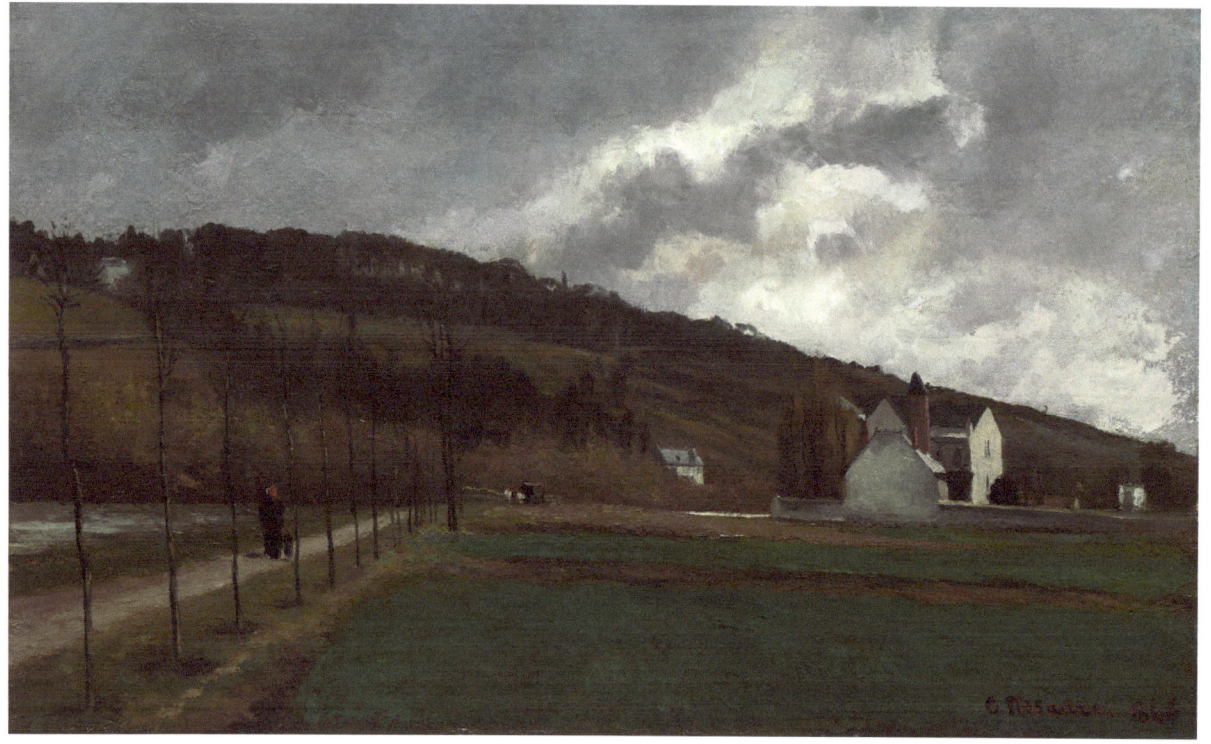

Fig. 89.
Banks of the Marne in Winter, 1866, The Art Institute of Chicago, Mr. and Mrs. Lewis Larned Coburn Memorial Collection [PDRS 107]

9. New York Studio School, September 26, 2018, "Joachim Pissarro in Conversation with Richard Shiff."

10. Author's communication with Heidi Colsman-Freyberger, executive director, The Barnett Newman Foundation, New York, October 11, 2017.

11. John P. O'Neill, ed., *Barnett Newman: Selected Writings and Interviews* (Berkeley: University of California Press, 1992), 44.

12. Richard R. Brettell, *Pissarro's People* (New York: Prestel, 2011), 32; Bailly-Herzberg, *Correspondance de Camille Pissarro*, 1:158; Ann Temkin et al., *Barnett Newman* (Philadelphia: Philadelphia Museum of Art, 2002), 22.

13. Brettell, *Pissarro's People*, 18; O'Neill, ed., *Barnett Newman: Selected Writings and Interviews*, xiii.

14. Rewald, ed., *Camille Pissarro: Letters to His Son Lucien*, 179-80; O'Neill, ed., *Barnett Newman: Selected Writings and Interviews*, xvi.

Pissarro was Newman's "favorite painter."[9] Newman's admiration for Pissarro is also evident in his personal library, which contains a copy of John Rewald's *Camille Pissarro: Letters to His Son Lucien*.[10] Like Pissarro, Newman also read the writings of Peter Kropotkin, the philosopher and anarchist. When Kropotkin's *Memoirs of a Revolutionist* was republished in 1968, Newman wrote the foreword.[11]

Any discussion of their commonalities might appropriately begin with their heritage. Both were nonpracticing Jews and atheists.[12] Both artists were highly intellectual, reading on a wide range of subjects and expressing their opinions in writing.[13] Both Pissarro and Newman were self-declared anarchists, valuing their independence and autonomy above all else.[14]

15. Joachim Pissarro, *Camille Pissarro* (New York: Harry N. Abrams, 1993), 8.

16. Quoted in Pissarro and Claire Durand-Ruel Snollaerts, *Pissarro: Catalogue Critique des Peintures*, 2:95-96.

17. Yve-Alain Bois, "On Two Paintings by Barnett Newman," *October* 108 (Spring 2004): 4.

18. Temkin et al., *Barnett Newman*, 158.

Fig. 90.
Barnett Newman,
Onement I, 1948,
The Museum of Modern Art,
New York

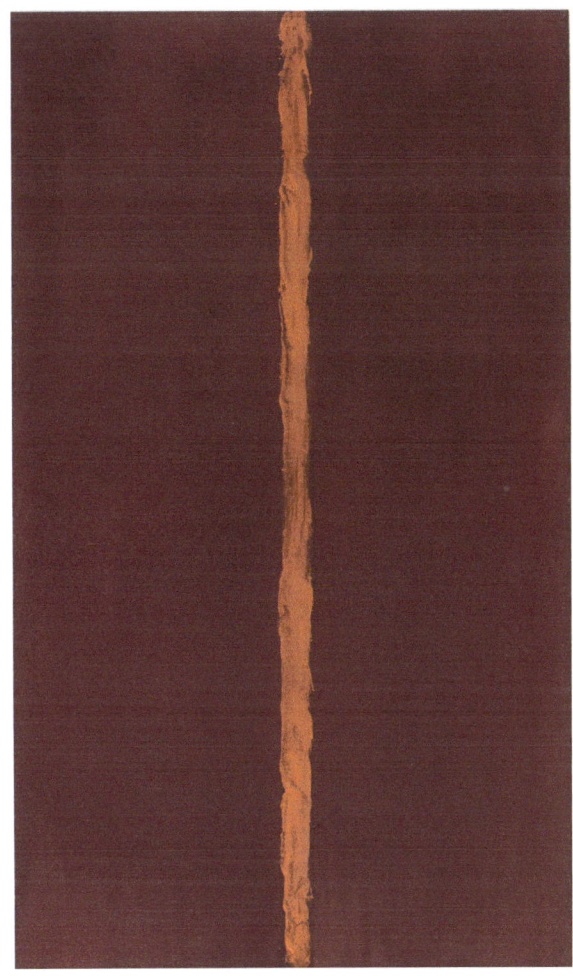

Pissarro's self-determination gave him the courage to oppose academic art and the "capacity to invent new rules and experiment with them."[15] When his painting *Banks of the Marne in Winter* (1866) was shown at the Salon of 1866, it was immediately clear that the artist intended to make **paintings**, not pictures. He set dark-green color fields with slivers of silver and beige against a dark-gray color field severed by white diagonals. Rough brushstrokes and palette knife ridges bespeak materiality. This inspired Émile Zola to write: "Not the least delectation for the eye. A grave and austere kind of painting, an extreme care for truth and rightness, an iron will."[16]

Likewise, Newman also asserted his freedom by opposing any suggestion of "formalist" art, stating: "Each painting to me, [each] new painting, is as if I had never painted before."[17] *Onement I*, a painting Newman made in 1948, reflects his determined independence and unique creativity. According to Ann Temkin, "It marked Newman's decisive move from what he called pictures to paintings, in which the object was an indivisible whole that represented nothing but itself."[18] He filled the canvas with two shades of red with low-value contrast. Richard Shiff pointed out the materiality evident in visible brushstrokes in the darker india red and marks of the palette knife in the zip of light cadmium red.[19]

While there is no obvious basis for comparison of these two paintings, there are some similarities in the use of large blocks of intense color and undisguised materiality. The Pissarro also exhibits one characteristic Newman would probably have appreciated—an evenness of light. During a visit to the Louvre in 1968, Newman praised Paolo Uccello's *The Battle of San Romano* (c. 1435-60), saying: "Fantastic. Absolute totality. One image. I suppose this is so because the light is even from corner to corner. No spotlights—Courbet and Pissarro are like that." He added: "Physically, it is a modern painting, a flat painting. You grasp the thing at once. What a fantastic sense of scale!"[20] That latter comment could also apply to the *Banks of the Marne in Winter*.

Yve-Alain Bois, who has written about Newman's paintings, recounted his conversations with Annalee Newman confirming that Newman "liked his [Pissarro's] work for the evenness of the light (the low contrast of value) and his ability to exalt color while working with a limited chromatic range." They specifically discussed how Pissarro, in his early paintings, used "10, 15, 20 different greens in a single painting."[21]

Newman's friend Robert Murray, the Canadian sculptor, recalls: "Barney talked about a quality of silvery light that interested him in Pissarro's work. And he was interested in light as color in his own work."[22]

After Newman's death, his wife Annalee purchased three paintings by Pissarro, one of which demonstrates that "silvery light" referred to by Murray. In *The Louvre, Foggy Morning* (Third Series) (1902), the pale grays and silvers are so close in value that they seem to meld together, creating a shimmering veil. This painting, along with works of art by Newman, his colleagues, and other artist friends, has now been given by the Barnett and Annalee Newman Foundation to the Jewish Museum in New York City.

19. New York Studio School, September 26, 2018, "Joachim Pissarro in Conversation with Richard Shiff."

20. O'Neill, ed., *Barnett Newman: Selected Writings and Interviews*, 292.

21. Author's communication with Yve-Alain Bois, September 16, 2018.

22. Robert Murray's communication with Heidi Colsman-Freyberger, October 30, 2017.

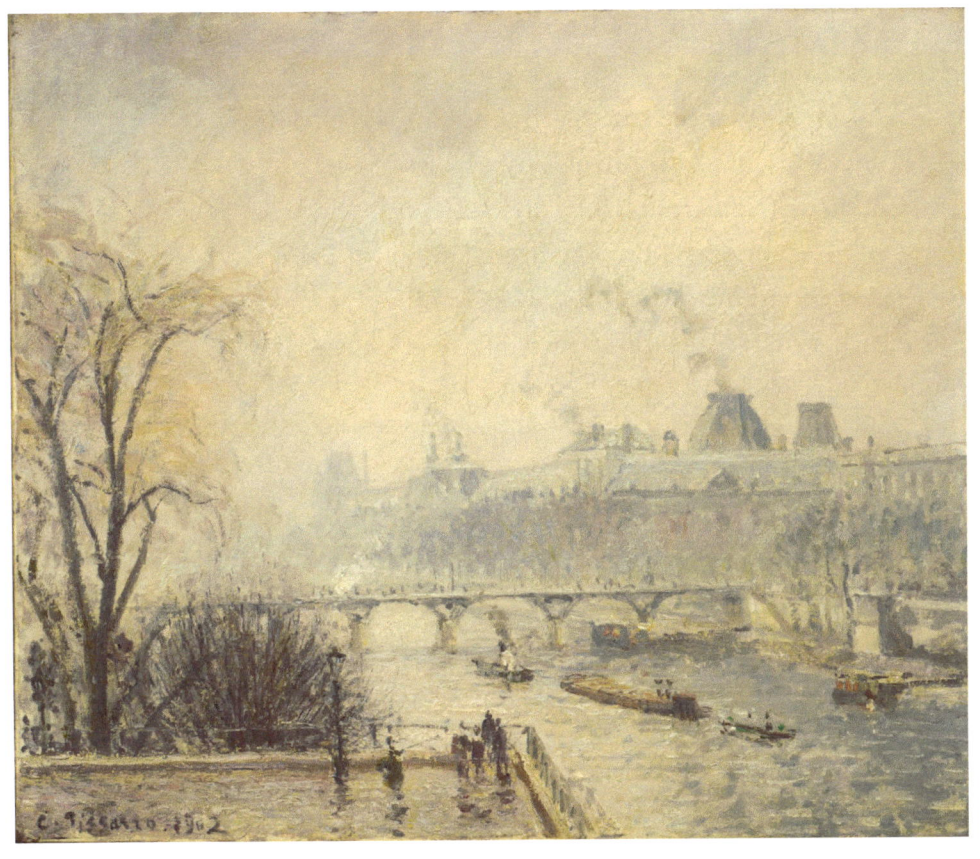

Fig. 91.
The Louvre, Foggy Morning (Third Series), 1902, The Jewish Museum, New York, Gift of The Barnett and Annalee Newman Foundation [PDRS 1475]

of elements now identified as "abstract" and determining why they were used, the evidence reveals Pissarro's leadership in the development of abstract art.

The Roger Fry Effect

Barnett Newman, whose writings are as profound as his art, was perhaps the first to question the Museum of Modern Art's position that modern art began with Post-Impressionism and specifically with Cézanne. In his 1944 review of MoMA's fifteenth-anniversary exhibition, he emphatically challenged that position: "Modern art really had its beginnings in the second half of the nineteenth century, when the Impressionists utilized the scientific discoveries concerning color prevalent at that time."[23] After a fuller explanation, he concluded, "It was therefore inexcusable that the Museum of Modern Art completely ignored this important beginning of the [Modern] movement."[24]

Today the markings of the Abstract Expressionists seem commonplace to us. It is perhaps impossible to "un-see" what is now familiar and to look at art through the eyes of the nineteenth century to understand how radical Pissarro's paintings were at that time. By tracing the use

23. O'Neill, ed., *Barnett Newman: Selected Writings and Interviews* (Berkeley: University of California Press, 1992), 68.

24. Ibid.

Nearly a decade later, Newman penned an open letter to William A.M. Burden, president of MoMA, when the museum purchased a Monet painting. He asked, "Is the museum that has, by dedicating itself to the myth of Post-Impressionism invented by the English critic, Roger Fry, promulgated the theory that the Impressionists were failures—mere experimenters—now renouncing this policy?"[25] Obviously, the answer was no.

The position of MoMA is not unique. Virtually all of art history now accepts the pronouncement made by Roger Fry in 1910: "It is generally admitted that the great and original genius, —for recent criticism has the courage to acclaim him as such—who really started this movement, the most promising and fruitful of modern times, was Cézanne."[26]

Fry first saw Cézanne's paintings in the 1906 Exhibition of the International Society of Sculptors, Painters, and Gravers in London.[27] Cézanne's work had gained prominence in France, largely due to the efforts of Pissarro, his first and most consistent supporter.[28] By 1904, he was well known in France and Germany.[29] In 1907, after Cézanne's death, the Symbolist artist Maurice Denis published his reflections on Cézanne. When Fry translated this article for *The Burlington Magazine* in 1910, he made his proclamation that modern art began with the work of Cézanne. He then promoted Cézanne in exhibitions in 1910 and 1912 and later wrote a monograph, *Cézanne: A Study of His Development.*[30]

During that time, Fry was also curator at the Metropolitan Museum of Art in New York.[31] His influence was international in scope, and in just five or six years, he firmly established Cézanne's position at the beginning of modern art not only in Europe but in the United States as well.

Barnett Newman questioned this position and its acceptance by MoMA and art historians with good reason. Cézanne's classicism appealed to Fry because it matched his own predilection for classical expression in

25. Ibid, 39.

26. Maurice Denis and Roger E. Fry, "Cézanne," *The Burlington Magazine for Connoisseurs,* 16, no. 82 (1910): 207.

27. Mary Ann Caws and Sarah Bird Wright, *Bloomsbury and France: Art and Friends* (New York: Oxford University Press, 1999), 25.

28. Cachin et al., *Cézanne,* 28. Note: The book *Cézanne* provides a comprehensive review of Cézanne criticism from 1865 to 1996.

29. Ibid., 36.

30. Christopher Green, ed., *Art Made Modern* (London: Merrell Holberton, 1999), 144-46.

31. Caws and Wright, *Bloomsbury and France: Art and Friends,* 25.

the arts. Fry appears to have dismissed the Impressionists as "unintelligible" primarily because they did not fit his own expectations. The Impressionists challenged the Salon and the archaic practices of the Paris academy in order to break away from classicism, and that was anathema to Fry's conservative perspective. Yet, it is Fry's pronouncement that continues to govern how art history is written. Despite its exceptional exhibition *Cézanne and Pissarro: Pioneering Modern Painting* (2005), curated by Joachim Pissarro, there is no indication of policy change at MoMA, which still does not own a Pissarro painting.[32]

The conundrum then is why many scholars are willing to accept this pronouncement as a canon of art history without considering the role played by the Impressionists, Pissarro chief among them, who actually created modern art with their rebellion against the Salon and the Paris academy and made lasting changes resulting in what we now recognize as abstract art.

32. A review of MoMA's collection online reveals no Pissarro paintings. See https://www.moma.org/collection/works/69741?classifications=any&date_begin=Pre_1850&date_end=2018&locale=en&page=1&g=camille+pissarro&with_images=1

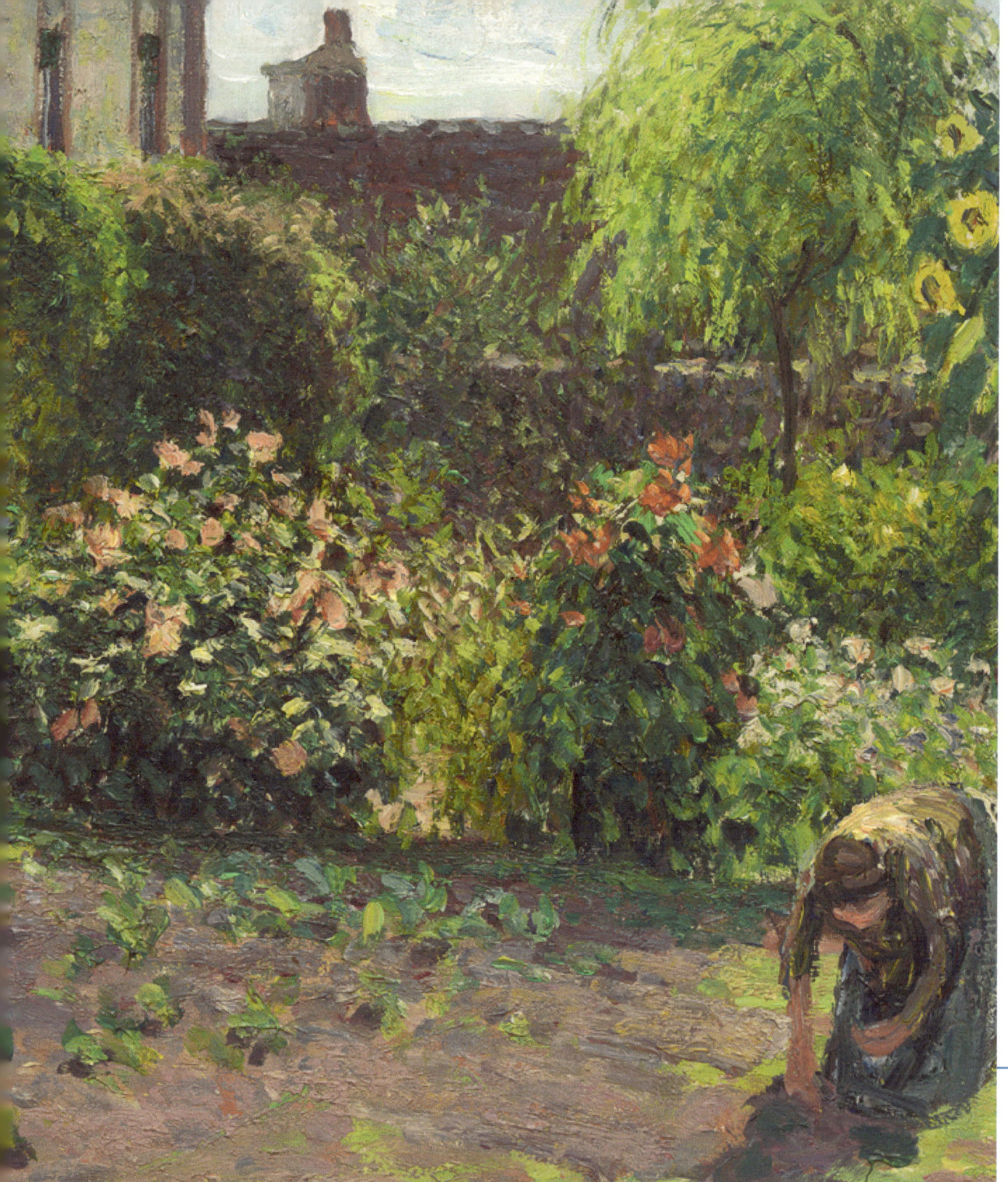

Fig. 92.
The Garden, Éragny, 1898,
National Gallery of Art,
Washington, D.C., Ailsa
Mellon Bruce Collection
[PDRS 1215]

10 Pissarro Reconsidered

Pissarro's art has been misunderstood and . . . this misunderstanding has been aided by the persistent clichés used to characterize the Impressionist movement as a whole.[1]

— Richard Brettell

Camille Pissarro is known first and foremost as an Impressionist, and that designation was well documented by art critics, even during his lifetime. He was a leader among the artists who became known as the Impressionists. He helped to organize the eight Impressionist exhibitions and was the only artist to take part in all of them. Occasionally, he painted side-by-side with the others, sharing with them his artistic techniques and innovations. Paul Cézanne probably assured the title with his proclamation that Pissarro was an Impressionist: In fact, he said, "It's he who was really the first Impressionist."[2]

But that is just part of Pissarro's story. While he was making Impressionist and Neo-Impressionist paintings, he was also creating art with unique elements that had no standard definition at that time. This was no accident; his use of these elements was intentional, because he signed his name, indicating that they were complete. He repeated these elements in variations and progression in every painting.

1. Cachin et al., *Pissarro*, 13.

2. Gasquet, *Joachim Gasquet's Cézanne: A Memoir with Conversations*, 164

A few paintings in the Pissarro catalogue raisonné have been designated as sketches or studies; they are either unsigned or simply have the initials "C.P." Those sketches or studies are not discussed in this book, with the exception of one painting, *Houses at Pontoise* (c. 1878), which, from the reproduction, appears to be complete (see fig. 12). It is not called a sketch or a study; but only the artist's initials are stamped in the lower right.[3]

In the 1860s, Pissarro made some paintings that, while reminiscent of Corot, also emphasize abstract elements in the contrast of color fields (sky and earth) and abstract shapes. He made paintings such as *Village Scene, Women Chatting* (1863), which feature strong geometric compositions, flattened structures, and overlapping planes with no depth—elements identified today as abstract.

Long before the group of artists known as the Impressionists came together, Pissarro made paintings that employed characteristics unique at the time. The painting

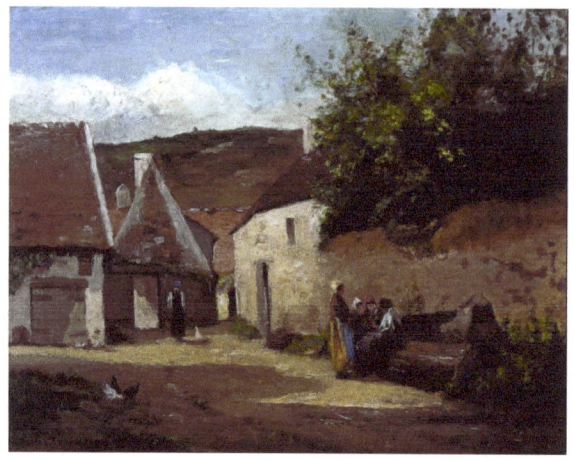

Fig. 93.
Village Scene, Women Chatting, 1863, Private collection [PDRS 70]

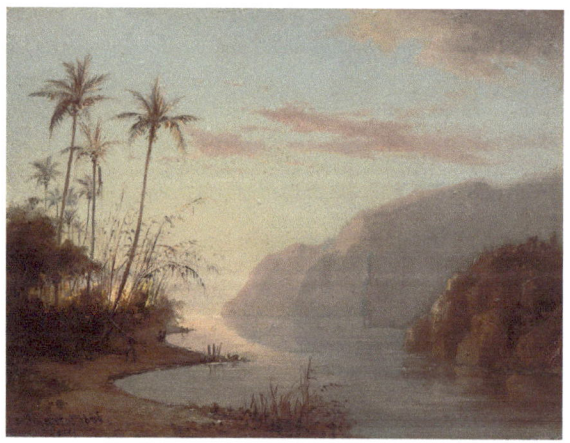

Fig. 94.
A Creek with Palm Trees, 1856, National Gallery of Art, Washington, D.C., Collection of Mr. and Mrs. Paul Mellon [PDRS 16]

A Creek with Palm Trees (1856) displays the clear colors and atmospheric sensibility that were eventually adopted by all the Impressionists.

3. Pissarro and Durand-Ruel Snollaerts, *Pissarro: Catalogue Critique des Peintures*, 2:376.

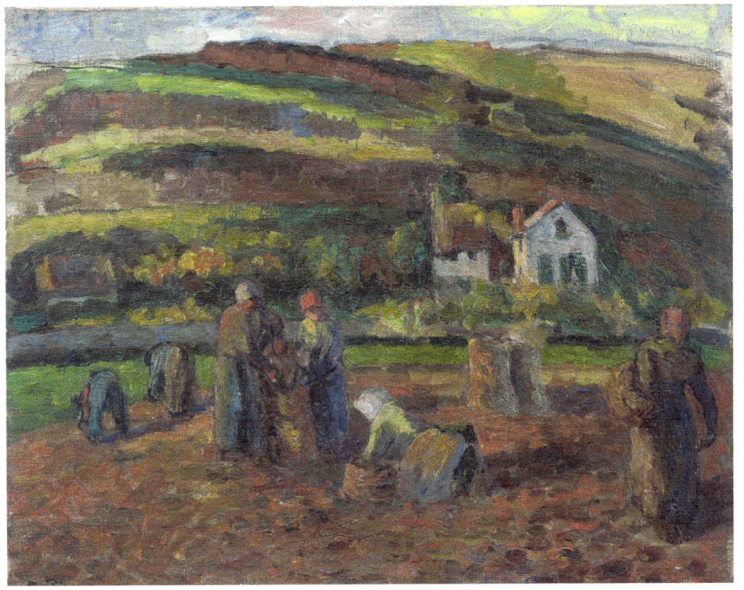

brushstrokes, and houses flattened against the canvas surface.

When Pissarro embraced Pointillism in the 1880s, he produced some paintings that were classic in their utilization of the technique. But he also used the Pointillist technique to experiment more exclusively with color blocks and shapes, setting light and dark-green fields against yellow grain and dark-purple shadow in *The Dieppe Railway* (1886). This is an allover painting with no focal point.

Fig. 95.
Harvesting Potatoes, Pontoise, 1874, Private collection [PDRS 360]

During the birth of Impressionism, Pissarro willingly shared his knowledge of color and brushstroke techniques with his younger colleagues. As they painted together and developed the new art, Pissarro made many paintings that are now considered icons of Impressionism. At the same time, he experimented with techniques that were far more daring. One startling example is *Harvesting Potatoes, Pontoise* (1874), with strips of color side-by-side, vivid tones on the distant hill causing it to push forward, figures composed of one or two

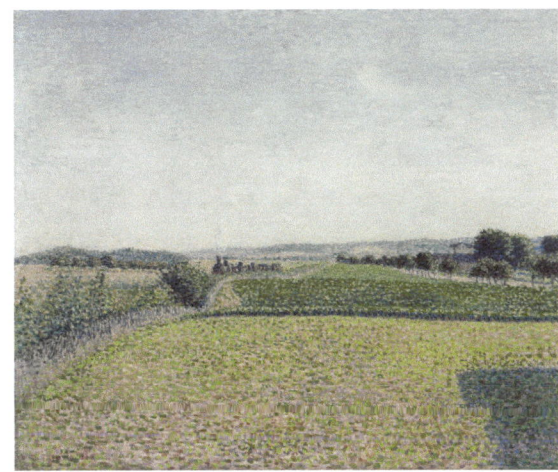

Fig. 96.
The Dieppe Railway, 1886, Philadelphia Museum of Art, Bequest of Helen Tyson Madeira, 2014 [PDRS 828]

After his experience with Pointillism, Pissarro once again turned to painting his "sensations" and found inspiration in his own backyard. The painting *The Garden, Éragny* (1898) reveals a variety of brushstrokes and a composition that recall some of his loveliest Impressionist paintings of the 1870s.

Just the year before, he composed a landscape filled with strong abstract references, *The Hills at Thierceville, Haystacks, Shepherd and Flock of Sheep* (1897). The painting is filled with stripes of different colors, set off by orange and green color blocks and accented by the sharp points of the haystacks. A huddle of tiny gray circles represents the sheep, with similar green circles forming the dark crowns of trees in the distance. The clouds are a plethora of lavender and yellow brushstrokes, some circular, some back-and-forth. The horizon stretches beyond the edge of the canvas, and there is no dominant focal point. The inventiveness of the pattern of clouds is extraordinary and is set off against the wavy pattern of the hills and the pattern of prickly trees on the mid-left.

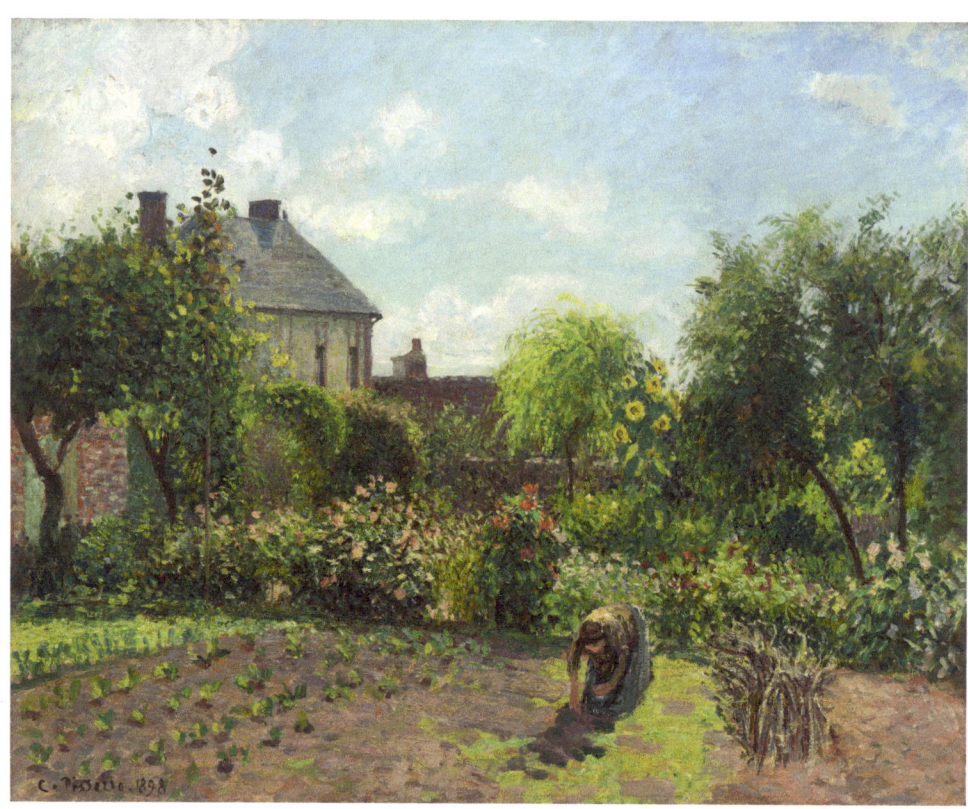

When he painted in Paris, Rouen, London, Le Havre, or Dieppe, Pissarro never lacked for ideas, and his late city paintings are justly celebrated. His imagination always searched for different, more interesting compositions, and his vision spurred him to create paintings with all-over composition such as this one, *Place du Théâtre-Français, the Omnibuses* (1898).

Fig. 97.
The Garden, Éragny, 1898, National Gallery of Art, Washington, D.C., Ailsa Mellon Bruce Collection [PDRS 1215]

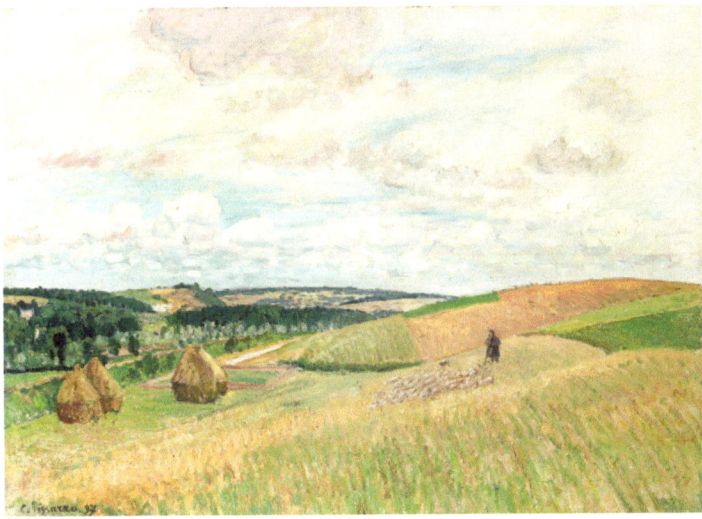

Fig. 98.
The Hills at Thierceville, Haystacks, Shepherd and Flock of Sheep, 1897, Private collection [PDRS 1189]

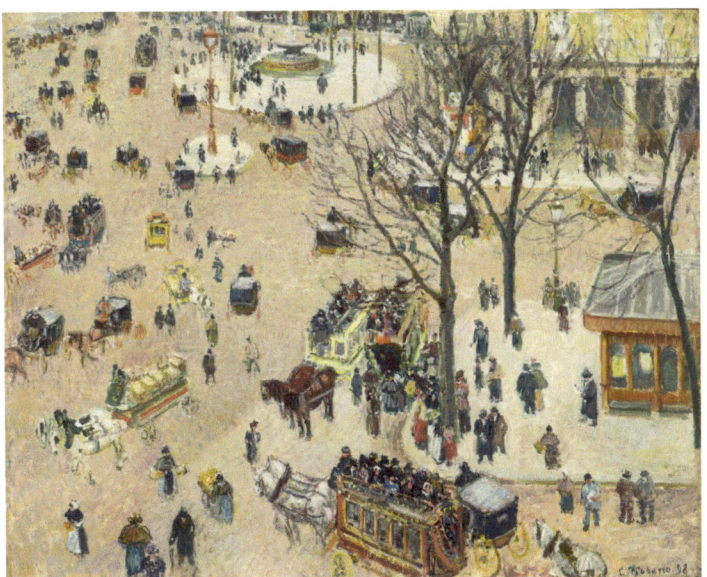

Fig. 99.
Place du Théâtre-Français, The Omnibuses, 1898, Los Angeles County Museum of Art, Mr. and Mrs. George Gard De Sylva Collection [PDRS 1208]

It is obvious that Camille Pissarro cannot be stuffed into a standard box labeled Impressionism. While he painted many brilliant masterpieces that were Impressionist, he also created many other paintings just as important for the abstract elements they display.

It is time to reconsider Pissarro—his artistic talent and the creative intelligence that pushed him to go beyond the accepted norm of the mid-nineteenth century and to develop innovative techniques well beyond what was deemed possible.

It is time to reconsider Pissarro's œuvre—the full body of **all** of his works, including those that in no way resemble Impressionism. His artistic techniques need to be re-examined to bring forward the abstract characteristics that make so many of his paintings unique.

It is time to reconsider Pissarro's legacy—
to recognize and acknowledge the influence
he had and continues to have on artists who
value artistic individuality and their own
"sensations." His influence was profound
for some of them, most of all for Cézanne.
In his later years, Pissarro touched the lives
of Matisse and others who were creating
new forms and pushing the boundaries of
the past. His influence can be seen today in
the freedom with which artists use abstract
elements. His legacy is still alive since it is
not bound by rules but by the ability of individual artists to follow their own "sensations,"
to seek their own artistic independence.

The year 2030 will mark the two-hundredth
anniversary of Pissarro's birth. The greatest honor that could be paid him would be
a considered review of his work that would
give equal importance to those paintings
that are not easily understood in impressionistic terms, those that do not fit within the
storyline of popular exhibitions, and those
that are rarely seen in public. Only then will
Pissarro's œuvre be fully understood.

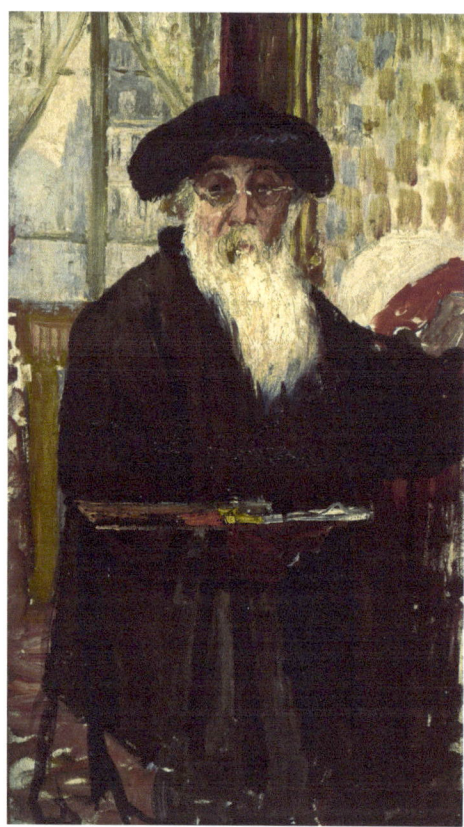

Fig. 100.
Self-Portrait with Palette, 1896, Dallas
Museum of Art, Wendy and Emery Reves
Collection [PDRS 1128]

Pissarro discovered a new subject central to art; the nature of the medium itself. He showed that all of painting's basic qualities— colors, brushstrokes, materiality, lines, shapes, composition—were meaningful in their own right, and in their potential to transform paint into purely visual poetry, as well as into illusionistic pictures. He was, in essence, the first abstract artist.[4]

—Dana Gordon

4. Gordon, *"An Intimate Exhibition That Rewards the Keen Eye."*

Brief Chronology

1830 On July 10, Camille Pissarro is born to Frédéric Pissarro and Rachel Manzana-Pomié in Charlotte Amalie, St. Thomas, Virgin Islands.

1834 Young Camille begins school at the Moravian Protestant school with the children of slaves.

1842 He is sent to Paris to study at the Pension Savary, located in Passy, a suburb where his grandparents, Joseph and Anne-Félicité Pissarro, live. He learns to draw, and, on Thursdays, Sundays, and holidays, when he is out of school, he visits the Louvre and the Paris Salons.

1848 Back in St. Thomas, Pissarro works with his father in the family business, where he supervises the loading and unloading of merchandise on the docks.

1850 Pissarro meets the Danish painter Fritz Melbye. Pissarro and Melbye travel together to the Dominican Republic and Haiti for a few weeks.

1852 Pissarro goes to Venezuela with Melbye in November. They establish an art studio in Caracas, where Pissarro sells drawings and paintings, until he is obliged to return home in August 1854.

1855 In October, Pissarro arrives in France just in time to visit the 1855 Exposition Universelle, where he sees works by Delacroix, Ingres, Corot, Courbet, and others.

1856 To please his father, Pissarro agrees to attend private classes by teachers from the École des Beaux-Arts for a short time. He lives with his family at 49 rue Notre-Dame de Lorette.

1857 Pissarro enrolls at the Académie Suisse. He meets Camille Corot and visits his studio to get a critical review of his own work.

1859 Pissarro has his first painting accepted by the Salon. He meets Claude Monet at the Académie Suisse.

1860 Julie Vellay begins work in the Pissarro household, and she and Camille begin a relationship. At the Académie Suisse, Pissarro meets Armand Guillaumin and Ludovic Piette, who was to become Pissarro's close friend.

1861 Pissarro registers as a copyist at the Louvre. He meets Paul Cézanne at the Académie Suisse.

1863 Monet introduces Pissarro to Frédéric Bazille, Alfred Sisley, and Auguste Renoir. Lucien, the first child of Camille and Julie, is born on February 20. Three of Pissarro's paintings are exhibited in the Salon des Refusés.

1864 Two of Pissarro's painting are accepted by the Paris Salon. Pissarro and his family visit the Piette family at Montfoucault for the first time.

1865 Two paintings by Pissarro are accepted for the Salon. Pissarro's second child, Jeanne-Rachel (Minette), is born on May 18.

1866 Pissarro moves his family to Pontoise. One of Pissarro's paintings is chosen for the Salon.

1868 Two Pissarro paintings are shown in the Salon.

1869 The Pissarro family moves to Louveciennes in the spring. One Pissarro painting is accepted for the Salon.

1870 Two Pissarro paintings are accepted for the Salon. In July, the Franco-Prussian War (1870-1871) begins. In September, Pissarro and his family flee to Montfoucault. Another daughter, Adèle Emma, is born and dies after three weeks. That December, the Pissarro family flees the war again, taking refuge in London.

1871 Pissarro meets art dealer Paul Durand-Ruel in London. Camille and Julie are married on June 14, before they return to Louveciennes. Their son Georges is born on November 22.

1872 In April, the Pissarro family moves back to Pontoise. Several of Pissarro's artist friends, including Cézanne, come to Pontoise to paint with him.

1874 The First Impressionist Exhibition opens in Paris on April 15. Minette dies on April 6 at the age of eight in Pontoise. Félix is born on July 24 in Pontoise. The Pissarro family spends the winter months at Montfoucault.

1875 The Pissarro family spends that fall and winter at Montfoucault.

1876 The Second Impressionist Exhibition runs from March 30 to April 30. The Pissarro family spends autumn at Montfoucault.

1877 The Third Impressionist Exhibition is held April 4 to 30.

1878 Pissarro's dear friend Ludovic Piette dies April 14 at Montfoucault. Pissarro's son Ludovic-Rodo is born in Paris on November 21.

1879 The Fourth Impressionist Exhibition opens on April 10 for a month.

1880 The Fifth Impressionist Exhibition is held April 1 to 30.

1881 The Sixth Impressionist Exhibition runs from April 2 to May 1. On August 27, his daughter, Jeanne-Marguerite (Cocotte) is born in Pontoise.

1882 The Seventh Impressionist Exhibition is held during March and runs until April 2.

1883 Durand-Ruel presents a solo exhibition of seventy works by Pissarro. In October and November, Pissarro makes his first painting expedition to Rouen.

1884 The Pissarro family moves to Éragny-sur-Epte in April. On August 22, his son Paul-Émile is born.

1885 Pissarro meets Paul Signac and Georges Seurat and begins painting in the Pointillist manner.

1886 The Eighth Impressionist Exhibition opens in Paris on May 15, and Pissarro's works are shown with the Neo-Impressionists.

1888 An eye infection, which began in 1880, interferes with Pissarro's painting.

1890 Pissarro decides to stop painting in the Pointillist manner. The Boussod & Valadon Gallery in Paris mounts a show of Pissarro's work. In May and June, Pissarro and Lucien travel to London to visit Georges Pissarro. Lucien moves to London in November.

1892 Durand-Ruel presents a retrospective of Pissarro's work. Pissarro travels to London to assist with Lucien's marriage. Julie borrows money from Monet to buy their house in Éragny.

1893 Confined to his hotel room in Paris with his eye infection, Pissarro paints a series of the Place du Havre. Durand-Ruel presents another solo exhibition of Pissarro's work.

1894 Durand-Ruel holds another exhibition of Pissarro's paintings. In June, Pissarro, Julie, and Félix go to Belgium, where Pissarro remains until October.

1896 Pissarro spends January 20 to March 30 in Rouen, painting the quays and bridges. In April and May, Durand-Ruel presents Pissarro's recent works at his gallery.

1897 In January, Pissarro returns to Paris to make more paintings of the Place du Havre. He spends February to April in Paris painting a series of the boulevard Montmartre. Durand-Ruel holds an exhibition of Pissarro's work in New York City. In May, Pissarro rushes to Lucien, who is seriously ill, and paints another London series. Félix dies of tuberculosis on November 25, in London. In December, Pissarro begins a new series of the Place du Théâtre-Français in Paris. Henri Matisse meets Pissarro at Durand-Ruel's gallery in Paris.

1898 Pissarro spends January to April painting in Paris. Publication on January 13 of Émile Zola's letter "J'accuse!" ignites the Dreyfus Affair. In July, Pissarro begins a three-month painting expedition in Rouen.

1899 Pissarro moves his family to rue de Rivoli in Paris for the winter and spring, where he paints a series of the Tuileries Gardens. The Pissarro family goes back to Éragny for the summer but returns to Paris in November.

1900 The following November, Pissarro moves his family to a flat on the corner of the Pont-Neuf to begin a new series of paintings.

1901 Pissarro makes a painting expedition to Dieppe in the summer. In October, he returns to Pont-Neuf for the winter.

1902 Pissarro paints in Dieppe from July to September. In November, the family returns to Pont-Neuf. Seeking variety, Pissarro rents a hotel room on the Quai Voltaire to use as a studio.

1903 From July to September, Pissarro paints in Le Havre. Soon after, the family moves to a new apartment in Paris. Pissarro becomes ill and dies on November 13, surrounded by his wife and children. He is buried on November 15, at Père-Lachaise.

This chronology is drawn from Joachim Pissarro and Claire Durand-Ruel Snollaerts, *Pissarro: Catalogue Critique des Peintures*, 3 vols. (Milan: Skira Editore S.p.A., 2005), 1:96-322.

Bibliography

Ambrosini, Lynne, Maite van Dijk, Michael Clarke, Frances Fowle, Nienke Bakker, and Renee Boitelle. *Inspiring Impressionism: Daubigny, Monet, Van Gogh*. Edinburgh: National Galleries of Scotland, 2015.

Bailly-Herzberg, Janine. *Correspondance de Camille Pissarro*. 5 vols. Paris: Valhermeil, 1986.

Barr, Jr., Alfred H. *Cubism and Abstract Art*. New York: The Museum of Modern Art, 1936.

Boime, Albert. *The Academy and French Painting in the Nineteenth Century*. London: Phaidon, 1971.

Bois, Yve-Alain. "On Two Paintings by Barnett Newman." *October* 108 (Spring 2004): 3-27.

Boulton, Alfredo. *Pissarro in Venezuela*. Translated by Stanton L. Catlin and Phyllis Freeman. New York: J. B. Watkins, 1968.

Brettell, Richard R. "Cat. 3 Snow at Louveciennes, c. 1870: Curatorial Entry." In *Pissarro Paintings and Works on Paper at the Art Institute of Chicago*. Chicago: The Art Institute of Chicago, 2015. https://publications.artic.edu/pissarro/reader/paintingsandpaper/section/12.

———. *Pissarro and Pontoise: The Painter in a Landscape*. New Haven, Conn.: Yale University Press, 1990.

———. *Pissarro's People*. New York: Prestel, 2011.

Brettell, Richard R., and Christopher Lloyd. *Catalogue of Drawings by Camille Pissarro in the Ashmolean Museum, Oxford*. Oxford: Oxford University Press, 1980.

Brettell, Richard R., and Joachim Pissarro. *The Impressionist and the City: Pissarro's Series Paintings*. New Haven, Conn.: Yale University Press, 1992.

Brettell, Richard R., and Karen Zukowski. *Camille Pissarro in the Caribbean, 1850-1855: Drawings from the Collection at Olana*. St. Thomas, U.S. Virgin Islands: Hebrew Congregation of St. Thomas, 1996.

Cachin, Françoise, Isabelle Cahn, Walter Feilchenfeldt, Henri Loyrette, and Joseph J. Rishel. *Cézanne*. Philadelphia: Philadelphia Museum of Art, 1996.

Cachin, Françoise, Anne Distel, Christopher Lloyd, Barbara Stern Shapiro, and John Walsh, Jr. *Pissarro*. Boston: Museum of Fine Arts, 1980.

Cachin, Françoise, and Charles S. Moffett. *Manet:1832-1883*. New York: Harry N. Abrams, 1983.

Castleman, Riva. *Jasper Johns: A Print Retrospective*. New York: Little, Brown, 1986.

Caws, Mary Ann, and Sarah Bird Wright. *Bloomsbury and France: Art and Friends*. New York: Oxford University Press, 1999.

Chu, Petra ten-Doesschate. *French Realism and the Dutch Masters: The Influence of Dutch Seventeenth-Century Painting on the Development of French Painting Between 1830 and 1870*. Ultrecht: Haentjens Dekker & Gumbert, 1974.

Colsman-Freyberger, Heidi. Correspondence with author.

Delacroix, Eugène. *The Journal of Eugène Delacroix*. Translated by Lucy Norton. New York: Phaidon, 1951.

Denis, Maurice, and Roger E. Fry. "Cézanne." *The Burlington Magazine for Connoisseurs* 16, no. 82 (1910): 207-9, 212, 215.

Duret, Théodore. *Manet and the French Impressionists*. Translated by J. E. Crawford Flitch. London: Grant Richards, 1910.

Gasquet, Joachim. *Joachim Gasquet's Cézanne: A Memoir with Conversations.* Translated by Christopher Pemberton. London: Thames and Hudson, 1991.

Gordon, Dana. "An Intimate Exhibition That Rewards the Keen Eye." *The Wall Street Journal,* October 17, 2007.

———. "The Moses of Modernism." Unpublished essay. 2005.

Green, Christopher, ed. *Art Made Modern: Roger Fry's Vision of Art.* London: Merrell Holberton, 1999.

Greenberg, Clement. "'American-Type' Painting." *Partisan Review* 22, no. 2 (1955): 179-96.

Halén, Widar. "Japan Revealed: Collecting of Japanese Art around the Opening of Japan." In *Perspectives on Japan and Korea: 2nd Nordic Symposium on Japanese and Korean Studies.* Copenhagen, 1991.

Hanson, Anne Coffin. *Manet and the Modern Tradition.* New Haven, Conn.: Yale University Press, 1977.

Haus, Mary. "Sign Here!" *ArtNews,* July 1, 2004. http://www.artnews.com/2004/07/01/sign-here/.

Herbert, Robert L., Françoise Cachin, Anne Distel, Susan A. Stein, and Gary Tinterow. *Georges Seurat: 1859-1891.* New York: Harry N. Abrams, 1991.

Janson, H. W., *History of Art,* 5th ed. New York: Harry N. Abrams, 1995.

Kunstler, Charles. *Pissarro: Landscapes and Cities.* Translated by Eva Kramer. New York: Justin K. Thannhauser Foundation, 1967.

Lloyd, Christopher. *Camille Pissarro (1830-1903): St. Thomas to Paris.* London: Stern Pissarro Gallery, 2003.

———. *Pissarro.* New York: Rizzoli, 1981.

Maloon, Terence, ed. *Camille Pissarro.* Sydney, Australia: Art Gallery of New South Wales, 2005.

———. *Paths to Abstraction, 1867-1917.* Sydney, Australia: Art Gallery of New South Wales, 2010.

Morton, Mary, and Charlotte Eyerman. *Courbet and the Modern Landscape.* Los Angeles: J. Paul Getty Museum, 2006.

Muller, Sheila D., ed. *Dutch Art: An Encyclopedia.* New York: Routledge, 1997.

New York Studio School, New York. "Joachim Pissarro in Conversation with Richard Shiff." September 26, 2018.

Noon, Patrick, and Christopher Riopelle. *Delacroix and the Rise of Modern Art.* London: The National Gallery, 2015.

O'Neill, John P., ed. *Barnett Newman: Selected Writings and Interviews.* Berkeley, Calif.: University of California Press, 1992.

Pissarro, Joachim. *Camille Pissarro.* New York: Harry N. Abrams, 1993.

———. *Cezanne and Pissarro: Pioneering Modern Painting, 1865-1885.* New York: The Museum of Modern Art, 2005.

Pissarro, Joachim, and Claire Durand-Ruel Snollaerts. *Pissarro: Catalogue Critique des Peintures.* 3 vols. Milan: Skira Editore S.p.A., 2005.

Pissarro, Joachim, and Stephanie Rachum. *Camille Pissarro: Impressionist Innovator.* Jerusalem: The Israel Museum, 1994.

Rabinow, Rebecca. "Édouard Manet (1832-1883)." October 2004. The Metropolitan Museum of Art, New York. http://www.metmuseum.org/toah/hd/mane/hd_mane.htm.

Reff, Theodore. "Cézanne's Constructive Stroke." *The Art Quarterly* 25, no. 5 (1962): 214-27.

Rewald, John. *Camille Pissarro*. New York: Harry N. Abrams, 1963.

———, ed. *Camille Pissarro: Letters to His Son Lucien*. New York: Pantheon, 1995.

——— . *The History of Impressionism,* 4th rev. ed. New York: The Museum of Modern Art, 1973.

Robert, F. "9ème Histoire [Paris]." http://www.neufhistoire.fr/articles.php?lng=fr&pg=1505&tconfig=0.

Rood, Ogden N. *Modern Chromatics: Students' Text-Book of Color with Applications to Art and Industry*. London: C. Kegan Paul, 1879.

Rothkopf, Katherine. *Pissarro: Creating the Impressionist Landscape*. London: Philip Wilson, 2006.

Sérullaz, Arlette, Vincent Pomarède, Joseph J. Rishel, Lee Johnson, Louis-Antoine Prat, and David Liot. *Delacroix: The Late Work*. London:Thames and Hudson, 1998.

Shikes, Ralph E., and Paula Harper. *Pissarro: His Life and Work*. New York. Horizon Press, 1980.

Slive, Seymour. "On the Meaning of Frans Hals' 'Malle Babbe.'" *The Burlington Magazine* 105, no. 727 (1963): 432-36.

Snollaerts, Claire Durand-Ruel, and Christophe Duvivier. *Camille Pissarro: The First among the Impressionists*. Vanves, France: Éditions Hazan, 2017.

Spurling, Hilary. *The Unknown Matisse: A Life of Henri Matisse, The Early Years, 1869-1908*. New York: Alfred A. Knopf, 1998.

Sullivan, Michael. *The Meeting of Eastern and Western Art,* rev. ed., Berkeley, Calif.: University of California Press, 1989.

Tabarant, Adolphe. *Pissarro*. Translated by J. Lewis May. London: John Lane; The Bodley Head, 1925.

Tatlock, Robert R. "Cézanne and the Nation," *The Burlington Magazine for Connoisseurs* 38, no. 218 (1921), 209.

Temkin, Ann, Richard Shiff, Suzanne Penn, and Melissa Ho. *Barnett Newman*. Philadelphia: Philadelphia Museum of Art, 2002.

Tinterow, Gary, and Henri Loyrette. *Origins of Impressionism*. New York: The Metropolitan Museum of Art, 1994.

Tinterow, Gary, Michael Pantazzi, and Vincent Pomarède. *Corot*. New York: The Metropolitan Museum of Art, 1996.

Varnedoe, Kirk. *Gustave Caillebotte*. New Haven, Conn.: Yale University Press, 1987.

———. *Jackson Pollock*. New York: The Museum of Modern Art, 2009.

Weisberg, Gabriel P., Phillip Dennis Cate, Gerald Needham, Martin Heidelberg, and William R. Johnston. *Japonisme: Japanese Influence on French Art, 1854-1910*. Cleveland, Oh.: The Cleveland Museum of Art, 1975.

Weiss, Jeffrey. "Art for the Nation." In *Art for the Nation*. National Gallery of Art, Washington, D. C. https://www.nga.gov/collection/art-object-page.106384.html.

Wright, Willard Huntington. *Modern Painting: Its Tendency and Meaning*. New York: Dodd, Mead, 1922.

Index

Photograph Credits

www.ingramcontent.com/pod-product-compliance
Lightning Source LLC
Chambersburg PA
CBHW041110170526

45159CB00009BA/2906